2-4-26
Kleidys

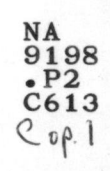

NA 9198 .P2 C613 Cop.1

Couperie, Pierre.

Paris through the ages

12.50

DATE			

**WOODSON REGIONAL CENTER
9525 SOUTH HALSTED ST.**

© THE BAKER & TAYLOR CO.

Paris through the ages

*an illustrated historical
atlas of urbanism and architecture
by Pierre Couperie*

NEW YORK / GEORGE BRAZILLER

Translated by Marilyn Low

Originally published in French under the title:
Paris au fil du temps
© Cuénot 1968

All rights reserved.
For information, address the publisher:
George Braziller, Inc. One Park Avenue New York, N.Y. 10016
Library of Congress Catalog Card Number: 77-104697
SBN 0. 8076. 0556. 5

Printed in Italy

Paris through the ages

The "Representation" of Cities

by André Chastel

● In what terms can a city be truthfully "represented"? The question assumes importance at a time when it has become clear that the future of societies and of the civilizations they sustain depends largely on a deeper understanding of the urban "phenomenon." ● The problem has never been studied more closely, or so it seems. Modern statistical devices and sociological investigation permit a constant scanning of community activities, of pressures, of population movements, of local and worldwide behavior, which constitute in some way the "content" of the city. Thus we have a sort of "instrument panel" available of inestimable interest and, sometimes, precision. But how do we deduce from it a "direction" to follow? This would presuppose a vision of the future, a hypothesis of the city's future development which would remain hopelessly abstracted from reality, as long as it did not rely on an intuition of the city as an historic ensemble, as an organism of multiple elements, interlocked but seldom interchangeable. Some are more deeply founded and more stable than others, but the total and simultaneous re-creation of all these elements is absolutely impossible. ● How can we make the fundamental data clear? Is there not an inherent difficulty in the representation of the city? The city is characterized not only by its environment and exchanges but also by the insertion of its ensemble into a certain ground space and the adoption of certain borders. It must be grasped from both the inside and the outside at the same time; it possesses both a "physiognomy" perceptible to novelists and poets and a "configuration" which must be read as a drawing, a treatment of masses, forms, and color. The way it occupies the ground, its adaptation to the site, the innumerable interrelations of its structures, its roads, and its squares, the entire physical aspect of the city, its "container," is at the heart of the problem. Nothing is more fallacious than the tendency to consider this physical container as a ready made object, being a more or less ordered collection of inherited elements, dear to many for sentimental reasons but by definition badly adapted to the needs of the present and future. Here precisely is the basic data which it is important to treat in historical perspective. For the configuration of a city, studied in its slow progress, analyzed through the rhythms of its development, is apt and perhaps uniquely suited to reveal the constant, the unusual, the accidental, the deliberate, to see the setbacks without which the present situation would remain quite unintelligible. Every society takes its form, in the true sense of the word, through architecture, which, be it monumental or commonplace, cannot be separated from the urban framework which it embellishes, defines, and submits to all at once. ● It has been said that "in the past the plan of the city corresponded to the structure of the totality of social groups and to the rapports which existed between the different classes of population. The society was written in the ground." (Chombard de Lauwe in La Vie urbaine, October 1963.) ● Even, and especially, if the city's form has ceased to project the social structure today, at least in explicit form it is all the more necessary to clarify the stages of the evolution which led from the former state to the one which we know, for the structures and their layout — partly or totally emptied of their former meaning — are still present and integrated into the urban mass. It is even reasonable to suppose that former generations often participated in the same belief and that the tendency to ascribe more coherence to a previous state of the city than exists now is not new. Thus there would be nothing more stimulating for the imagination nor more revealing under analysis than a "cinematographic" representation of the urban evolution. ● This solution was thought of long ago. One of those great administrators typical of the ancien régime, Delemare, King's Conseiller and Commissaire au Châtelet de Paris, published an imposing treatise "de la Police" at the beginning of the 18th century, one of the most precious documents in the history of municipal institutions. He had the sensible idea of preceding his study with an "historical and topographical description of the city of Paris seen in all the different states through which she has passed until now and which serves as an introduction to the understanding of her police" (Book I, Heading VI). In fact, he presents eight maps by Nicolas de Fer (1708), accompanied by captions which present a synthesis of urban data for each period and which amplify the appropriate chapters. These maps, all on the same scale, plot the essentials of an evolution leading from legendary origins to contemporary problems.

● The effectivness of this solution is remarkable and suffices to demonstrate the interest inherent in a systematic translation of urban structures into graphic form, divided by well-chosen stages. The first map represents Lutetia with information drawn from "Caesar, Strabo, the Emperor Julian, and Ammianus Marcellinus" and constitutes a naïve "archaeological" representation of the site. Certain noteworthy sites are included, their transformations revealed in the subsequent maps. On the site of the temple of Isis, located on the left bank toward the southwest, will appear the abbey of St-Germain-des-Prés on the 3rd map. On the 2nd map the church of Notre-Dame-des-Champs rises where the temple of Mercury or Esus once stood to the south of La Cité. These maps carefully specify the introduction of key buildings, such as the castle of the Louvre, "built," we are told, "by Louis the Fat to serve as a principal manor of the crown's fiefs" (3rd map) and the appearance of successive walls, their purposes and later stages duly indicated (4th and 5th maps). The interest in representative monuments, which is characteristic of modern times and began with the Renaissance, is duly emphasized: "a real feeling for the quality of buildings did not appear before the reign of François I" (6th map); at the same time were faced some specific problems which were still important for the following reigns: "There still remained several empty places in the ring of walls around Paris which deformed this great city," and the space was not completely utilized until the time of Henri IV and Louis XIII (8th map). It was these walls, finally, which produced the great density of occupancy in the city, the extremely tight web of population in the center, and the necessary expansion to the suburbs just when the 20 arrondissements were created in the 18th century. Attempts were made to correct or to reorient by vast new projects this difficult problem. "One need only cast one's gaze on the last map of Paris and on the preceeding one to see how much this city grew and was embellished under the reign of Louis the Great. The magnificence of this Prince and the zeal of his subjects for glory bursts forth from all directions... . One will see eighty-two streets opened and built in different areas..., four new bridges for the convenience of commerce, a "châtelet" (small fortification) for the exercise of justice, a salt storehouse, etc..., all the places needed for his officers to exercise their functions, an Hôtel de Mars with a church of formidable structure for his disabled officers and soldiers. ..."(8th map)

● Never before, perhaps, had the constant relationship between architecture and city planning, the reciprocal play of their requirements, the inescapable pressure of the site, of previous layouts, of the present state of occupation, and of the nature of buildings been rendered more explicitly. Each régime, each generation, whatever its innovative ambitions, always takes a city in hand at a given moment of its evolution. What one calls the structure of a city at a particular date is nothing but a slice cut through a complex organism, to be accurate, the most complex that exists in the cultural order. The particular elements — thoroughfares, blocks, buildings — can by themselves be seen as having unequal importance; needs, more or less clearly formulated, can invite modifications, even upheavals in detail. But they do not affect the main point. It is the sum that has importance, the totality of all the data, human and material, social and architectural, which makes up the original character of the city, with its own seductions, its aptitudes, its own prestige. This specific aspect, this "face" of the great city, presents itself as a "constant" or perennial trait dependent on the "long term" to which Fernand Braudel discerningly drew attention. This perhaps, is the essential issue today. At each stage there is an unstable and sometimes suspenseful equilibrium of contrary pressures and opposed requirements, of which all analysis of "circumstances" must retrospectively try to render account. Nothing is more difficult and nothing more necessary than to make it understood that every large city and, most of all, every capital has always had its problems. And when we have reconstituted, thanks to the help of the interpretative map, the problems of each period, there is a better chance of understanding the problems of today. The mode of representation of the urban reality adopted by this new collection will surely be provocative in its return to the past and its presentation of the factors of inertia and the conditions of change. As a productive focusing of the historic "perception," it will surely make the reader more aware of what is possible and how things evolve. It is in this context that one will be able to understand and extend to all great cities the well-known proposition of Le Corbusier: "Paris is good if you know how to thrust to her roots; if you remain at the surface, you are done for."

Introduction

● *The conventions of this atlas are as simple as its principle: to show the progressive growth of the organism called Paris — that is, its area of construction and its principal arteries — by a succession of maps of constant scale in which the agglomeration grows and branches out into the surrounding valleys, in which swamps dry up and retreat little by little, in which country roads become streets. The monuments and installations which appeared in the era illustrated by a map are shown by names and red dots. Depending on whether they exist or have been destroyed, their name is printed in red or in black, respectively.* ● *The red holds an increasing position, which becomes substantial only in the comparatively recent maps, for Paris is a ravaged city which has preserved very few of its monuments. Nevertheless, while fires, earthquakes, and bombs destroyed London, Lisbon, Copenhagen, Chicago, San Francisco, Berlin, Dresden, Tokyo, Warsaw, and Hiroshima, no major disaster, accidental or military, has touched Paris since the Viking raids in the 9th century. No fire has spread beyond the most immediate vicinity of its origin. The only wartime damages since those of the Danes were incurred during the civil war of 1871. Paris has been destroyed only by her own inhabitants, but this destruction has been extensive, even more extensive perhaps than would be inevitably called for by the life of a city whose growth has never ceased. Depending on the period, these destructions resulted from the aggravated poverty of some, or from the wealthy changing tastes of others. Destruction was thrust on Paris as a capital in the form of monumental government ventures and as the country's principal artistic center in the form of architects' ambitions to innovate. How much the destruction was a reflection of character traits defining the psychology of the people is a question we shall not pursue.* ● *Destruction was not limited to buildings. Documents, already deficient in some areas, perished too. The population of Paris before 1801 is unknown. The fiscal records that would have permitted a demographic, economic, and social exploration of the city under the ancien régime burned with the Chambre des Comptes in 1737. The parish registers since 1515, kept in the Hôtel de Ville, were destroyed in 1871 by the Communards. Quite luckily, Colbert had had statistics published since 1670 on births, marriages, and deaths, allowing an estimate of the size of the population. Fiscal and property inventories drawn up in 1637 and 1684 are of some value. For the 16th century, two countings or estimates of 1549 and 1590 are known only through chronicled hearsay. For the Middle Ages we are reduced to suppositions, supported by more or less consistent fiscal registers of around 1300, but confused by a completely contradictory census of households in the kingdom said to be "of 1328." Here and there information surfaces bearing ironic precision: we know how many wolves and birds of prey were killed each year within its walls, thanks to treasury accounts of bounties paid to hunters. For the same reason — the chance preservation of accounts of the city's payments to gravediggers — we know the exact number of corpses pulled from the Seine after the St Bartholomew massacre in 1572. Moreover, the existence of a very detailed report of an inspection of diocesan hospitals and leperhouses in 1356-57 does not compensate for the disappearance of death records for the Hôtel-Dieu, kept since the Middle Ages and recording several centuries of epidemics. Happily the researcher does have access to enormous collections of long-standing archives of "notaires," sometimes reaching back to the 15th century, now entrusted to the Minutier Central. They offer inventories of estates, object by object, marriage contracts, leases, appraisals, etc.; the entire life of a people resides in these millions of documents. But despite their somewhat crushing mass, they cannot furnish the trustworthy conclusions of a complete census. While recourse to "notaires" for documents was much more common then than it is today, it was nevertheless dependent on social class. What is more, several such archives have disap-*

peared, and with them the documents on certain sections of the city, such as the two offices that were swept away in 1658 when the Pont Marie collapsed along with the houses on it. Still, these sources are the only hope of piercing the mystery of the economic life of Paris before the last century.

● The physical form of the city is scarcely better known. There is no plan of Paris before the 16th century, no serious plan before 1652, no scientifically established plan before 1787, no relief map before Napoleon III. But a masterpiece does exist, the so-called Turgot map of 1739, a bird's-eye view of all the houses correctly represented, a tour de force so remarkable that it was held suspect for a long time. It is the only plan that gives a precise picture of the true area of construction, since this was not represented at all on the 1787 plan by Verniquet. For the Middle Ages, scholarship has established the dates of origin for numerous streets and allowed the expansion of construction to be plotted. But the reader must not forget the uncertainty surrounding these maps as well as the relief, the slopes of which are now altered by fill. We must also add that the lower stream of the Bièvre is poorly known. We have adopted the solution of two mouths, seeing the canal of St-Victor as a harnessed natural branch (Map IV). For why would the monks have cut a canal to Notre-Dame, going through the hostile rival domain of Ste-Geneviève, when they could have it shorter, as was actually done when it had to be diverted in the 14th century (Map VII)? If it is still necessary to specify it, the "Grange-Batelière" is not represented in this atlas because the river never existed. ● In a work such as this, intended for the public and not for specialists, there is a traditional approach to the history of Paris, never weary of celebrating the sojourn of the Emperor Julian, the tournaments of the Place Royale, and the taking of the Bastille. We have resolutely strayed from that course in hopes of drawing attention to more fundamental realities: population, the role of site and location, sanitation, rent, transportation, and so on. Through patiently gathered studies, particularly under the auspices of the Société pour l'Histoire de Paris et de l'Ile-de-France, ambitious recent investigations, some still in progress, have been conducted on the socio-professional makeup of neighborhoods in the 17th century and during the Revolution, on marriage contracts, on housing, on leases, on immigration, on the life of neighboring regions. For the contemporary era, studies by sociologists and geographers have culminated in the appearence of an enormous and invaluable geographic atlas of the Paris region. All these works, of which the principal ones can be found in the bibliography, have constructed little by little a new image of the substance of Paris history. We hope we have given an idea of it to the public. If as a result there is abundant discussion of problems, of insufficient sanitation, and of poverty, this is not a denigration. It is the lot of all large cities. While the Bièvre contaminated Paris, the Fleet in London had been blocked by sewage as early as the 13th century. Captain Bourke, describing the manure heaps of a small town in Arizona in 1870, concluded, " the streets ... were every bit as filthy as those of New York." Such a story shows the terrible inertia of things and of peoples. The removal of Les Halles, desired by Napoleon I, took more than 160 years to accomplish. That of the Hôtel-Dieu was envisioned by Louis XV; nothing has moved. The Ministry of Finance " provisionally" occupied part of the Louvre in 1871 and has succeeded in defending this position more magnificently than Montluc at Siena. The reader may be amused to find some constant themes in this history. The Duke of Saint-Simon was struck by the fact that so many excellent laws were never enforced. Today's Parisian still sees many laws flouted — by the public services themselves — against air pollution, noise and disorder, the strict enforcement of which could only benefit everyone. And what fine illustrations of Parkinson's laws. For example:" A perfection of planned layout is achieved only by institutions on the point of collapse." The Louvre was finished, perfect after 600 years of labor, 13 years before the fall of the last king. The Ministry of War was magnificently relocated just before the disaster of 1870. To return to the special features of this book, it must be remembered that most of the noble town houses (hôtels) are known by names that would have been anachronisms on the maps where they appear, names often derived from their late-18th-century or even Restoration occupants. We have tried to return them to their first owner or at least to their first tenant insofar as these were known. The aristocracy was unsentimental about its residences and readily abandoned them for newer, more fashionable quarters. For example, there were numerous Hôtels d'Aumont; the one that bears the name today is in fact a Hôtel Scarron. Some great notables had several hôtels simultaneously, for example, rental property, a residence for show, and the family residence. Some buildings changed function, while some changed name several times, for example, the older churches. Most religious orders were known by nicknames, sometimes inherited from predecessors: the hermits of St-Guillaume, dressed in black, were called Blancs-Manteaux (White Cloaks) because they succeeded the Serfs de la Vierge, who wore white. Along this line, it is amusing to see the center of parliamentarianism, the " Bourbon" Palace, perpetuate the name of the last dynasty, in a city that pushed revolutionary logic to the point of changing the name of Rue Chantereine (singing Queen) so as not to give a flattering musical image to the monarchy, when it had in fact referred to the croaking frogs ("raines" in Old French) of the former swamps. Finally, words such as " Opéra," " Comédie-Française," and so on, have applied to successive monuments variously situated, some of which still exist under other names. For all these reasons, cross references between old and modern names have been included as much as possible in the index. They will help the reader to disentangle the constant changes of an organism in perpetual evolution.

I *Formation of the site and prehistory*

II *Lutetia under the Roman Empire 52 B.C. – A.D. 253*

III *The late Empire, the Merovingians and Carolingians 253-987*

IV *From Hugh Capet to Louis VII 987-1180*

V *The reign of Philippe Auguste 1180-1223*

VI *Louis VIII and Saint Louis 1223-1270*

VII *From Philip the Fair to Charles V 1270-1380*

VIII *From Charles VI to Louis XII 1380-1515*

IX *From François I to Henri III 1515-1589*

X *Henri IV and Louis XIII 1589-1643*

XI *The reign of Louis XIV 1643-1715*

XII *Louis XV and Louis XVI 1715-1789*

XIII *From the Revolution to Louis-Philippe 1789-1848*

XIV *The 2nd Republic and Napoléon III 1848-1870*   XV *The Commune 1871*

XVI *The 3rd Republic 1871-1914*

XVII *The 3rd Republic 1914-1940*

XVIII *The War, the 4th and 5th Republics 1940-1968*

Chronological scale

I Formation of the site and prehistory

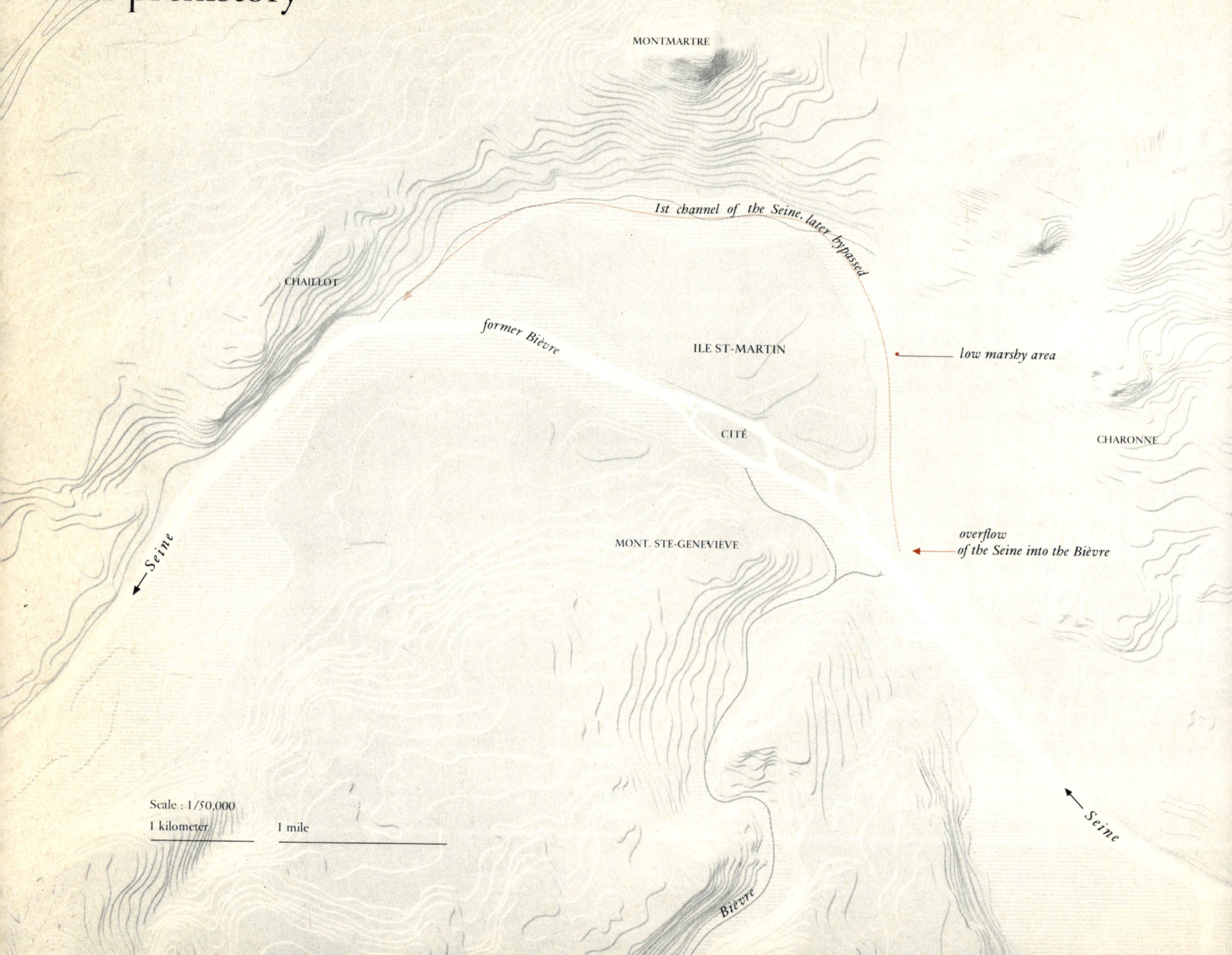

The site of Paris, which had been a seabed in the Tertiary period, was formed during the Quaternary glacial period by an enormous Siberian-type river. 30,000 or 40,000 years ago this river, fed by melting snow and summer rain, cut the basin that extends from Chaillot to Charonne and deposited a thick layer of gravel. The mellowing of the climate (ca 10,000 B.C.) reduced the Seine to its present size, creating a stream underfit for its riverbed. It meandered to the north along the foot of the hills and joined the Bièvre approximately at the present Place de l'Alma. During a flood, the Seine broke through the narrow isthmus that separated it from the Bièvre (around the present Gare d'Austerlitz) and emptied into the lower stream of its tributary, annexing and rearranging it. This cut off the island, La Cité, which was a fragment of the plain rather than a composite layer of silt, while the north bank was eroded away into steep slopes at the center. Confined by a new bed, the waters slowly eroded and graded La Cité, until its surface was finally below the level of high floods. The old riverbed became silted and stagnated. By the end of the Neolithic period the site of Paris, which was to govern the development of the city until the 17th century, had been determined: a platform of insubmergible gravel formed an island (the Ile St-Martin in the Middle Ages) between the two arms of the river; a general slope ran from Mont. Ste-Geneviève to the foot of Montmartre rather than to the present Seine, a ring of swamp (5 mi long, 220-330 yds wide), refilled by each big flood, blocked access to the NE and NW hills; an easily flooded island, La Cité emerged especially to the SE; and on the high side of the right bank a notch of gentle slope formed the future Grève.

Having been initially populated in the Lower Paleolithic period, the region of Paris was deserted in the Upper Paleolithic period because of the severe climate; only hunting expeditions went through (an ecampment found at Pincevent). In the Neolithic period La Cité was occupied; the first village was on the Villejuif slopes, far from the humid land (3rd millenium B.C.). In the 3rd century B.C. the Quarisii Celts (later Parisii) invaded the region, introducing iron and destroying the so-called Seine-Oise-Marne copper civilization, which had already been in contact with the Mediterranean and the North Sea. While part of the Parisii pushed all the way to Yorkshire, the rest established their huts on La Cité, at the center of their territory (ca 250 B.C.); in their eyes, the defensive advantages outweighed the problems of dampness. (During the same era Melun and Sens were also begun on islands). They borrowed from the indigenous pre-Celts, the name of Lucotecia, later Lutetia. Fishermen, foresters, herdsmen, and boatmen, the Parisii were seldom farmers. They grew rich exploiting passage on and across the Seine (wooden toll bridges to La Cité), the principal crossroad of northern Gaul. Their territory seems to have been already one of the most heavily populated; they sent 8,000 men to the chieftain Vercingetorix, as many as the Helvetii, to fight against Caesar. With four times the territory, the Senones sent only 12,000. In 52 B.C., Lutetia, its two bridges, its cult site (perhaps situated to the southeast of La Cité), and its fortress (even more, hypothetically, to the west) were burned by the inhabitants to stop the Roman troops. In 51 B.C. the Romans finally occupied Lutetia.

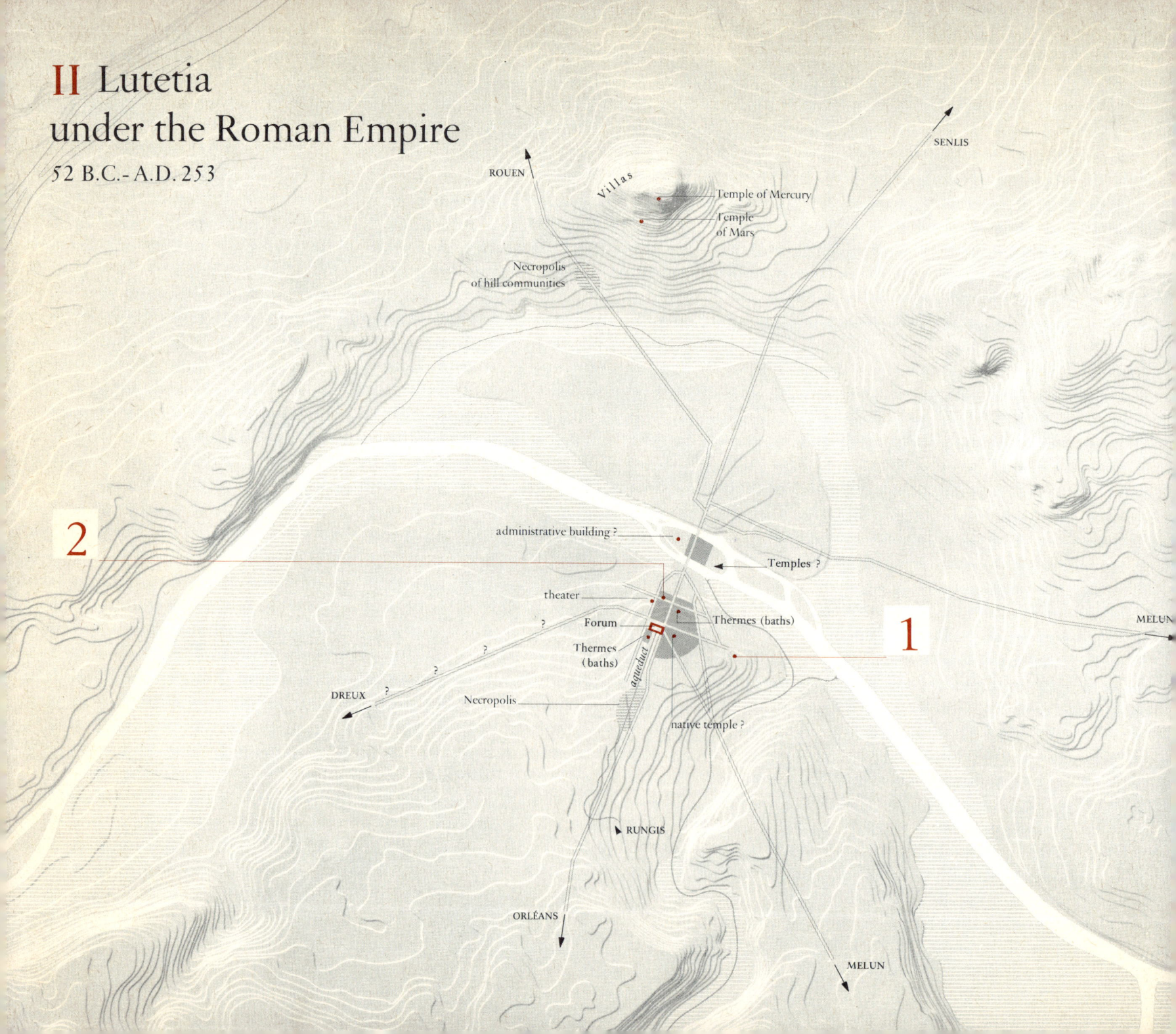

Rebuilt in the 1st century A.D., Lutetia was a prosperous city, though of modest size for the Roman Empire. Integrated into a political ensemble with a distant capital, it lost its strategic role. The great crossroads were at Reims, and Lutetia was only the junction between roads from the south and the important Troyes-Rouen river-road axis. The roads from the north appear to have been of secondary importance. Lutetia's boatmen (nautes) brought wealth to the city, the capital of the Parisii and doubtless the agricultural marketplace of a region where the indigenous peasantry seems to have been particularly dense. Lutetia, then, was a settlement with two separate poles. Little is known about one: La Cité. Two wooden bridges and an official building to the west are certain, but no one knows where the port was. The Roman city planners established the other pole at the summit of the closest hill, thus avoiding the marshy lowlands. A forum (originally an open square, then in the 2nd century an enclosure of shops under a colonnade) and baths (thermae) formed the nucleus of the upper town, with, perhaps, a circular Gallic temple above. A small 10-mi aqueduct furnished it with water. Because they were places for the dead, the amphitheater and necropolis were placed outside the city limits. A long straight road (the future Rue St-Jacques) received traffic via the steepest slope, led it north to the bridges uniting the two sections of the city. Under the Roman veneer, Lutetia maintained Gallic customs and language and spread toward the Seine. In the 2nd and 3rd centuries the urban front descended toward the river; a small theater, and the east (2nd century) and north thermae mark out its boundaries. With its rich monuments, Lutetia covered 370 acres and counted 10,000 inhabitants at the same time that Rome's population had reached 1,000,000. The exact population figures for Lyon are unknown, but it is estimated that its aqueducts carried 20,000,000 gallons per day, compared to 530,000 for Lutetia.

1 ARENES DE LUTECE. (Lutetia Arena, 1st century). Amphitheater with stage, a hybrid provincial type for a medium-size city combining theater and amphitheater in one building. The one at Lutetia, nevertheless, is one of the largest known: it is oval shaped, 417 by 327 ft, and surrounds an oval track, 173 by 160 ft. No tiers of seats were found; those today are modern. On about one third of the perimeter, a theater stage replaces the tiers. A portico of arcades enclosed the stone amphitheater, and the entrance consisted of two long corridors.

2 THERMES DE CLUNY. (Cluny Baths, end 2nd beginning 3rd centuries). A large building (320 by 213 ft), built of stone with brick ties. On the edge of marshy meadows, the Baths — today known as "Cluny" or "north baths" — follow the symmetrical prototype that was realized in Rome about the end of the 1st century (Baths of Trajan) and that was copied throughout the Empire. The cold waters (to the north), the warm and the hot waters (the latter traditionally placed to the southwest), and their many annexes, in particular their furnaces, are arranged around an axis passing through a large hall with a pool (Frigi-

darium). The Frigidarium, 65 by 36 ft, was covered by two tunnels vaults, whose intersection formed a groin vault. This type of construction and the remarkable solidity of the building were the result of specific requirements: the need to eliminate fire hazards, to conserve the heat, and to isolate various sections all called for very thick walls (6 1/2 ft) and vaults, instead of timber roofs. These vaults, in turn, required thick supporting walls. Ruined at the end of the 3rd century, the Baths never disappeared, but served throughout later centuries as housing and sheds.

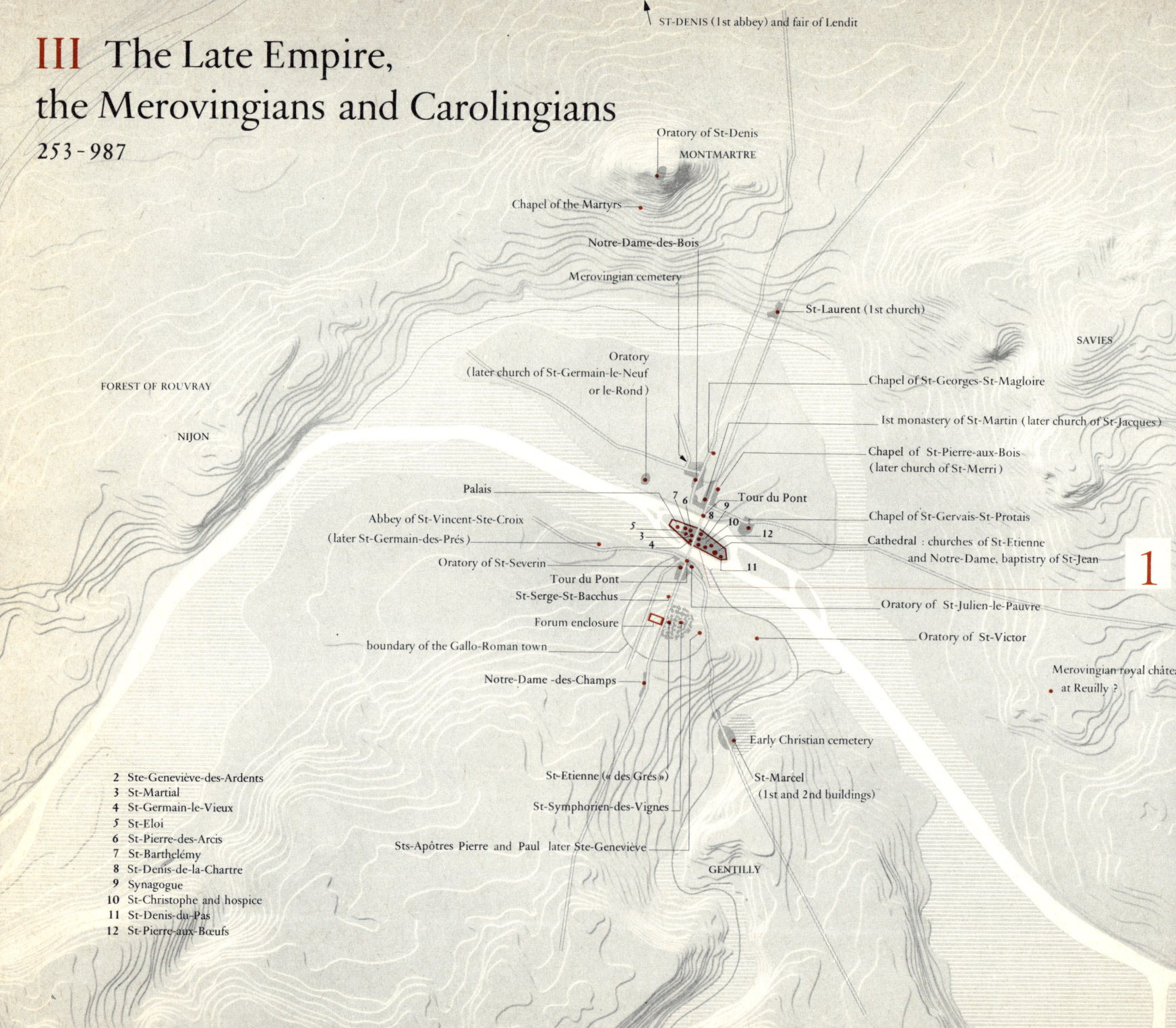

Between 253 and 280 the barbarians broke the defenses of the Empire. They ravaged the upper town of Lutetia, but La Cité escaped the raids. It was the emperors' creation of a defense in depth that relieved the situation. Lutetia acquired a new life in her role as a strategic crossroads grew. La Cité was enclosed by a wall, the ground level of the island having greatly risen. The upper town was reoccupied. Surrounded by a wall, the forum served as a citadel. The swamp was filled in and built up in the vicinity of the bridge, and a modest district developed on the north bank above the beach. Lutetia becoming a military town, the base for a river squadron patrolling on the Oise and the Marne. It changed, became Latinized and Christian. After the preaching of St. Denis (250-51), the first church appeared in the village near the Bièvre quarries (the future Bourg St-Marcel), accompanied by a vast necropolis. A major church seems to have been built on La Cité as early as the 4th century. It was dependent on the see of Sens, the capital of the province. As was the custom in Gaul, the town took the name of its people: Lutetia became Paris ca 360. In the 5th century the Empire collapsed. The strength from its new Romanization and dense population made the Paris region a Gallo-Roman state, a region that the Franks did not conquer until 486. Isolated, Paris was led by its bishop, St Marcel and by Ste Geneviève. A strategic reversal restored its importance: leaving Soissons, Clovis took up residence in Paris (508) in order to oversee the south, which he had just conquered. Unlike the other barbarian kings who were Arian heretics, Clovis made Paris an orthodox Christian center, rivaling the then-dominant Tours. He founded the Sts-Apôtres church, and his son Childebert would build St-Vincent. Religious expansion in Merovingian Paris is most evident in the success of monasticism (St-Martial, St-Christophe, St-Martin, the Sts-Apôtres) and in the increasing number of churches in the upper town, on the buttes of the north bank, and on La Cité especially, where a complex of three separate churches made up the cathedral. The conversion of the region was complete ca 600. The political supremacy of Paris was made clear when Caribert's brothers divided the kingdom but kept Paris in joint estate. But Soissons, Orléans, Reims, and Tours contested this preeminence, ans St-Denis, with a palace, the mint, and the royal necropolis, became a new and nearby rival. In a region alive with great land-clearing projects, where Franks did not settle and Latin was spoken until ca 700, Paris seems to have prospered. It was filled with activity, open to foreign influences through its Syrian and Jewish colonies. The upper town remained the principal district, but construction flourished on La Cité, now sheltered from floods by accumulated fill which doubled its height. Small settlements developed on the higher buttes of the north bank. St-Denis and Paris formed the beginning of a double organism, linked by the St-Denis fairground situated on the bypassed riverbed near St-Laurent. Thus, the Carolingians inherited a town of 20,000 or 30,000 inhabitants. Because the Empire encompassed Germany and Italy, Paris lost its central position and its growth abated, although its economic importance persisted. Aix-la-Chapelle became the imperial residence, while in Gaul, St-Denis and Laon gained favor. An inventory of the property of St-Germain-des-Prés shows that the population south of the city was, in 806-29, already one half of what it would be in 1835. This local overpopulation found its outlet in Paris, requiring the town to seek provisions from outside. An active riverboat trade united it with Rouen and the Channel, but that in turn attracted the Vikings, who, as organized units and using their naval superiority to advantage, inflicted far more damage than the barbarians of the 3rd century. Paris was pillaged, ransomed, and finally won in 885-86 after a long series of attacks. The city emerged changed by the Danish invasions: on the south bank, farmland overgrew the destroyed upper town; the severely damaged north bank managed to survive. With the Vikings established in Normandy, Paris became a frontier post. Strengthened by this position and by the remoteness of the Emperor, the successive local rulers — dukes of the Franks and counts of Paris — became royalty, for they began to assume the crown in 987.

1 ENCEINTE DE LA CITE (Cité wall, excavations in front of Notre-Dame, 1965-66). This wall, hastily constructed about AD 280 using stone from buildings on the left bank, enclosed about 21 acres. In the same period, 70 other Gallic cities were fortified: the walls of Bordeaux enclosed 79 acres, those of Reims 150 or 160. But the wall of La Cité was only the defensive retreat of Lutetia. When the Vikings appeared, they took La Cité without striking a blow. After 600 years, probably only the base remained, but it allowed the erection of a rampart, scarcely finished for the siege of 885. The wall disappeared during the 12th century, but remains were still apparent in the 16th century.

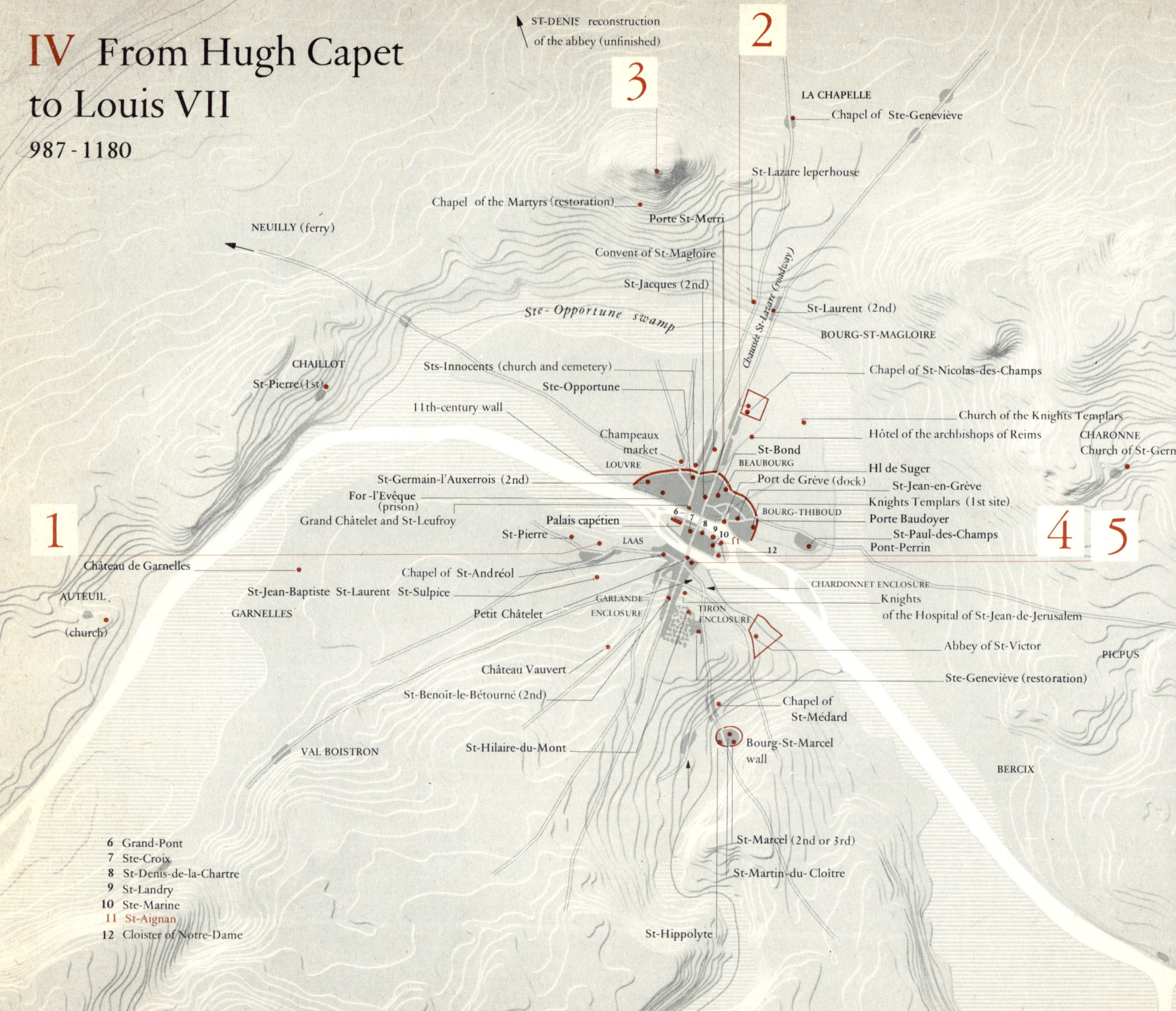

The rebirth of Paris was a slow process, coinciding with the economic and demographic renewal of the West. It was in Champagne rather than in Paris that international commerce was established. The schools of Laon and Chartres eclipsed those of La Cité. The tranquillity of the Normans caused Paris to lose its military importance as well as its royal residence to Orléans, but the new Norman threat after 1050 returned strategic importance to Paris and brought back the King, Philippe I. Anglo-Angevin power and imperial designs in Champagne definitively established Louis VI and Louis VII at Paris: this sealed the destiny of the city. Thanks to the King, Paris escaped being stifled by the feudal lords in the area, but it also missed the commune movement. The King's return revived the town and launched a campaign of restoration and construction. The livelier growth on the north bank (Outre-Pont) was marked by the transfer of the Grève market to Les Champeaux, later to be the site of Les Halles central markets; by the concession of the Grève port to the merchants in 1141; and by the shifting of the population toward the St-Denis road, newly opened by a bridge (itself evidence of the rebuilt palace). Butchers and the company of "marchands de l'eau" appeared as constitued groups. A wall of unknown dimensions sheltered this activity, perhaps about the end of the 11th century. Stimulated by palace works and the new cathedral, La Cité remained the heart of the city, but its market declined, and its commotion was detrimental to the monasteries, some of which left (St-Magloire). Some of its students emigrated to Ste-Geneviève and St-Victor. The left bank regained its life slowly. The Laas and the vineyard enclosures at the foot of the slopes began to be parceled out, but the active centers were the villages of St-Marcel and St-Germain, quite separate from Paris. 12th-century Paris also acquired intellectual renown with William of Champeaux and Abélard. At the same time, a capital effort began which would, little by little, facilitate access to the city: the canons of Ste-Opportune, feudal lords of the old riverbed, began its drainage and exploitation.

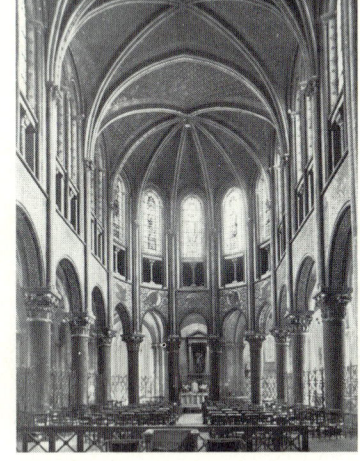

2 ST-MARTIN-DES-CHAMPS, tower (12th century) and apse (1130-40). The transition from Romanesque to Gothic is represented: semicircular arches in the tower and chapels, buttressed walls, groin vaults, and irregular, poorly adapted rib vaults.

3 ST-PIERRE-DE-MONTMARTRE, chevet. Consecrated in 1147, the church belonged to a Benedictine abbey founded in 1133-34. The ogival vault at the entrance to the choir is the earliest Gothic vault in Paris that can be dated.

1 ST-GERMAIN-DES-PRES, tower and choir. Between 900 and 1014 the Abbey began construction of a new Romanesque church reminiscent of the Carolingian period: the nave was flanked by three towers, two framing the chevet and a tower-portal, one of the earliest in France. The nave, finished after 1050, was vaulted in the 17th century. A new choir, for the growing number of monks, was consecrated in 1163. Inspired by St-Denis and Noyon, it included galleries and, for the first time in Paris, a successfully vaulted ambulatory. At that time, an upper story was added to the tower, as well as a portal, under the porch.

4 NOTRE-DAME, choir and ambulatory. Gothic architecture first appeared in the Parisian region; it was contemporaneous with the last Romanesque churches (Cluny in 1130, the nave of Vézelay in 1140, Worms in 1181, Bamberg after 1200). After 1137, great Gothic cathedrals — St-Denis, Sens, Senlis, Noyon, Laon, Poitiers — preceded Notre-Dame. As a manifestation of the renaissance in Paris of royal power, the new cathedral was undertaken in 1163, beginning with the choir, which was consecrated in 1182. The double ambulatory, a novelty, recalls that of Cluny.

5 ST-JULIEN-LE-PAUVRE (ca 1165-70). A small country church of an early Gothic type, without flying buttresses, still essentially Romanesque.

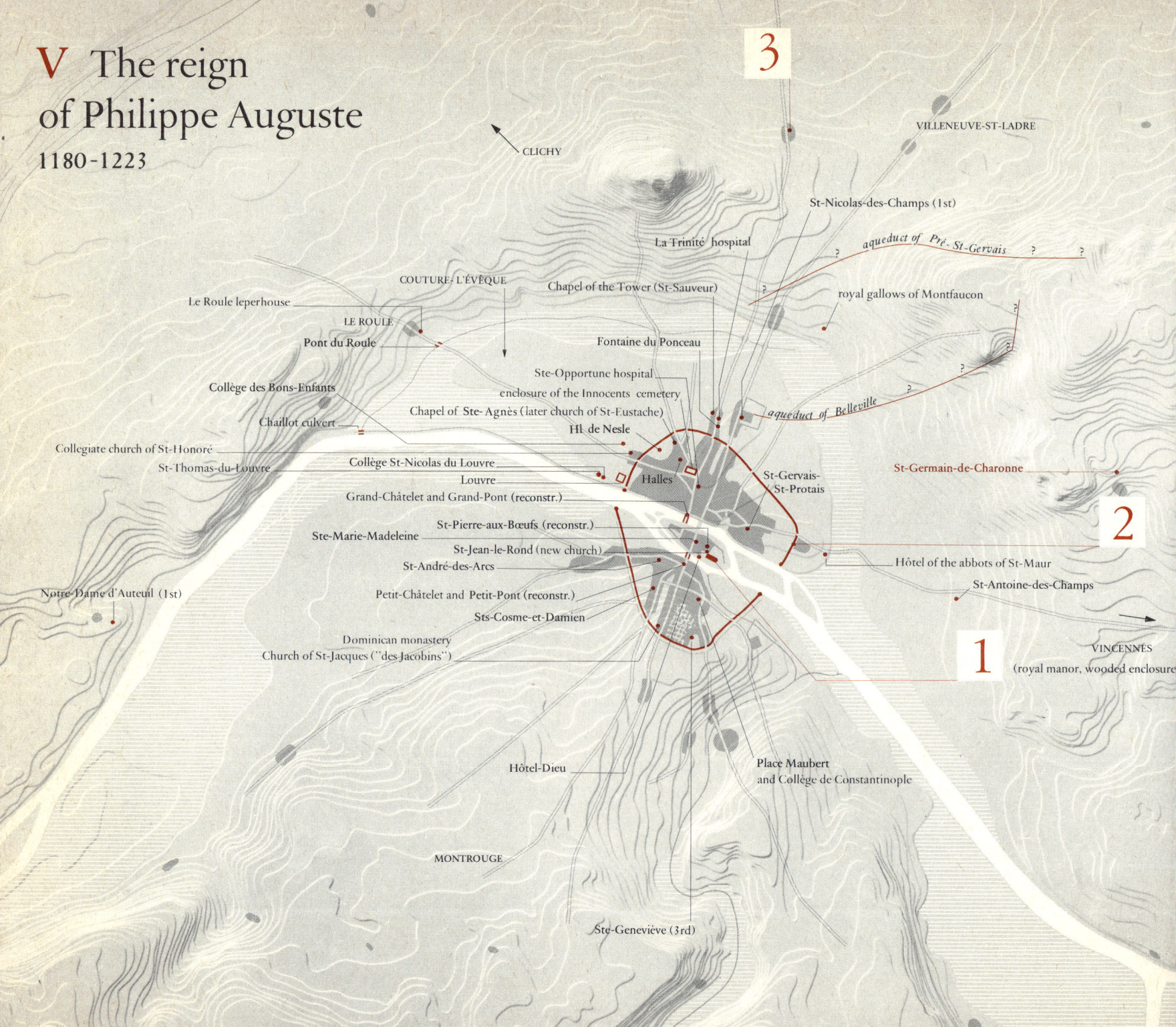

With the reign of Philippe Auguste, Paris had not yet become the capital of France, but it was already outstanding. Its strategic position and the decisions of an authoritarian king gave it renewed momentum. The English garrisons 40 mi away (Gisors) and the possibility of raids by Richard the Lion-Hearted caused the King to order the fortification of Paris: 3.3 mi of walls, protected by the Louvre castle, encompassed more than 620 acres and brought about a unified town. This protection attracted population, and the construction area expanded. The King encouraged this, ordering that the left bank be "filled to the walls with houses" (an order not carried out until the 14th century). The city was reorganized: 4 new districts and several parishes were added, determined by the growth of the right bank and by the wall, which had cut through old parishes. The King had streets paved, two enclosed markets built at Champeaux, the Innocents' cemetery enclosed (it would better have been moved outside the city), the "châtelets" (bridge fortifications) rebuilt. Although the left bank remained pastoral, Paris expanded over the grain fields of the Ile St-Martin Swamp drainage continued, permitting cultivation of grain, the basis of the food production. Communication was improved by new bridges over the former riverbed. The religious and intellectual role of Paris was strengthened when the incorporation of masters and students (universitas) was officially recognized by the Pope (1209-10). To house students, collèges multiplied. The King relied on the bourgeoisie and entrusted the treasury to them during his crusade. He wanted Paris to become a center of royal function. The wall, the depositing of archives permanently after 1194, and the custom of appealing to the King for justice all contributed to this. The conquest of Normandy ended the English threat and assured access to the sea, but it also launched a long-lived economic rivalry between Paris and Rouen.

1 NOTRE-DAME, nave and façade. The nave was vaulted 1180-1200, the façade begun in 1200, the Gallery of Kings completed by 1220, and the rose window zone finished in 1225. The towers followed between 1225 and 1250. The original plan was maintained from start to finish except for the tower spires, which were never executed, since the façade attains a remarkable equilibrium without them. The interior of the church is 427 ft long, 157 ft wide, the vaults 115 ft high, 226 ft in all with the towers. It has a capacity of 9,000 persons. The structure remains Romanesque: the nave is supported — and darkened — by tribunes, the solution of St-Denis and the great Norman churches being applied here for the last time. The six-part vaults are typical of the Ile-de-France.

1 NOTRE-DAME, nave and tribunes. Originally, round windows crowned the bays under tiny, high lancets. In some bays Viollet-le-Duc reconstructed this arrangement, but the rose openings had been blind, covered by the tribune roofs, now destroyed.

2 CITY WALL (1190-1209). From 29 to 32 ft high, and 9 ft wide at the base (rubble between cut-stone façades). Crenelated parapet, 67 towers, 20 ft in diameter; in some of these, ground-level passages served as gates. There were no moats.

3 ST-DENIS-DE-LA-CHAPELLE (nave ca 1200). A small village church still far from Paris. The nave is roofed in timber; the façade and choir are modern.

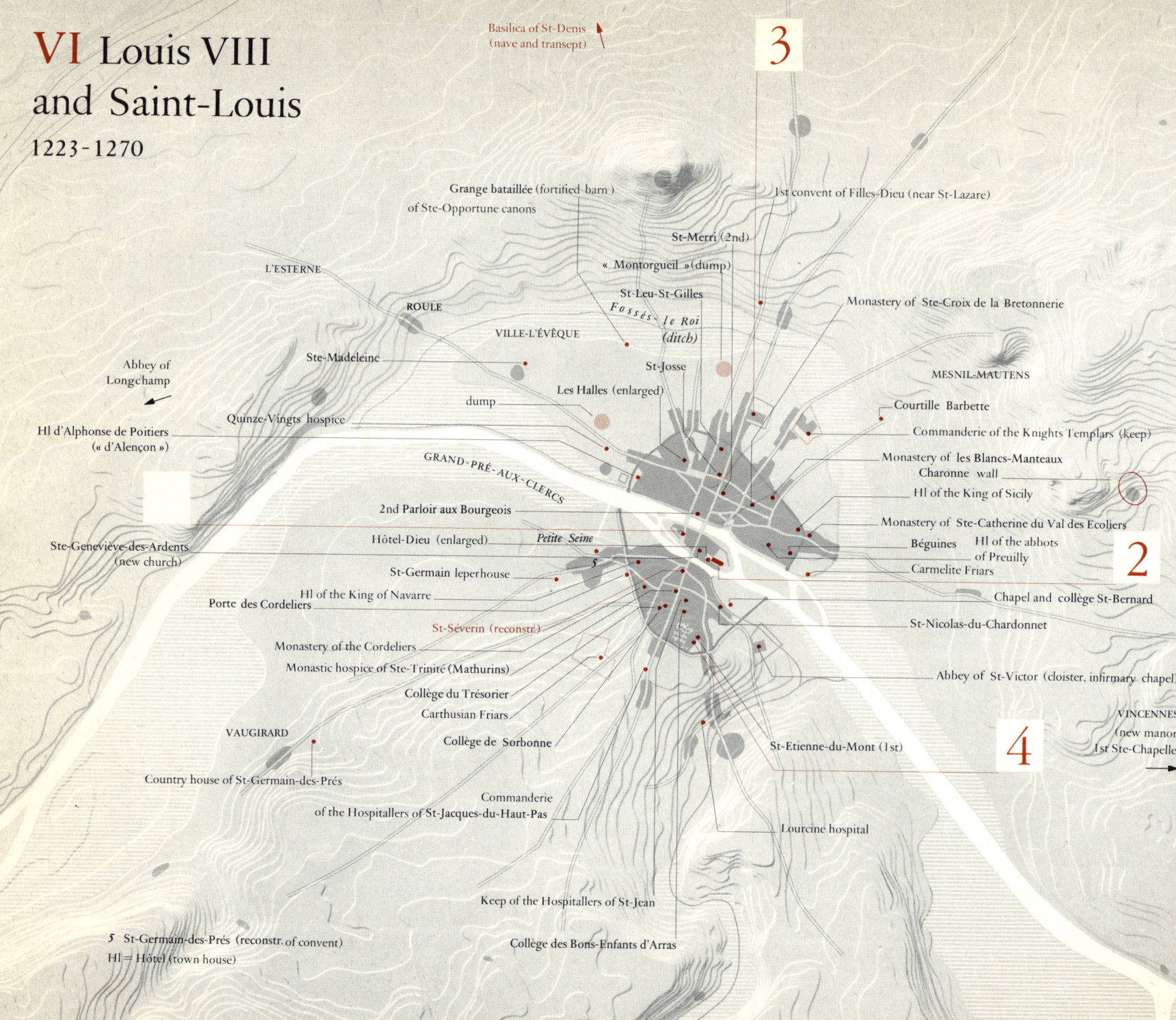

Though hardly finished, the new wall was inadequate for the expansion of Paris along the major roads. The King had to grant permission to build beyond the walls in 1240. (At the gates were formed small mountains of refuse, dumps which would become a part of Parisian topography). Renewed activity animated the Paris basin and its hills. The Commanderie of the Temple and the Seigneurie of the Bishop outside the Porte St-Honoré (gate) formed new population centers. The swamp was used more profitably for vegetable production, rather than grain. In 1260 the King had a sewer (Fossés-le-Roi) cut through the swamp for the waste water of the city. The hill villages across the swamp, now better linked to Paris, began to use it as an outlet. Their growth and that of Les Halles (markets) went hand in hand. The King reorganized the city's administration in 1261; it was divided between the provost of the King (affairs of state) and the provost of the merchants (local affairs). The enlargement of the palace, the work on the cathedral, two new pavilions at Les Halles, the excellence of the university in particular, the proliferation of collèges and convents, the installation of mendicant orders, and the flowering of the Gothic — all contribute to the physiognomy of 13th-century Paris. With St Thomas Aquinas, St Bonaventura, and the foundation of the Collège de Sorbonne, Paris became the capital of high theology. Supported by the Pope and the King, the university was free of the bishop's authority. The renown of the King also made Paris a center of European diplomatic arbitration. Certain fundamental traits took shape; the Parisian countryside would barely change until the 19th century. The role as capital was established, as was government of France, by the Parisians. Ruined by the crusades, the knights of the Ile-de-France entered into the royal administration. Finally, it seems that the change from the ancient Lyon-centered road network to the modern Paris-centered one was realized as early as the 13th century.

1 SAINTE-CHAPELLE. A reconstruction of the old palace chapel, Sainte-Chapelle (The Holy Chapel) was constructed in 33 months, perhaps by Pierre de Montreuil, and was finished and consecrated in 1248. The upper, royal chapel, which sheltered relics of the Passion which were recently bought by Saint Louis from Baudoin, French emperor of Constantinople, was superimposed on a lower, massive chapel for the household. The upper chapel represents the complete mastery of Gothic architecture: the perfect channeling of the weight from the vaults into thin supports allowed the elimination of the walls. They were replaced by windows (49 ft high) which are the oldest and by far the most beautiful in Paris. The famous relics were exhibited on a raised platform in the choir. The façade of Sainte-Chapelle was altered in the 15th and 19th centuries, and the present spire dates from 1857.

2 NOTRE-DAME south transept façade (1258) and north transept portal (1250). With chapels added along the nave, the transepts then became too short and had to be lengthened. Their new façades with immense rose windows (59 by 43 ft open surface) demonstrated the architects' skill and increased the light in the church, a major concern of 13th-century architecture. At this time the upper windows of the nave were enlarged.

3 ST-MARTIN-DES-CHAMPS, monks' refectory (now library of the Conservatoire des Arts et Métiers). The Benedictine abbey of St-Martin was one of the largest religious establishments in Paris. The two-aisled refectory, where the reader's chair still exists, typifies the architecture of the time of Saint Louis in its etheral proportions and abundance of light. It is often attributed to Pierre de Montreuil, but without proof.

4 ABBAYE STE-GENEVIEVE, monks' refectory. It is constructed above the abbey kitchens and has vaults. Today it is the chapel of the Lycée Henri IV and the only remains of the interior arrangement of the medieval abbey.

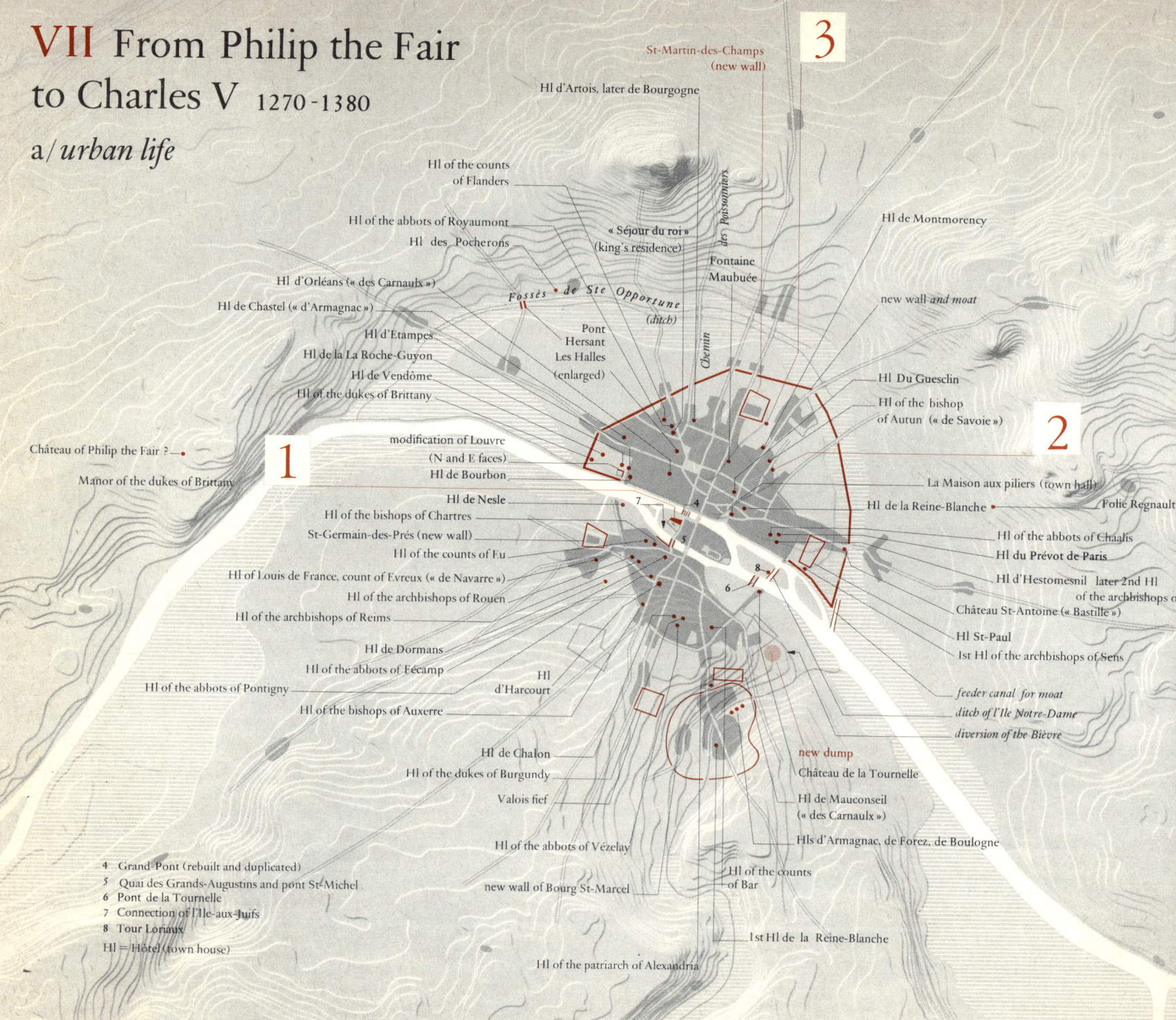

VII From Philip the Fair to Charles V 1270-1380

a/ *urban life*

4 Grand-Pont (rebuilt and duplicated)
5 Quai des Grands-Augustins and pont St-Michel
6 Pont de la Tournelle
7 Connection of l'Ile-aux-Juifs
8 Tour Loriaux
Hl = Hôtel (town house)

The influence of Paris asserted itself under Philip the Fair and his sons, who strengthened centralization. The development of administrative services involved a total reorganization of the palace (1294-1324), followed by an enlargement under Jean le Bon. The war quickly rendered these improvements inadequate by expanding the financial and judiciary functions. Administrative advances furnished data on the city: lists of taxpayers and a census of "hearths" (households) of 1328, the figures of which must bee a copyist's error (61,098 households of 3 or 4 persons; therefore 203,000 people, or 240 per acre against 145 today). The fiscal registers indicate a population of about 80,000 (including roughly 10,000 students), or 74 per acre, a high density for the Middle Ages. Venice, Milan, and Paris were the three big cities of Europe (Ghent had 56,000, London 35-45,000). The works of G. Fourquin confirm the exceptional population of the region: "the greatest density in the entire kingdom, perhaps in the West" (12 per square mile versus 3 for the entire kingdom). The same documents and a record of tithes for 1352 furnish an economic geography of the city: 4/5 of the taxpayers and taxable wealth were on the north bank; the wealthy district extended from the Grève to St-Germain-l'Auxerrois, bypassing La Cité, whose parishes were not much richer than those on the south bank. The trades were spread over a wide area and not tightly grouped on particular streets. Paris experienced a "belle époque," full of expansion: 51 streets outside the walls in 1300, a proliferation of noble houses in the outskirts — near the Louvre, in the Marais, and Mont. Ste-Geneviève. Although the swamps were cultivated, no one dared live in them. Paris took over the fairs of Champagne and from 1300 to 1360 became a center of international finance. As the capital of the only large state in the West, Paris became the principal diplomatic center, the seat of the most renowned university and of a learned administration in which

1 PALAIS DU ROI (Ile de la Cité), magistrates' entrance towers (called Tour de César and Tour d'Argent in the 17th century). Built ca 1301-15 under Philip the Fair, the vaulted five-story towers housed civil and criminal proceedings. Upper part restored, 19th century.

1 PALAIS DU ROI (Ile de la Cité), Salle des Gens d'Armes and kitchens. In remodeling the palace, Philip the Fair replaced the King's chamber and hall with the double-aisled Great Hall (1301-15), below which the lower Great Hall, or Salle des Gens d'Armes, served as foyer and refectory for the servants of the King's household. At that time it was at ground level and opened into the kitchen courtyard. 65 columns support the hall, creating 4 aisles (226 ft long). In 1350 Jean le Bon built new square kitchens, divided into 4 sections, each with a fireplace. Despite the legend, Saint Louis had no part in this construction.

2 HOTEL DE CLISSON (1371). In a cantwall at the corner of a street which has since disappeared, the entrance to the residence of the King's high constable, Olivier de Clisson, is one of the oldest remains of private architecture in Paris, as well as a landmark of the first Marais district, where the nobility established itself near the Hôtel St-Paul

3 HOUSE, RUE VOLTA (ca 1300). The oldest in Paris. Two shops, four floors, a gable (no longer existent). It is a half-timbered house, the most common type in Paris until the middle of the 17th century.

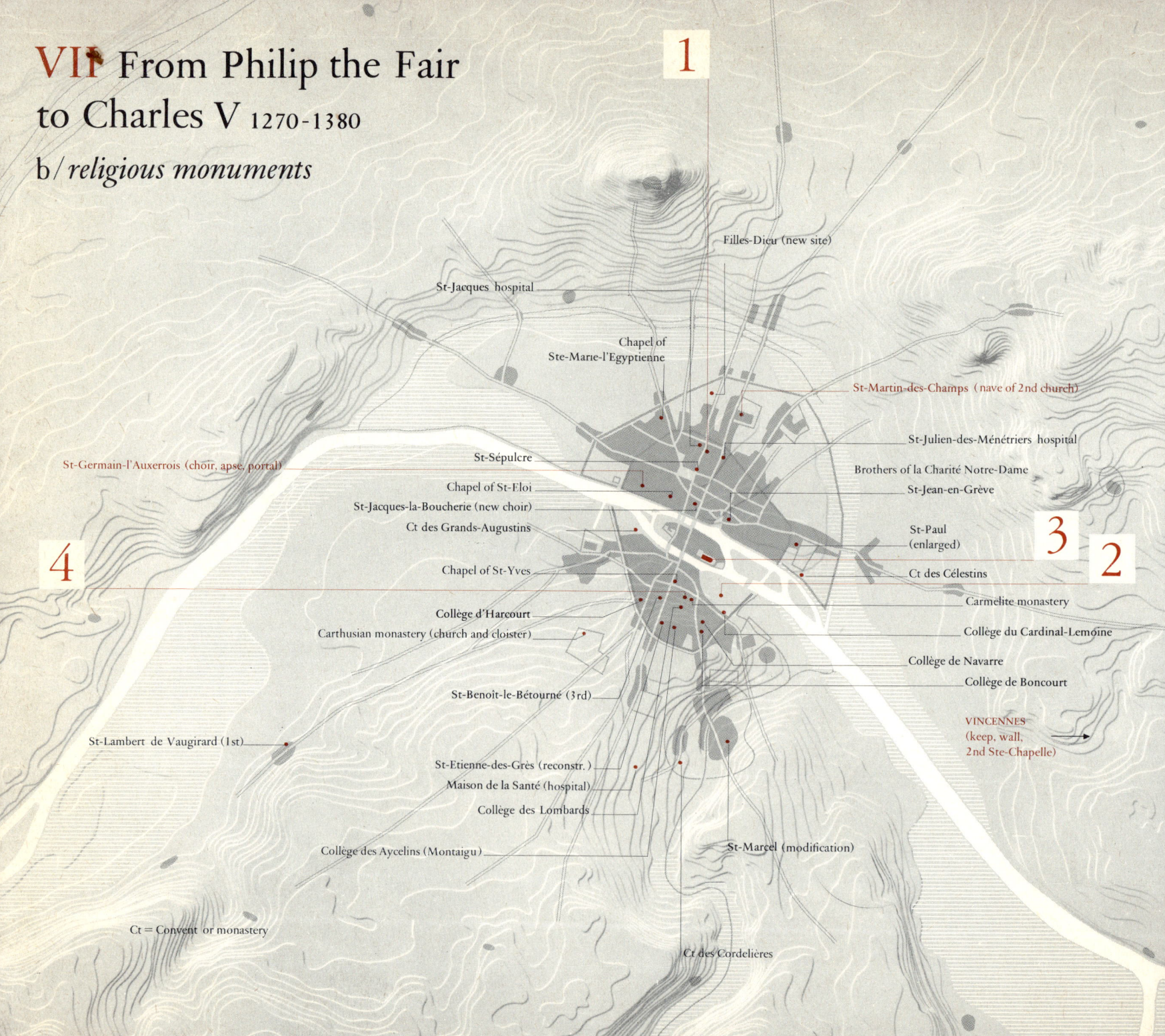

would develop under Charles VI a literate movement heralding the Renaissance (with all that, Paris remained a simple bishopric despite the efforts of Charles V). Plague, war, and troubles tarnished this brilliance. While leprosy disappeared (31 lepers in the 35 diocesan leper hospitals in 1351), the Black Death arrived. No one knows the number of deaths (50 percent of the population of Albi, 70 percent at Bremen, 40-45 percent for the West in general), we know only that in the parish of St-Germain-l'Auxerrois there were 49 times more deaths from June 1348 to March 1350. The importance of Paris made it the political and military stake of the war. From 1356, the provost of merchants, Etienne Marcel, began a new wall on the north bank, continued by Charles V. A wall 26 to 33 ft high, reinforced by 6 bastilles (small fortresses) and a double moat, encompassed 430 acres outside the wall of Philippe Auguste. On the south bank, the wall of Philippe Auguste was modernized (fortified gates, moats requiring the diverting of the Bièvre). Paris now covered 1,084 acres. On the east the wall acted as a dike and isolated a part of the swamp, providing low-cost land for royal and noble residences. The old riverbed protected —and obstructed— Paris until the 17th century. The Parisians gained an awareness of their importance as a support as well as a threat to the King. The municipality was installed in the place de Grève (for which the "Maison aux Piliers" was bought). The first riot of 1306, the intrigues of Etienne Marcel forced Charles V to abandon the palace, which was too central. He enlarged the Louvre but it was locked within the new walls. Thus he prefered the Hôtel St-Paul, near the Bastille, a virtual escape hatch. It was at this time that the idea of installing the King outside Paris was adopted. The château at Vincennes was transformed into a base fortified against Paris.

1 ST-LEU-ST-GILLES (1320 and after). The expiatory offerings of 1315, a year of disasters (storms, famine, epidemic), permitted reconstruction of the church. An example of construction financing in the Middle Ages.

2 COLLEGE ST-BERNARD (1346 and after). It was to house the monks of Citeaux ("Bernardins") sent by their order to the University of Paris to pursue their studies. This "college" was thus a virtual cloistered monastery, with a large chapel (now disappeared) and an immense refectory (262 by 49 ft) with three rib-vaulted aisles, built over a vast cellar. In 1709 the latter was purposely filled in as a precaution against floods from the Seine.

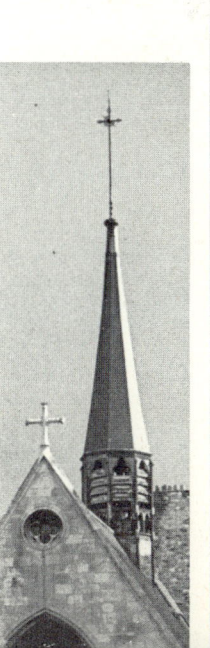

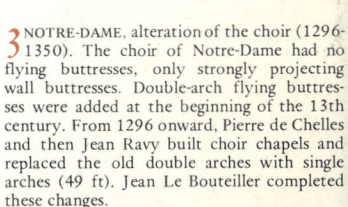

3 NOTRE-DAME, alteration of the choir (1296-1350). The choir of Notre-Dame had no flying buttresses, only strongly projecting wall buttresses. Double-arch flying buttresses were added at the beginning of the 13th century. From 1296 onward, Pierre de Chelles and then Jean Ravy built choir chapels and replaced the old double arches with single arches (49 ft). Jean Le Bouteiller completed these changes.

4 COLLEGE DE BEAUVAIS, or "de Dormans" (1375-80, Raymond du Temple). The 14th-century spire of the much-restored chapel is all that remains of the numerous collèges from this era.

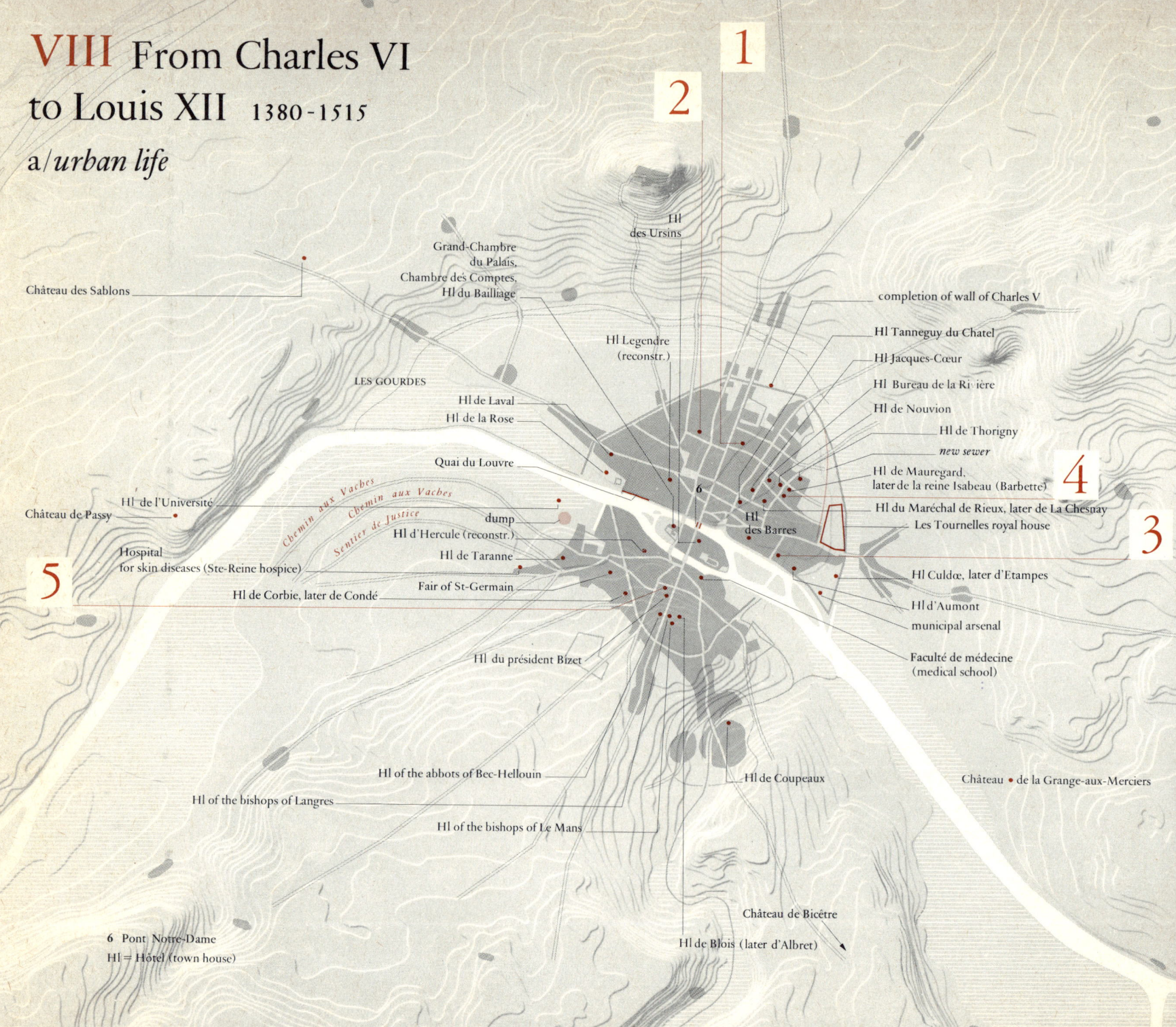

The letters of pardon accorded by Charles VII
show crimes of larceny by the common people,
who were dying of starvation. Meanwhile
the court abandoned the Hôtel St-Paul, too filled
with past drama, for the Hôtel des Tournelles.
Economic recovery began after 1450.
Although the demographic evolution of the city
is unknown, we do know that the region
revived under the initiative of the great landowners
(especially the Chapter of Notre-Dame).
About 1500 the density was again very great,
the rural emigration to Paris renewed. Despite
the efforts of Louis XI, the fair of Lendit
remained only a regional market, and
Paris remained the economic center of a region
with only a 30-125 mi radius. It was a
wine-producing center, shipping wine and wheat
to the Channel and receiving salt, fish, butter, eggs,
and fruit in exchange. Lacking industry,
it attempted a new operation, textile dyeing
(by the Gobelins and the Canaglias on the Bièvre).
Again it outstripped the regional capitals
(Rouen, Bourges, Arras, etc.) revived during
the war. Paris had no bank but was a center of
investment. The land fortunes of the
nobility had escaped the difficulties of the war;
thus the Parisian bourgeoisie could not
invest in land. It put its money into the commerce
of Toulouse, Marseille, and above all Rouen,
whose seagoing aspirations it backed.
The Notre-Dame bridge (1506-12) marked
its return to prosperity. The King held Paris under
his domination (the Provost of merchants
was one of his officers). He intervened
in municipal elections and bridled the university
which, having cast its lot with the English
and Burgundians, had lost its autonomy. This was
the moment when Paris was recognized
as capital of the kingdom (the expression first
appeared in 1415). The King left to live on
the Loire, but the administration remained in Paris.

1 MAISON DE NICOLAS FLAMEL (1407). A rich burgher created this pious foundation which offered lodging to the poor who paid with a daily prayer for the dead. Much restored.

2 HOTEL OF THE DUKES OF BURGUNDY, tower of Jean sans Peur (ca 1400). An addition to the already fortified residence which, in its position alongside the city wall, constituted a fortress thrust into the aristocratic quarter north of St-Eustache.

4 HOTEL HEROUET (ca 1510). The overhanging corner turret, housing a staircase or forming a balcony overlooking an intersection, expanded the house into public space and conferred on it an aristocratic prestige, as in the Hôtel of the Abbots of Fécamp.

3 HOTEL OF THE ARCHBISHOPS OF SENS (1475-1519). Like many dignitaries often called to present themselves at court, the Archbishop of Sens acquired a Parisian residence at an early date. The residence of Archbishop Tristan de Salazar is the third Hôtel de Sens. The defensive appearance of the high walls is not purely ornamental; a loophole is hidden above the gate. The main building housed a spiral stair in a tower dominating the district. That this Gothic residence is contemporaneous with the Renaissance palace of the Duke of Urbino indicates the conservatism of Parisian architecture in the later Middle Ages.

5 HOTEL OF THE ABBOTS OF CLUNY (1485-98), constructed for Abbot Jacques d'Amboise. The great monasteries had residences in Paris for their abbots. With three main buildings, an arcaded courtyard, a chapel, 6 stairways — one in a projecting tower on the façade, following the model established at the Louvre under Charles V — the Hôtel de Cluny is a noble and comfortable residence and a beautiful example of Flamboyant Gothic. The departure of the Court had made Paris a provincial artistic center trailing the Loire valley, and especially Italy: in 1485 the Rucellai, Medici, and Pitti palaces in Florence had existed respectively for 39, 40, and 45 years. This residence is contemporaneous with, yet remote from, the Palazzo della Cancelleria in Rome.

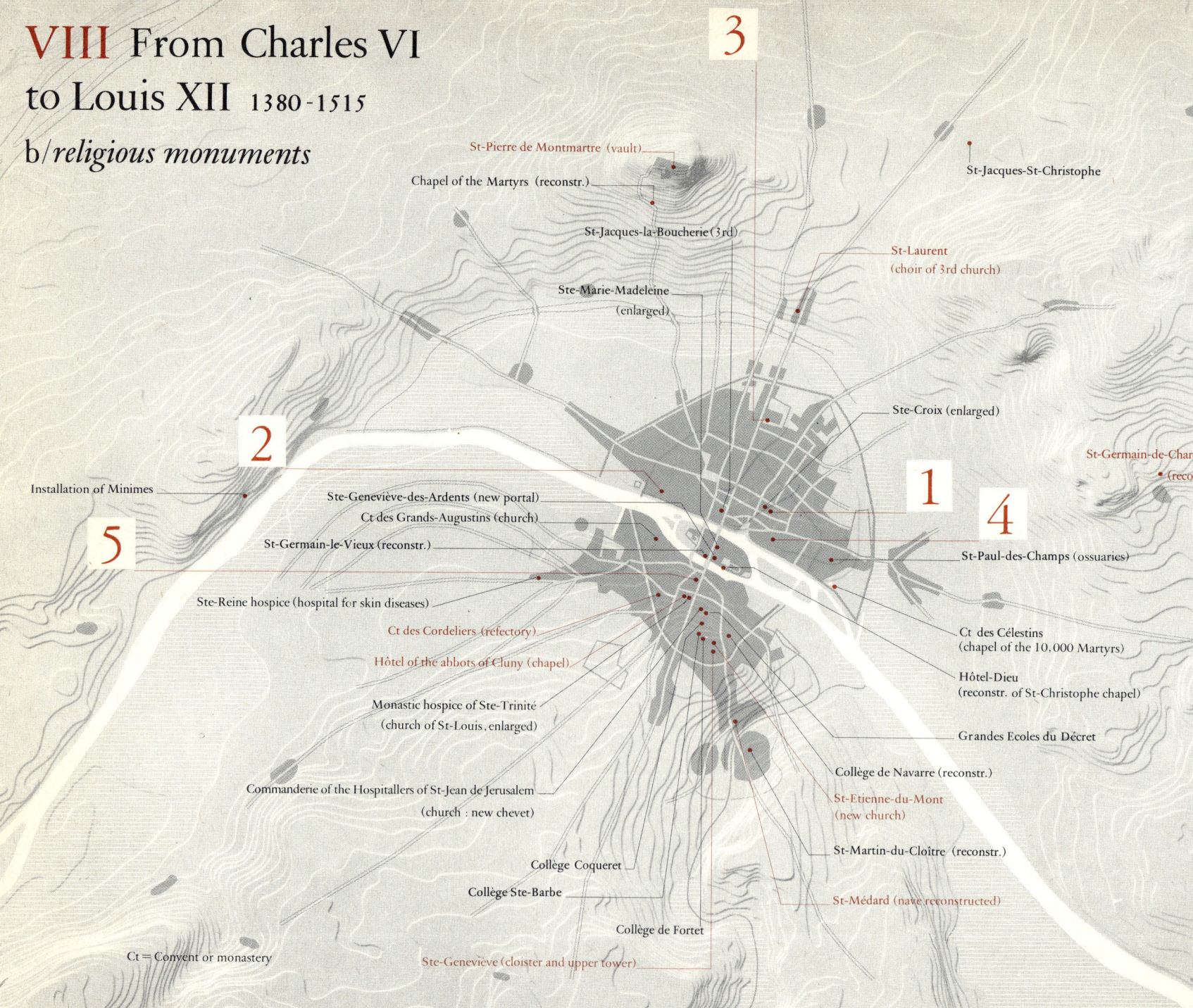

With Charles V dead, riots against the taxes erupted everywhere. As a sanction against the revolt, Paris saw the provostship of merchants and the magistracy suppressed from 1382 to 1411. The public wrath turned on the Jews, who were finally driven out in 1394. But until 1411 the veneer was still brilliant. The new St-Michel bridge linked the palace to the St-André-des-Arts district, peopled by the King's retinue and Parliament. The Pont-Neuf was already being contemplated. An important economic factor was the court, which lived on a grand scale at the Hôtel St-Paul, enlivening business and raising prices (the King's household alone consumed 1/5 to 1/3 of the meat eaten in Paris). There was one problem: inadequate sewage disposal poisoned the Seine, and the dumps, which towered over the ramparts, weakened the defense of the city. The Anglo-Burgundian domination and the civil war ended a Parisian era (1411-36). The return of the city to the King of France (1436) did not clarify the situation. Paris lived for 30 years in an atmosphere of siege, with some of its gates permanently walled up; a generation did not leave the city until adulthood. Still living but ruined by raids, the exhausted countryside was inadequate to provide for Paris; to supplement this, the abounding Seine was intensively fished. Parliament, in the name of public interest, intervened throughout the region to ensure the arrival of provisions, thereby extending the predominance of the city. The English domination of the Seine facilitated a period of provisioning, then proved an impediment when Paris escaped it. Creameries, taverns, and bakers made fortunes, but scarcity, monetary instability, and the affluence of the English garrison made life very expensive. The return of the plague, banishment, and military losses (from escorting convoys) diminished the population. Property declined and abandoned houses, in ruins, were destroyed.

1 MONASTERY OF THE FRERES DE LA CHARITE NOTRE-DAME (Billettes), after 1427. Four galleries in Flamboyant Gothic style, the only remaining medieval cloister in Paris.

2 ST-GERMAIN-L'AUXERROIS, porch (1435-39, J. Gaussel). Borrowed from Burgundian architecture, it is, with that of Sainte-Chapelle, the only church porch in Paris. With its Flamboyant decoration, its five unequal doorways, its complicated vaults, it is contemporary with Brunelleschi's Pazzi Chapel in Florence.

3 ST-NICOLAS-DES-CHAMPS (1420-80). Cautious and rather dull reconstruction in the Flamboyant style, at a very difficult period in the history of Paris.

4 ST-SEVERIN, ossuaries (1428-1608). The cemetery surrounded by cloister galleries is a common type (the Innocents' cemetery). These covered walks were then busy public places.

4 ST-SEVERIN, ambulatory (1489-94). Anti-rational treatment at the conclusion of Gothic: obliteration of functional divisions (moldings fusing into piers), suggestions of movement and lack of balance (ribs obliquely placed).

5 ST-GERVAIS-ST-PROTAIS (1494-1620, Martin Chambiges?). On the threshold of the Renaissance, the pure Gothic of St-Gervais illustrates the weak influence in France of the Flamboyant style.

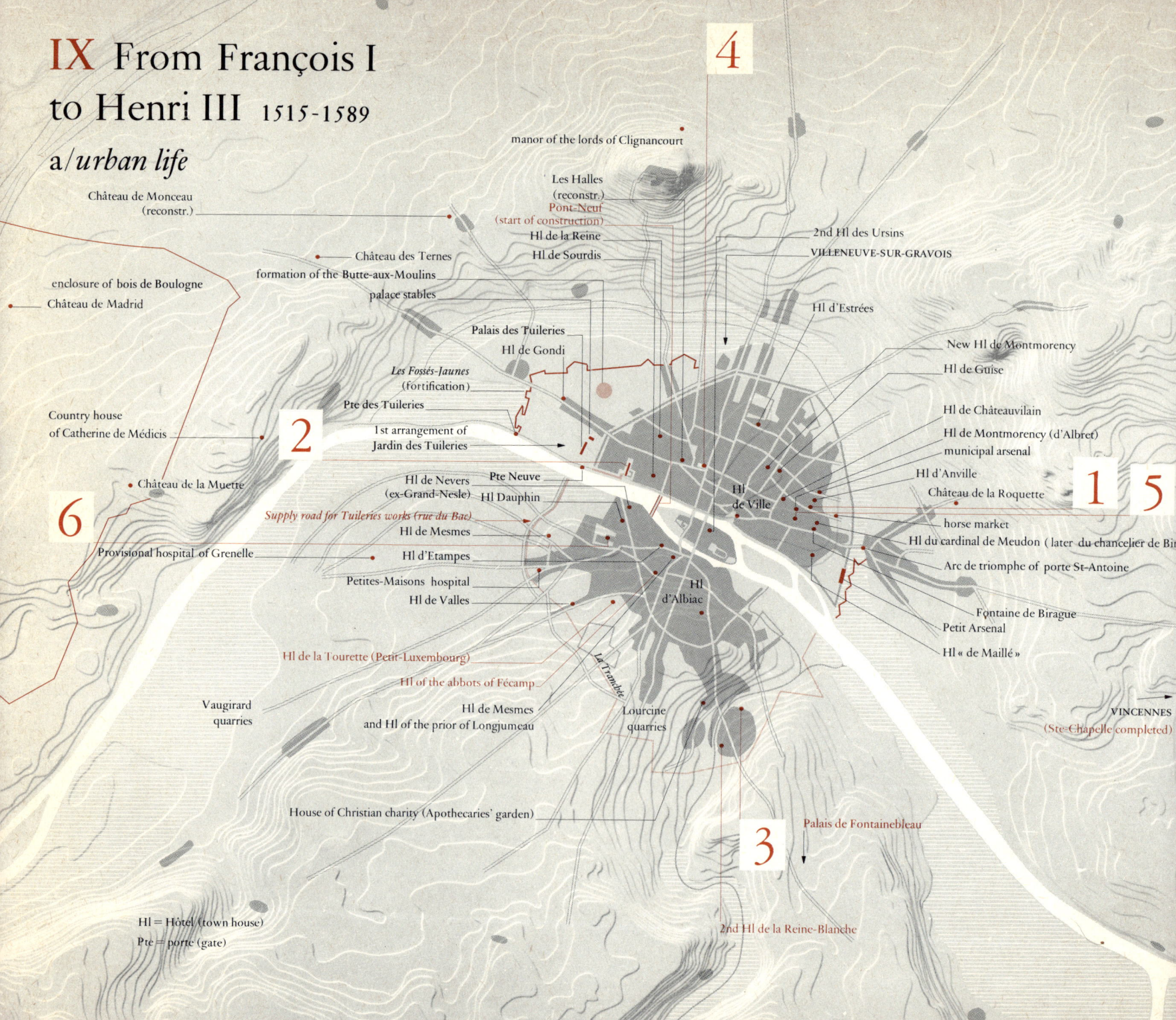

The 16th century witnessed the crisis of medieval Paris, too small for its population, too vast for its defense, too crowded for sanitation, too tortuous for traffic. The city was stifled within its walls, and more important, it reached its physical limit, the swamp on the east and north. The authorities became aware of the problems of the large city (150,000 or 200,000 inhabitants?), the difficulties of provisioning, of police, and of the cost of maintaining an agglomeration growing faster than the revenue. The King tried to check the expansion of the suburbs toward which the Parisians, too, were hostile (they destroyed the surrounding truck farms and sheltered the artisans escaping the fees of the urban trades). Paris expanded within at the expense of its free space. The King liquidated his numerous town houses, from Hôtel St-Paul (1516) to the Hôtel des Tournelles (1565). All these were parceled out without coordinated plan. Even dumps became building sites (Villeneuve-sur-Gravois). Still the suburbs extended to the south and west, where a long evolution began with the renovation of the Louvre (1531 and after) and especially with the construction of the Tuileries palace, the latter outside the walls on a swamp embankment (1563 and after). The protection built for the palace opened up the western extension of the city. With the Hapsburgs in Artois, Paris was close to the northern frontier and therefore, with its arsenal, a principal military base. But the wall was outdated. Shrinking from the cost of a new one, they tried to repair the old by partial modernizations following each alarm (the excavated material creating the Butte-aux-Moulins). But when the wars of religion exposed the Tuileries to raids, a fortified front called the "fossés jaunes" (yellow trenches) was begun (1566), forming a dam at the end of the palace gardens. Rents rose. Even by 1550 a modest salary could no longer rent a complete house.

1 HOTEL DE LIGNERIS, later Kernevenoy, called Carnavalet (1544, Pierre Lescot?). French-style town house, between court and garden, with decorative emphasis (J. Goujon).

2 PALAIS DU LOUVRE, wings of François I and Henri II (1546 and after, Goujon and Lescot). The Louvre had been abandoned since 1380 when François I began its modernization by tearing down the keep. He already had three Renaissance palaces: Amboise, Blois, Chambord. As superintendant of the palace (1547-63), Lescot directed the remodeling, perhaps from a distance, assisted by Goujon (the real originator?). Entirely new, without Italian precedent, the façade superimposes antique forms with mastery. In 1594 the similar wing of Henri II was incomplete, the small gallery limited to a ground floor and only the foundations of the large gallery done.

2 PALAIS DU LOUVRE (1550, Lescot, Goujon). Musicians' Tribune. Michelangelo and J. Martin's translation of Vitruvius (illustrated by Goujon) had restored caryatids to fashion.

3 HOTEL SCIPION SARDINI (1565). Constructed by the Italian financier in the style of his country: semicircular arcades, walls decorated with medallions. Last splendid building in the Bièvre valley.

4 FONTAINE DES INNOCENTS (1548-49, Goujon). Situated on a street corner, originally a tribune of three loggias on a tall base. Its decoration made it a manifesto of the Renaissance in a center of medieval grimness.

5 HOTEL D'ANGOULEME, called Hôtel Lamoignon (1584-86, J. Thiriot). Its façade reveals the groping of the architect in dealing with antique forms. A correct colossal Order extends to two floors, but the entablature is truncated by third-floor windows, while the pediment is virtually destroyed by a low window which penetrates it.

6 ST-GERMAIN-DES-PRES, Abbey Palace (1586, G. Marchant). Appearance of a more severe style, in which Renaissance decoration is canceled by coloristic effects (stone, slate, brick).

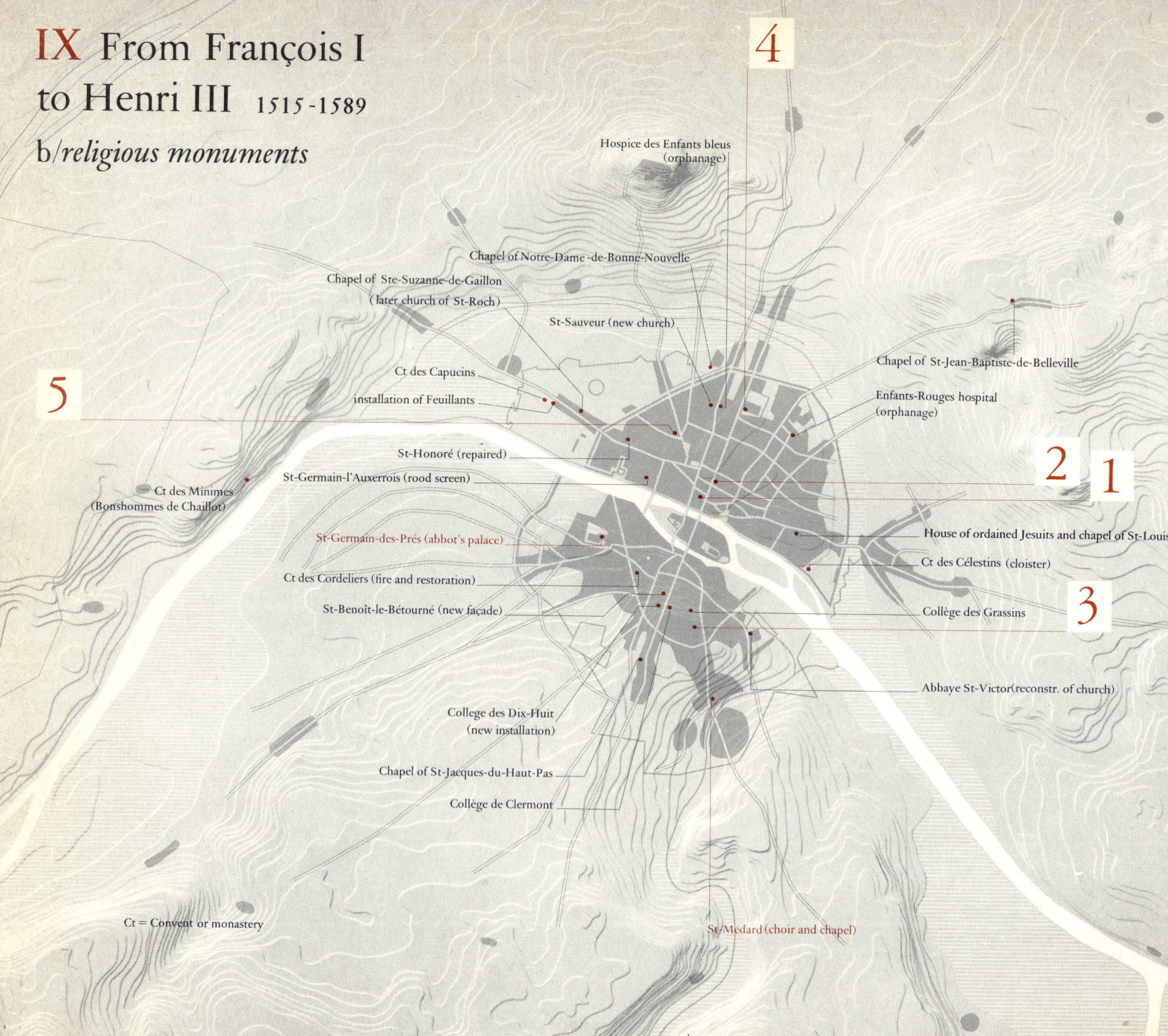

Paris lacked sufficient water; there was no fountain on the south bank. Medieval customs with regard to cleanliness disappeared. Certain districts were foul-smelling: Les Tournelles because of the sewer, Maubert of the old Bièvre. The example of modern hospitals in Italy and the return of epidemics led to the creation of a contagious disease ward at the Hôtel-Dieu (1532) and a provisional hospital at Grenelle (1580). Traffic became choked; François I called for straight, aligned streets and had a wide stone quay built from the Louvre to the Châtelet. The bridge project at the end of La Cité was resumed in 1577, then stopped. In 1563 Parliament called for the prohibition of private carriages. Economic activity seems to have declined; Paris now exported nothing and redistributed little. Textile dyeing disappeared. Nevertheless Paris remained a major investment center (in Rouen, Marseille, Antwerp markets), but its capital was turned to land purchases and rent. In 1522 the King sold the city the right to revenues which he had formerly collected there. With these, the city established municipal bonds (rentes de l'Hôtel de Ville) which were very profitable after 1551. The Parisian civil servant and bond-holding classes formed at this time an unfavorable development for the economic dynamism of the city. Paris lent money to the King, prided itself on the new Hôtel de Ville, and resented the increasing fiscal burden. At the same time, it lost its religious unity: the first execution of Protestants was in 1523, the first barricades in 1557. The population lost patience with the King's tolerance; most executions were mob lynchings. The fight against Protestantism revived the declining Sorbonne, but it also roused fanatic preachers who urged the people to massacre (some 2,000 killed at St-Barthélemy and to organize militarily against Protestants. In 1588 Paris revolted against the King, who tried to stop these preachers. In 1589 the city was besieged by the King. Declared guilty of felony, it was stripped of all rights and privileges.

1 ST-JACQUES-DE-LA-BOUCHERIE, south tower (1509-23 Jean de Felin). Serving a bourgeois parish with traditional tastes: pure Flamboyant style at the time of Raphael and Bramante.

2 ST-MERRI (1510-52). Reconstruction of the church in Flamboyant Gothic, at the zenith of the St-Merri district, when the rich bourgeoisie acceded to the nobility.

3 ST-ETIENNE-DU-MONT, nave (1492-1584). A church of an exceptional transitional type: a general Gothic plan without pronounced transept, an ogival choir (1537-40), semicircular Renaissance nave arcades (1580-84), aisles almost as high as the nave — realizing the German type of hall-church — a late Gothic asymmetrical tower, a rood screen (1525-35) and walkway. The views from the ambulatory toward the upper parts of the transept reveal a complex space, in which screens of openwork interweave (piers, rood screen, walkway and windows).

4 ST-NICOLAS-DES-CHAMPS, South portal (1575). Repeating a portal for Les Tournelles by Delorme, it introduced the purest High Renaissance style to Paris, a distant echo of the façades of Alberti (S. Andrea of Mantua).

5 ST-EUSTACHE (1532-1640). The conception of the Gothic ensemble gives the building its grandeur. Only the details of the forms carry the imprint of the Renaissance: semicircular arches, pilasters, fluted columns — incongruities in a Gothic structure, considering that the true Renaissance church was inspired by Roman, Byzantine, or Romanesque structures.

5 ST-EUSTACHE, south portal. Built a little after 1532. Renaissance motifs are awkwardly applied to the schema of a still traditional ensemble. The portal evokes the Gothic style too much not to seem dry in comparison; illogically, statues decorate the lateral pilasters like the buttresses separating cathedral portals.

X Henri IV and Louis XIII 1589-1643

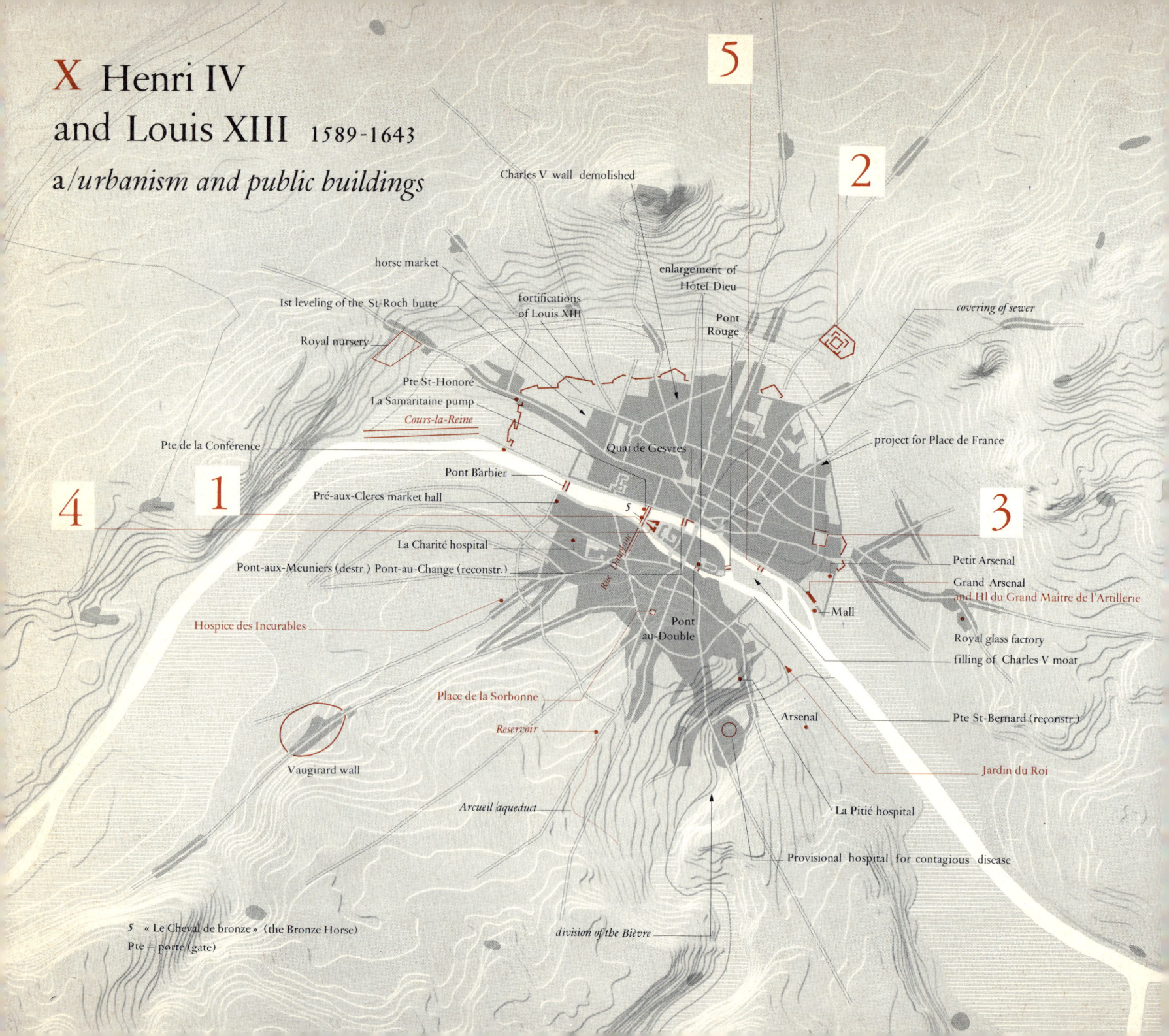

a/urbanism and public buildings

- Charles V wall demolished
- horse market
- 1st leveling of the St-Roch butte
- fortifications of Louis XIII
- enlargement of Hôtel-Dieu
- Royal nursery
- covering of sewer
- Pte St-Honoré
- La Samaritaine pump
- Pont Rouge
- Cours-la-Reine
- Pte de la Conférence
- Quai de Gesvres
- project for Place de France
- Pont Barbier
- Pré-aux-Clercs market hall
- La Charité hospital
- Rue Dauphine
- Pont-aux-Meuniers (destr.) Pont-au-Change (reconstr.)
- Petit Arsenal
- Grand Arsenal and Hl du Grand Maître de l'Artillerie
- Mall
- Hospice des Incurables
- Pont au-Double
- Royal glass factory
- filling of Charles V moat
- Place de la Sorbonne
- Reservoir
- Arsenal
- Pte St-Bernard (reconstr.)
- Vaugirard wall
- Jardin du Roi
- Arcueil aqueduct
- La Pitié hospital
- Provisional hospital for contagious disease
- division of the Bièvre

5 « Le Cheval de bronze » (the Bronze Horse)
Pte = porte (gate)

A general urban growth occurred from the end of the wars of religion until 1640, reflecting perhaps a population increase. At the same time, until about 1630-40, the economic situation improved. Paris experienced one of its greatest expansions; its territory grew by 1/3. According to the figures of the times, its population was 200,000 in 1590 and 400,000 in 1637. Henri IV, entering Paris in 1594, had inherited a ruined city: razed suburbs, rents reduced by 1/3 and even unpaid, poverty-stricken mobs ready for anything. A custom of violence had provoked merciless repression by the King and his comrade, the provost of merchants François Miron. Henri IV was unable to establish a controlling plan such as that which Amsterdam had after 1607, but he had a public-works program which revived the city as well as enhanced the King's prestige. His principle was to juxtapose the old districts with more open and ordered ensembles linked to the old city. Work on the Pont-Neuf was resumed (freed of houses to preserve the view of the Louvre) which was extended by the rue Dauphine to the south. The Place Dauphine and its quays rose at the center on an embankment over the little island at the end of La Cité. To the north it was impossible to penetrate the urban fabric; the Pont-Neuf was less a bridge than a public square. In the Marais, there were two big operations: the Place Royale on the unsold lots of Les Tournelles, which was to have been an economic center (silk manufacturing), became instead a monumental promenade sheltered from traffic, the center of an aristocratic district; the projected Place de France would have been the monumental entrance to Paris. The King made the alignment of houses obligatory in 1607 and prohibited overhanging stories and wood construction. But these restrictions went largely unheeded. He tried to reestablish the balance between the two banks (35 new streets on the right bank, 33 on the left).

1 PONT DES AUGUSTINS, or Pont-Neuf bridge (1578-1606). Begun in 1578, the south part by Jean-Baptiste Androuet du Cerceau and the north part by Des Illes, the work was soon interrupted, then brought to completion from 1598 to 1606. Built on 12 round arches, it gave Parisians the spectacle of the Seine, hidden by houses on the other bridges.

2 HOPITAL ST-LOUIS (1607-11, Vellefaux?). A rural annex of the Hôtel-Dieu for victims of the plague, its buildings were carefully isolated. It was open only in times of epidemics.

3 PLACE ROYALE, called Place des Vosges (1607-12, Vellefaux?). The first planned square in Paris; previously there had been only intersections. On the site of the horse market, the square took its present form in 1608 (after the failure of a silk factory which bordered it): a square of 321-ft sides surrounded by 38 pavilions, on arcades, of stone and roughcast rubble imitating brick. Enclosed within itself, sheltered from traffic, the square was a meeting place for social promenade, not a crossroads. It recalls certain medieval collective courts, the tradition of which was likewise pursued in England (i.e., Gray's Inn, 1600, in London). Severe constraints have preserved its unity.

4 PLACE DAUPHINE (1607 and after). For the first work on the Pont-Neuf, the water-level islets at the end of La Cité had been filled in. In 1607 the King ceded the land to the Président de Harlay, who was commissioned to create a regular square there. A triangle bordered by 32 uniform houses, the Place Dauphine was a forum sheltered from city traffic; access was through only two narrow passages. With no subsequent restrictions imposed, the square gradually lost its original aspect.

5 PONT-MARIE (bridge, 1618-35, Marie). With the development of the Ile St-Louis, the bridge partially collapsed in 1658 and was rebuilt. This rebuilt bridge supported houses.

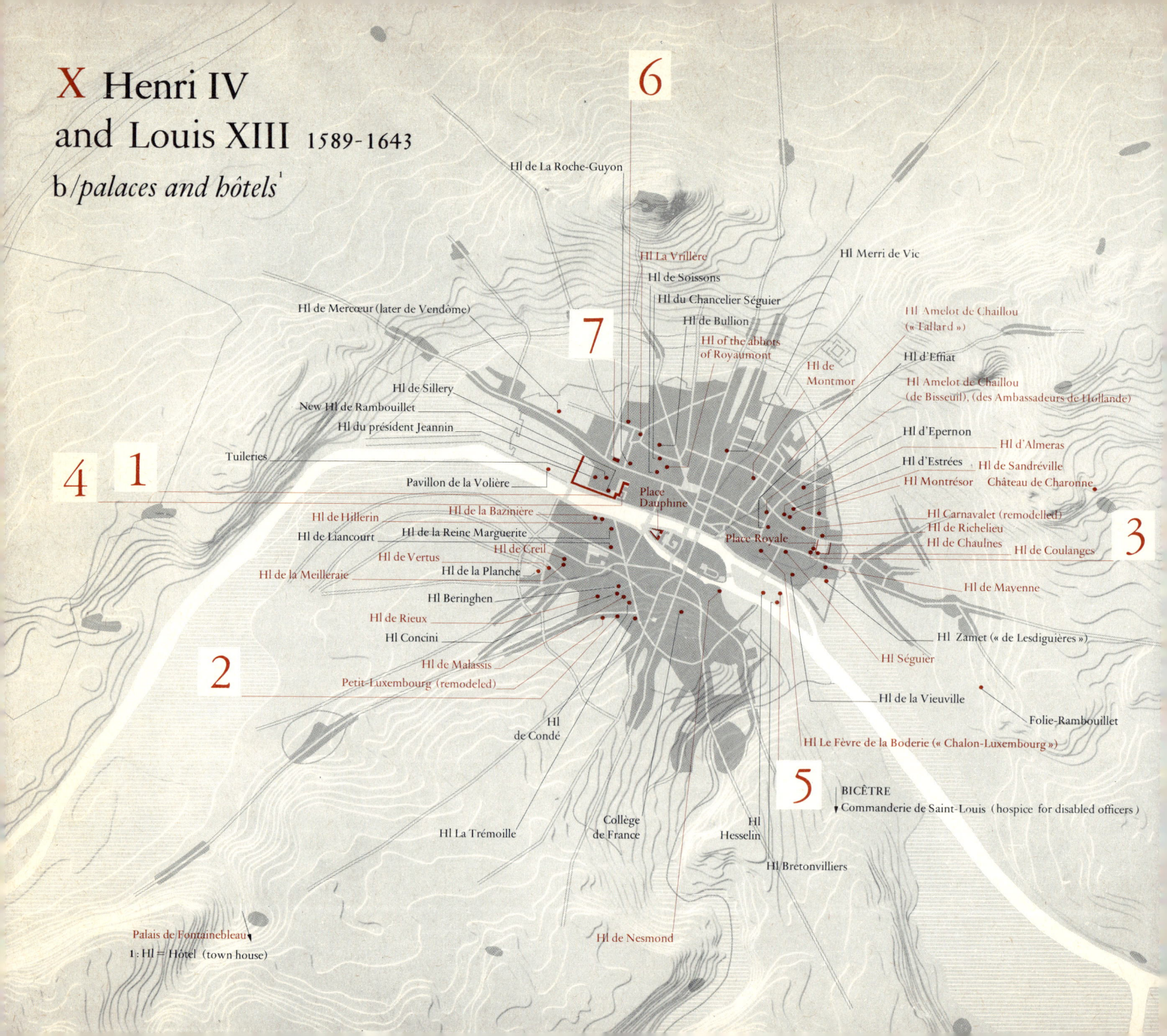

X Henri IV and Louis XIII 1589-1643
b/*palaces and hôtels*[1]

Hl de La Roche-Guyon

Hl La Vrillère
Hl de Soissons
Hl Merri de Vic
Hl du Chancelier Séguier
Hl de Mercœur (later de Vendôme)
Hl de Bullion
Hl Amelot de Chaillou (« Tallard »)
Hl of the abbots of Royaumont
Hl d'Effiat
Hl de Montmor
Hl Amelot de Chaillou (de Bisseuil), (des Ambassadeurs de Hollande)
Hl de Sillery
New Hl de Rambouillet
Hl du président Jeannin
Hl d'Epernon
Tuileries
Hl d'Almeras
Hl d'Estrées
Hl de Sandréville
Pavillon de la Volière
Place Dauphine
Hl Montrésor Château de Charonne
Hl de Hillerin Hl de la Bazinière
Hl Carnavalet (remodelled)
Hl de Liancourt Hl de la Reine Marguerite
Place Royale
Hl de Richelieu
Hl de Creil
Hl de Chaulnes
Hl de Vertus
Hl de Coulanges
Hl de la Meilleraie Hl de la Planche
Hl Beringhen
Hl de Mayenne
Hl de Rieux
Hl Concini
Hl Zamet (« de Lesdiguières »)
Hl de Malassis
Hl Séguier
Petit-Luxembourg (remodeled)
Hl de la Vieuville
Folie-Rambouillet
Hl de Condé
Hl Le Fèvre de la Boderie (« Chalon-Luxembourg »)

BICÊTRE
↓ Commanderie de Saint-Louis (hospice for disabled officers)

Hl La Trémoille Collège de France Hl Hesselin
Hl Bretonvilliers

↓ Palais de Fontainebleau
1: Hl = Hôtel (town house)

Hl de Nesmond

but in joining the Louvre to the Tuileries he created
a half-mile separation. Public irresponsibility
broke down his efforts to pave the streets
and organize the disposal of waste. The Pont-Neuf
pump (Samaritaine) relieved the water
shortage slightly. Efforts to improve hospitalization
culminated in the creation of the St-Louis
hospital, with isolated buildings, outside the city.
Under Louis XIII, expansion was uncontrolled
and explosive, dominated by speculators
such as Barbier or Marie. They parceled out
the Pré-aux-Clercs, despite the university's
resistance, and the Ile-aux-Vaches (Ile St-Louis),
despite that of the cathedral chapter.
By resuming the rampart of the yellow trenches
and destroying the wall of Charles V behind
it, they laid their hands on the new district (now
Palais-Royal) where Richelieu built his
palace. The encircling truck farms were overrun
and the dumps transferred beyond the swamp.
In 40 years rents multiplied 5 and 10 times, the
price of land 60 times. Monasteries invested
in property, since construction was cheap. Constant
complaints were directed against speculators,
the owners of 20 or 30 houses who raised
their rents even higher when the court was absent
to turn their loss to a gain. The south bank
was revived by the construction of the Medici
palace (Luxembourg); the Arcueil
aqueduct which supplied it put an end to the lack
of water paralyzing the district. But the Bièvre,
whose water was reduced by the aqueduct
and by the first draining at Versailles, silted up,
poisoning the Seine. They considered diverting it
toward Chaillot. Hydraulics were fashionable,
and to the north they wanted to reinstall the old
riverbed as a canal. One problem irritated
the Parisians: the proliferation of coaches (325 in
1610). Noisy and cumbersome, they circulated
with much difficulty. Thus the promenade
reserved for coaches appeared (Cours-la-Reine).

1 PALAIS DU LOUVRE, Galerie du bord de l'eau (along the Seine). After 1594 the small gallery was finished and the large gallery connecting the Louvre and the unfinished Tuileries resumed (L. Métezeau and J. Du Cerceau architects). Henri IV planned a symmetrical north wing and the razing of houses between the Louvre and Tuileries palaces.

2 PALAIS MEDICIS (1615-25, Salomon de Brosse, a typically Parisian plan, despite some Italian touches: ashlar masonry, entrance with cupola (third dome in Paris).

3 HOTEL MESME GALLET, later Hôtel Sully (1624, J. du Cerceau). Renaissance in its sculptured decoration, luxurious in its use of large dressed stones, costly and exceptional in Paris.

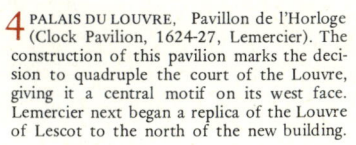

4 PALAIS DU LOUVRE, Pavillon de l'Horloge (Clock Pavilion, 1624-27, Lemercier). The construction of this pavilion marks the decision to quadruple the court of the Louvre, giving it a central motif on its west face. Lemercier next began a replica of the Louvre of Lescot to the north of the new building.

5 HOTEL LAMBERT DE THORIGNY (1640, Le Vau). Distinction between the showy court and stairway and the comfortable garden suite.

6 HOTEL DURET DE CHEVRY, later Hôtel Tubeuf (1635-42, J. Thircot). In a fashionable district, its construction in brick and stone reflects the owner's country château.

7 PALAIS CARDINAL (1624-45, Lemercier). Of Richelieu's town house, with its severe exterior and pointed roofs, only the gallery of prows remains.

X Henri IV and Louis XIII 1589-1643

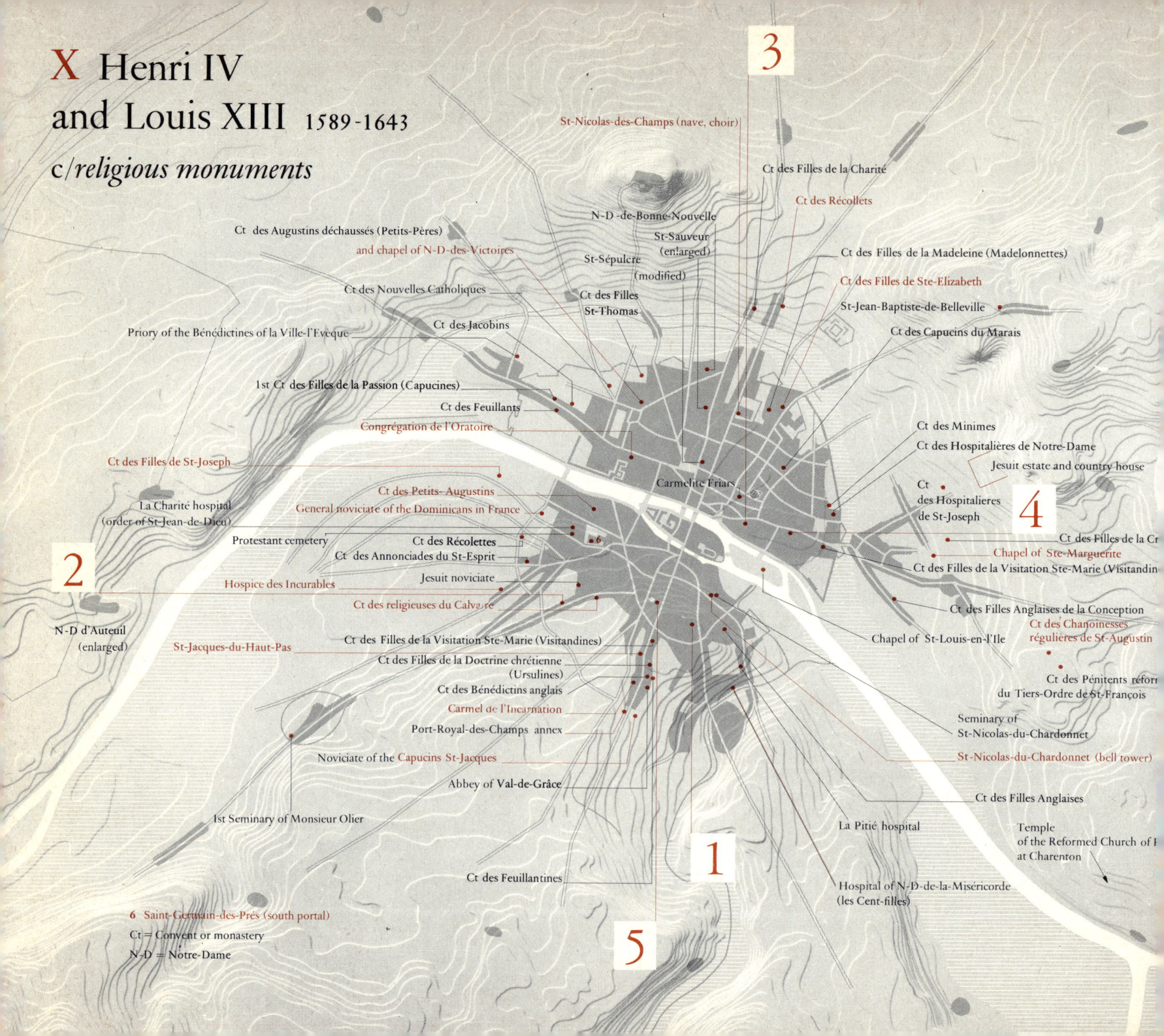

c/*religious monuments*

St-Nicolas-des-Champs (nave, choir)

Ct des Filles de la Charité

Ct des Récollets

Ct des Augustins déchaussés (Petits-Pères) and chapel of N-D-des-Victoires

N-D-de-Bonne-Nouvelle
St-Sauveur (enlarged)
St-Sépulcre (modified)

Ct des Filles de la Madeleine (Madelonnettes)

Ct des Nouvelles Catholiques

Ct des Filles Ste-Elizabeth

Ct des Filles St-Thomas

St-Jean-Baptiste-de-Belleville

Priory of the Bénédictines of la Ville-l'Evêque

Ct des Jacobins

Ct des Capucins du Marais

1st Ct des Filles de la Passion (Capucines)

Ct des Feuillants

Congrégation de l'Oratoire

Ct des Minimes
Ct des Hospitalières de Notre-Dame

Ct des Filles de St-Joseph

Jesuit estate and country house

La Charité hospital (order of St-Jean-de-Dieu)

Ct des Petits-Augustins
General noviciate of the Dominicans in France

Carmelite Friars

Ct des Hospitalières de St-Joseph

Protestant cemetery

Ct des Récolettes
Ct des Annonciades du St-Esprit

Ct des Filles de la Cr
Chapel of Ste-Marguerite
Ct des Filles de la Visitation Ste-Marie (Visitandin

Hospice des Incurables

Jesuit noviciate

Ct des religieuses du Calvaire

Ct des Filles Anglaises de la Conception

N-D d'Auteuil (enlarged)

St-Jacques-du-Haut-Pas

Ct des Filles de la Visitation Ste-Marie (Visitandines)

Chapel of St-Louis-en-l'Ile

Ct des Chanoinesses régulières de St-Augustin

Ct des Filles de la Doctrine chrétienne (Ursulines)

Ct des Pénitents réforr du Tiers-Ordre de St-François

Ct des Bénédictins anglais

Carmel de l'Incarnation

Seminary of St-Nicolas-du-Chardonnet

Port-Royal-des-Champs annex

St-Nicolas-du-Chardonnet (bell tower)

Noviciate of the Capucins St-Jacques

Abbey of Val-de-Grâce

Ct des Filles Anglaises

1st Seminary of Monsieur Olier

La Pitié hospital

Temple of the Reformed Church of at Charenton

Ct des Feuillantines

Hospital of N-D-de-la-Miséricorde (les Cent-filles)

6 Saint-Germain-des-Prés (south portal)

Ct = Convent or monastery
N-D = Notre-Dame

Despite the Edict of Nantes, religious peace remained precarious. The Protestants – about 20,000 in the region – could not practice their worship in Paris; their church was at Grigny first, then at Ablon, finally at Charenton (1606). They encountered great intolerance. Every Sunday evening they were awaited at Rue St-Antoine by rabble and students spoiling for a fight. Custom and the flogger's whip took a long time to quiet the provocateurs. Badly impeded, Protestantism stagnated and lost followers. On the contrary, Catholic dynamism was remarkable, renovating the very appearance of the city. Foreign orders were introduced (Carmelites, Ursulines, Oratorians), new ones created (the Visitandines by St Francis de Sales), great monasteries reformed (Ste-Geneviève, Montmartre, St-Germain-des-Prés, etc.). From 1600 to 1639, 60 monasteries were founded, creating entire religious districts. Great efforts were made to educate girls (Ursulines, Filles de la Croix), to aid the poor (Filles de la Charité founded 1633 by St Vincent de Paul), and to convert. Paris was a center of missions organized by the mendicants, by St Vincent de Paul and by Abbé Bourdoise, the priest of St-Nicolas-du-Chardonnet. The religious difficulties had revealed not only the primitive and superficial character of popular religion but also the weaknesses in the training of the parish clergy; seminaries appeared from 1629 to 1642, the date of the seminary of the priest Olier at Vaugirard, later at St-Sulpice. A renewed clergy and the spread of a religious spirit throughout the austere Parisian bourgeoisie revived parish life. Paris, elevated to an archbishopric in 1622, was also the refuge and capital of the persecuted English Catholics, who made important contributions.

1 ST-ETIENNE-DU-MONT, façade (1606-1622, Cl. Guérin). The illogical and sprightly combination of antique forms reveals the architect's inexperience with Italian novelty and does not hide the fundamentally Gothic structure of the church.

2 ST-JOSEPH-DES-CARMES (1613-20). The first domes in Paris (Petits-Augustins in 1608, then the Carmelite Friars) were artificial wooden and plaster shells, timidly imitating the much earlier stone domes of Italy (Cathedral of Florence, 1420-34; St-Peter's in Rome, 1558-90).

3 ST-GERVAIS, façade (1616-20, Clément Métezeau). A decisive stage following the groping of St-Etienne-du-Mont. All traces of Gothic have disappeared. The stories are clearly articulated in the façade, the Orders correctly superimposed: Tuscan, Ionic and Corinthian.

4 ST-LOUIS-DES-JESUITES, façade (1627-41, R.P. Derrand). It imitates the façade of St-Gervais, not that of Il Gesù in Rome as has often been said. Its height completely obscures the dôme.

4 ST-LOUIS-DES-JESUITES, nave (1627-41, R.P. Martellange). An aisleless nave, covered by a dome over the crossing of the transepts. It followed the plan of Il Gesù, prototype of the style wrongly called Jesuit, and introduced Roman Baroque to Paris.

5 STE-URSULE DE LA SORBONNE (1635-42, Lemercier). This church introduced to Paris the Baroque façade (in Rome, Il Gesù, 1575, and Santa Susanna, 1597) and was taller than its models. For the first time, the dome crowns the façade. There is a second façade, the portico of which is inspired by that of the Panthéon.

XI The reign of Louis XIV 1643-1715
a/urbanism

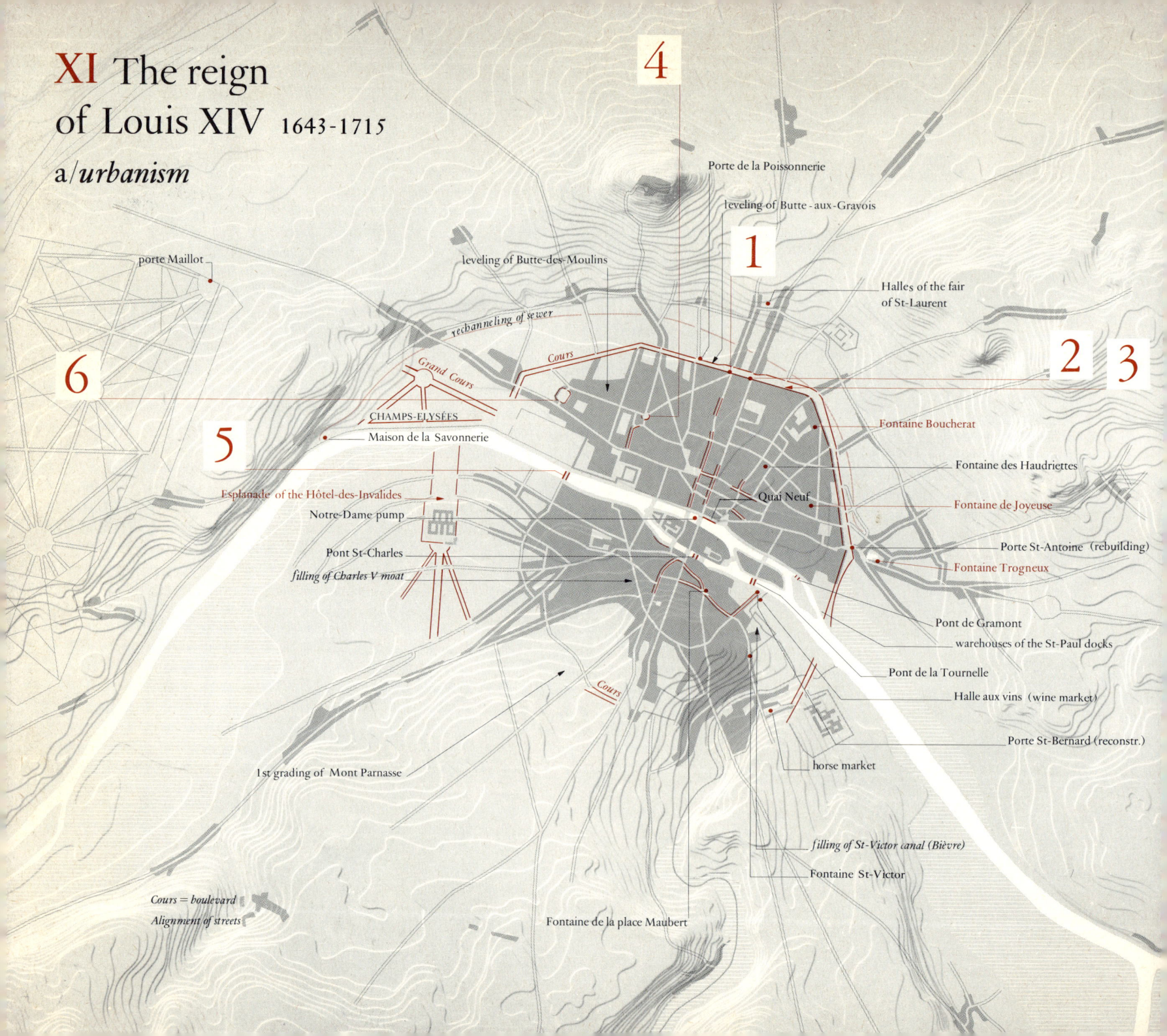

porte Maillot

Porte de la Poissonnerie

leveling of Butte-aux-Gravois

leveling of Butte-des-Moulins

Halles of the fair of St-Laurent

rechanneling of sewer

Grand Cours

Cours

Fontaine Boucherat

CHAMPS-ÉLYSÉES

Maison de la Savonnerie

Fontaine des Haudriettes

Esplanade of the Hôtel-des-Invalides

Quai Neuf

Fontaine de Joyeuse

Notre-Dame pump

Pont St-Charles

Porte St-Antoine (rebuilding)

filling of Charles V moat

Fontaine Trogneux

Pont de Gramont

warehouses of the St-Paul docks

Pont de la Tournelle

Halle aux vins (wine market)

Cours

Porte St-Bernard (reconstr.)

1st grading of Mont Parnasse

horse market

filling of St-Victor canal (Bièvre)

Fontaine St-Victor

Cours = boulevard
Alignment of streets

Fontaine de la place Maubert

As part of the general European slump beginning about 1630-40 and the depression of 1650-1730, the growth of Paris slowed under Louis XIV after making extraordinary strides under Henri IV and Louis XIII. The Fronde insurrection coincided with the general deterioration. The outskirts of Paris were ravaged (the bourgeoisie profited from this by buying abandoned lands), and the city remained much affected during the 1650s. The middle classes and the religious orders — especially female — suffered more than the artisans, who maintained their high prices. The greediness of the merchants increased the high cost of living. Rents went down again. Caught with declining revenues (farms and houses) when the city was overrun by the poor, the hospital system could not help them. A group organization, the general hospital of Paris, housed 10,000 out of 48,000 beggars and tried to give them trades (1657). Charity dried up. St Vincent de Paul had to refuse help to the provinces but took the Protestants under his protection, handicapped as they were by their small numbers and disorganization. Each year 300 or 400 children were abandoned, and an inquest revealed that 600 infanticides were confessed in one year. The King and Colbert took the city in hand and beautified it.
To reestablish order, the post of lieutenant de police was created in 1667 for the energetic La Reynie, who inherited the police functions of the provost of Paris. He suppressed the traditional places of asylum (the Temple, the Hôtel de Soissons) and assaulted the last 'cour des miracles", another refuge for robbers. He required sewers and latrines, which most houses lacked, and offensive factories were banished to Chaillot and St-Marcel. City lighting (6,500 lamps) and paving were extended. But the inertia of the inhabitants and their unwillingness to do their share compromised these efforts. Paris remained dirty, its stench stretching for 10 miles. One could get around only in boots,

1 2 PORTES ST-DENIS AND ST-MARTIN (gates; 1672, Blondel; 1674, Bullet). The triumphal arch had been known to Paris since the 16th century, both as a temporary structure built on the occasion of royal entries and in permanent form recalling the fortified gate (Porte St-Antoine) or following a nonclassical design with two openings (Porte St-Bernard by Blondel). With St-Martin and St-Denis gates, these entries became true triumphal arches.

3 COURS (boulevard, 1670-1705). The demolition of the wall of Charles V was accompanied by the creation of a semicircle of boulevards planted with trees on the rampart embankment. New gates dominating a road on a lower level were built. Since merging with the present boulevards, the gates are now located in the middle of the roadway.

4 PLACE DES VICTOIRES (J. Hardouin-Mansart, 1685). Italian type of square previously unknown in Paris. Conceived entirely to set off a statue of the King, the height of which determined the radius of the square. The intention was to fix the pedestrian's ideal vantage point close to the façades, which consist of walled arcades, not covered walks.

5 PONT-ROYAL (bridge, 1685-89, P. Romain, Jacques Gabriel). Replacing the Barbier bridge (wooden), it connected the Tuileries palace to the new St-Germain suburb, where a part of the King's household overflowed (1st Company of Musketeers, rue du Bac).

6 PLACE LOUIS-LE-GRAND (Place Vendôme). Louvois projected a monumental official center (containing academies, the mint, and so on) on the site of the Hôtel de Vendôme. In 1686 Hardouin-Mansart began a three-sided square, open to the south. To increase the building (and resalable) perimeter, it became a closed octagon in 1699, completed on the axis of its two openings by the façade of the Feuillants (F. Mansart, 1667) on the south and by that of the Capucines (d'Orbay, 1688) on the north, and serving to frame an equestrian statue of the King. Always hard-pressed to mobilize large sums, the landowning nobility left to the financiers the very costly lots of the square.

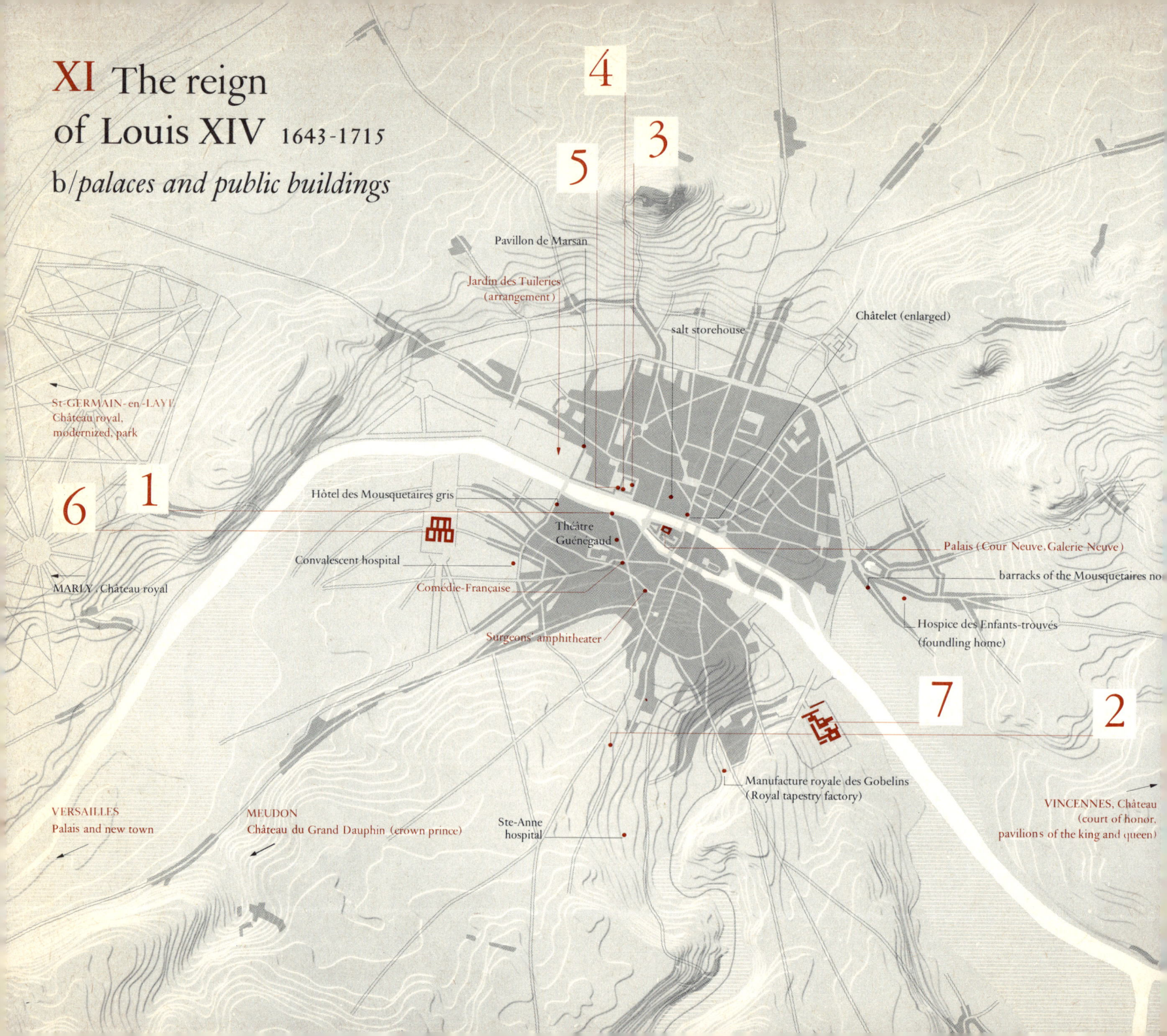

XI The reign of Louis XIV 1643-1715
b/ *palaces and public buildings*

Pavillon de Marsan

Jardin des Tuileries (arrangement)

salt storehouse

Châtelet (enlarged)

St-GERMAIN-en-LAYE
Château royal, modernized, park

Hôtel des Mousquetaires gris

Théâtre Guénégaud

Palais (Cour Neuve, Galerie Neuve)

Convalescent hospital

Comédie-Française

MARLY, Château royal

barracks of the Mousquetaires no[irs]

Surgeons' amphitheater

Hospice des Enfants-trouvés (foundling home)

Manufacture royale des Gobelins (Royal tapestry factory)

VERSAILLES
Palais and new town

MEUDON
Château du Grand Dauphin (crown prince)

Ste-Anne hospital

VINCENNES, Château (court of honor, pavilions of the king and queen)

in a corrosive slime which rotted fabrics. In the summer the Bièvre, clogged with sewage, was foul smelling. The King had the St-Victor canal filled, but the riverside dwellers refused to help clean up the Bièvre. Two new pumps at the Pont Notre-Dame (1670) and 15 fountains supplied only a partial remedy to the constant shortage of water. In every domain the authorities tried to clarify matters. In theory, Paris was still a complex of feudal seigniories, with private property nonexistent within them. In practice "effective" property was indistinguishable from actual property. But when the King tried to abolish seigniorial justices to clarify the situation (1674), he encountered strong resistance from the large abbeys. This same care for clarity and precision produced statistics and the first correct maps. Starting in 1670, Colbert had an annual records of births, marriages, and deaths published Births, when multiplied by the coefficient 30 (defined in the 18th century), give the population figures: 500,000 to 510,000 in 1715. This figure is confirmed by a 1684 record of housing: 23,086 houses, each sheltered an average of 20 or 21 residents; thus about 485,000 inhabitants in 1684. The enormous mortality, constantly higher than the birth rate, is also evident from the figures (21,461 deaths versus 16,816 baptisms in 1670). Paris, as all the old cities, was sustained only by rural immigration. Succeeding the bird's-eye views and rather symbolic maps of the 16th century, the first reasonably precise plans of Paris appeared after the Gomboust plan (1652). They allow us to follow the expansion of the city: from 2,000 acres in 1652, it covered more than 2,750 at the end of the reign, during which 123 streets were opened. Under Louis XIV, Paris escaped its

1 COLLEGE DES QUATRE-NATIONS 1663-91, Le Vau, then François d'Orbay). Founded by a bequest of Cardinal Mazarin to receive students from conquered provinces. The long concave-convex façade, the Greek-cross church, its oval nave and atrium, make it the only truly Baroque monument in Paris, related, though with great originality, to Santa Maria della Pace by Pietro da Cortona. The collège echoed the south façade of the Louvre, which had three pavilions and a dome.

2 OBSERVATORY (1668-72, Claude Perrault). A prestige building, it was palatial. Lacking specialized installations and departments, it represented a strong reaction to the model observatory built by Tycho Brahé as early as 1575 in Denmark. Equipped with five telescopes, one 130 ft, it housed unaffiliated researchers, working freely without a director.

3 4 PALAIS DU LOUVRE, east and south façades (1667-80, Perrault). The abandonment of Le Vau's and Bernini's plans marked the rejection of Baroque and the transition to the finest Classicism. Paris no longer took its inspiration from Rome. A colossal peristyle of double columns constructed on a metal armature, the colonnade had no precedent. Its length required doubling the width of the south wing, whose new façade hid that of Le Vau.

5 PALAIS DU LOUVRE, Gallery of Apollo (1661-80, Le Brun). Type of hall characteristic of the French palaces and rich town houses since the 16th century (Fontainebleau).

6 HOTEL DES INVALIDES (residence, 1671-76, Libéral Bruant). Disabled soldiers had customarily been housed by monasteries. This custom explains the majestic austerity and plan of the residence which could house 7,000 men: a vast cloistered court with large openings, on the axis of the soldiers' church; attendance at all services was required. The general checkerboard plan (six other large courts) relates Les Invalides to Jesuit collèges.

7 HOPITAL GENERAL DE LA SALPETRIERE (hospital, 1657 and after, Le Vau, then Bruant). An austere building for compulsory lodging and correction of the vagabonds and poor of Paris, enlarged little by little.

XI The reign of Louis XIV 1643-1715

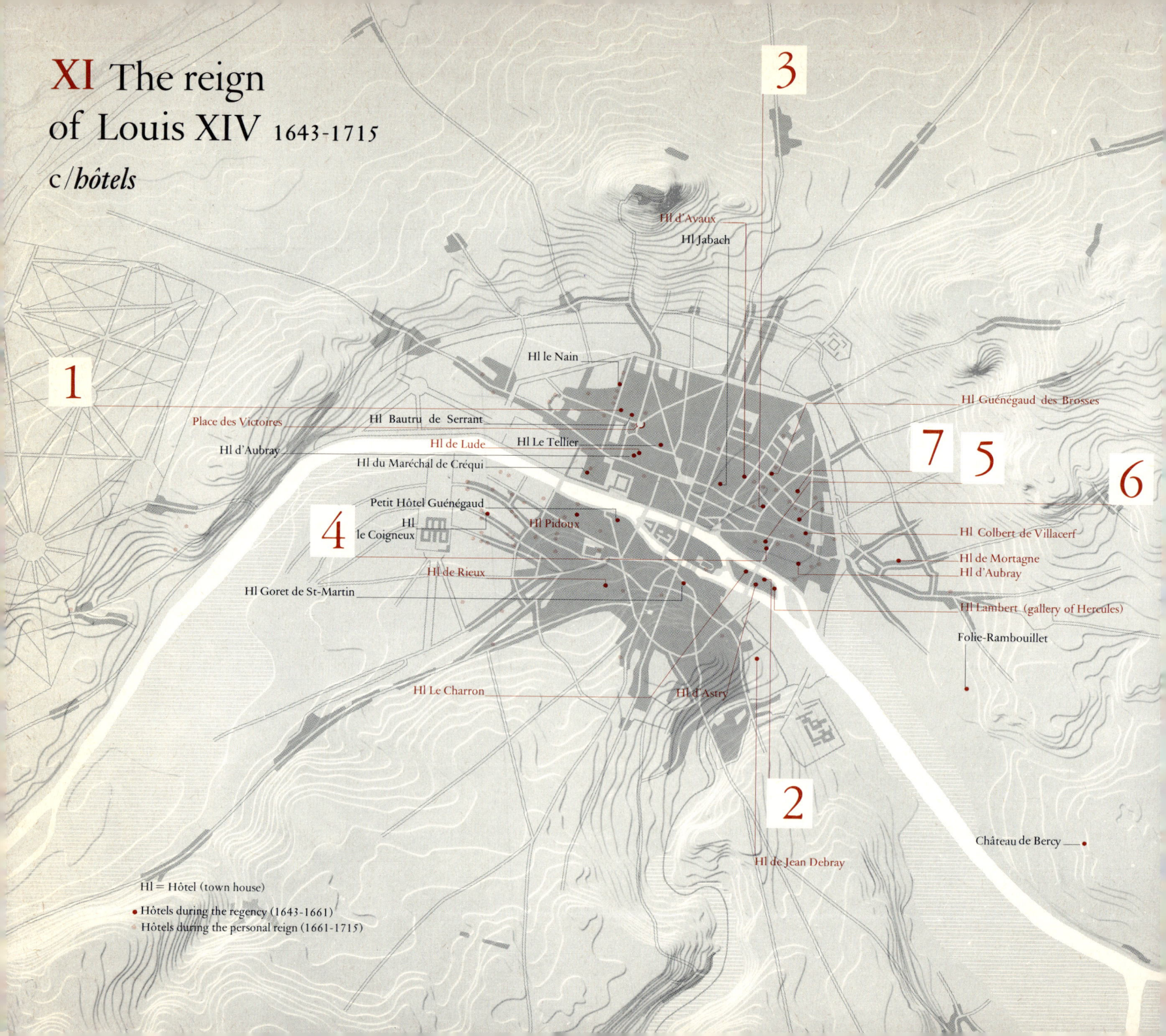

c/hôtels

- Hl d'Avaux
- Hl Jabach
- Hl le Nain
- Hl Guénégaud des Brosses
- Place des Victoires
- Hl Bautru de Serrant
- Hl d'Aubray
- Hl de Lude
- Hl Le Tellier
- Hl du Maréchal de Créqui
- Hl Colbert de Villacerf
- Petit Hôtel Guénégaud
- Hl le Coigneux
- Hl Pidoux
- Hl de Mortagne
- Hl d'Aubray
- Hl de Rieux
- Hl Lambert (gallery of Hercules)
- Hl Goret de St-Martin
- Folie-Rambouillet
- Hl Le Charron
- Hl d'Astry
- Château de Bercy
- Hl de Jean Debray

Hl = Hôtel (town house)
- Hôtels during the regency (1643-1661)
- Hôtels during the personal reign (1661-1715)

two barriers: the swamp, which it began to cross, and the wall. Paris became an open city.
The conquest of Artois and of Flanders finally put the border at a distance, fortified by Vauban. "The capital, which was almost at the frontier, is today at the center of the kingdom." Nevertheless Vauban was disturbed to see Paris without proper defense. To shelter it from heavy mortars, he proposed a distant wall on the heights, which extended almost to the line of the future Thiers wall. The King refused, considering the project useless and mistrusting the Parisians. This decision was to be fatal for Napoleon I in 1814, by his own acknowledgment. Meanwhile, the wall of Charles V was destroyed (only the Bastille St-Antoine survived), the yellow trenches quickly deteriorated, and the wall of Philippe Auguste on the left bank disappeared into houses. A semicircle of boulevards, the Cours, encircled the city to the north, already making it easier to go around the city than to cross it. Expropriation was nonexistent under the ancien régime, and efforts to pierce the central core of Paris were limited to the alignment and widening of streets. Their layout and narrowness (15-25 ft at the widest) were unfavorable to the first attempt at public transport, 5-sou coaches (1662-79). But 5 lines of 35 vehicles with 8 places provided an inadequate capacity, causing the project to fail. Paris expanded in all directions but particularly in the St-Germain and St-Honoré suburbs to the west, due to the King's presence in the Tuileries. There the Place Vendôme represented a vast speculative venture which enjoyed little immediate success. The biggest city of the West, with London close behind, Paris was not only the capital but also the principal economic power of the kingdom. A securities market appeared at the end of the reign, prefiguring the Bourse (stock exchange). State industries such as Gobelins and Savonnerie and royal industries, which were private but privileged and subsidized,

1 PALAIS MAZARIN (1645, F. Mansart). As in the Cardinal palace, the Hôtel Lambert, and so on, two galleries were superimposed. Here the lower gallery housed the Cardinal's collections, the upper gallery served as a library.

2 HOTEL GRUYN DES BORDES ("de Lauzun," 1656-57, Le Vau). The decoration signals a change of custom: rented property and removable decoration gave way to the fixed installation.

3 HOTEL AMELOT DE BISSEUIL, called Hôtel des Ambassadeurs de Hollande (1655-60, Pierre Cottard). The gate was made large to form a monument, both for the owner's prestige and to correspond to the scale of the house.

4 HOTEL SCARRON, later Hôtel d'Aumont (1646-49). Le Vau built a house of three parts which F. Mansart had to remodel, extending the garden façade (1656-62).

5 HOTEL DE BEAUVAIS (1655, Le Pautre). Unusual plan to fit the trapezoidal shape of the land: the residence built over its stables at the end of a half-oval court, with a rented house on the street. Ingenuity for varying plans characterized Parisian architects throughout this period.

6 HOTEL CARNAVALET, remodeled 1655-61. F. Mansart carried to two stories the façade on the street and in the wings, which held only a gallery. Unity of appearance, the ideal of Clacissism, had not always been realized in the 16th century.

7 HOTEL AUBERT-DE-FONTENAY, called Hôtel Salé (1656, Boullier). The Baroque sense of movement in space made the grand stairway a piece of bravura for the architect, an element of prestige for the owner.

XI The reign of Louis XIV 1643-1715
d/*hôtels*

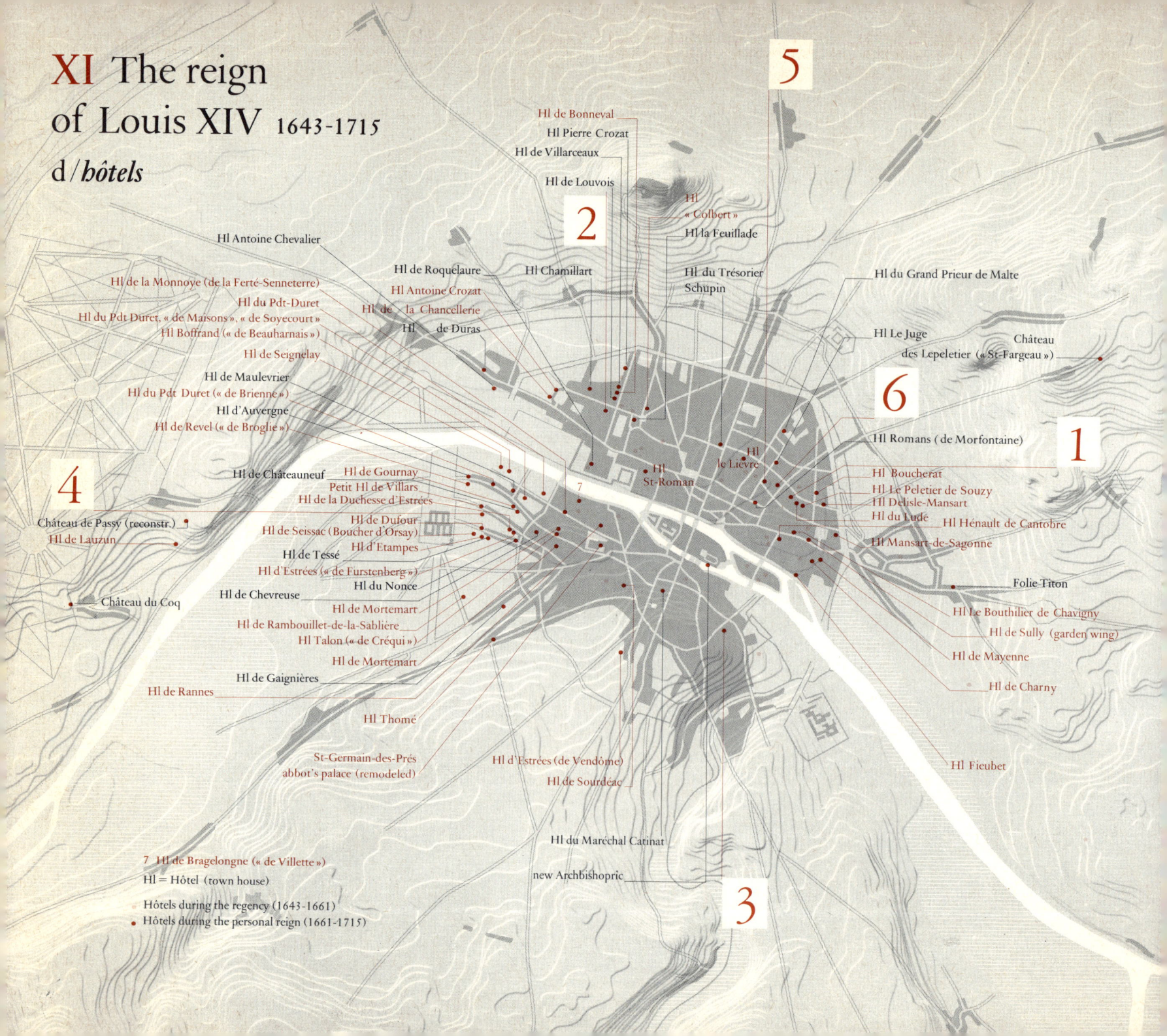

Hl de Bonneval
Hl Pierre Crozat
Hl de Villarceaux
Hl de Louvois
Hl Antoine Chevalier
Hl « Colbert »
Hl la Feuillade
Hl de la Monnoye (de la Ferté-Senneterre)
Hl de Roquelaure
Hl Chamillart
Hl du Trésorier Schupin
Hl du Grand Prieur de Malte
Hl du Pdt-Duret
Hl Antoine Crozat
Hl du Pdt Duret, « de Maisons », « de Soyecourt »
Hl de la Chancellerie
Hl Boffrand (« de Beauharnais »)
Hl de Duras
Hl Le Juge
Hl de Seignelay
Château des Lepeletier (« St-Fargeau »)
Hl de Maulevrier
Hl du Pdt Duret (« de Brienne »)
Hl d'Auvergne
Hl de Revel (« de Broglie »)
Hl Romans (de Morfontaine)
Hl de Châteauneuf
Hl de Gournay
Hl St-Roman
Hl le Lièvre
Petit Hl de Villars
Hl Boucherat
Hl de la Duchesse d'Estrées
Hl Le Peletier de Souzy
Château de Passy (reconstr.)
Hl Delisle-Mansart
Hl de Lauzun
Hl de Dufour
Hl du Ludé
Hl de Seissac (Boucher d'Orsay)
Hl Hénault de Cantobre
Hl de Tessé
Hl d'Etampes
Hl Mansart-de-Sagonne
Hl d'Estrées (« de Furstenberg »)
Hl du Nonce
Folie Titon
Château du Coq
Hl de Chevreuse
Hl de Mortemart
Hl Le Bouthilier de Chavigny
Hl de Rambouillet-de-la-Sablière
Hl de Sully (garden wing)
Hl Talon (« de Créqui »)
Hl de Mayenne
Hl de Mortemart
Hl de Gaignières
Hl de Charny
Hl de Rannes
Hl Thomé
St-Germain-des-Prés abbot's palace (remodeled)
Hl d'Estrées (de Vendôme)
Hl de Sourdéac
Hl Fieubet
Hl du Maréchal Catinat
new Archbishopric

7 Hl de Bragelongne (« de Villette »)
Hl = Hôtel (town house)
Hôtels during the regency (1643-1661)
• Hôtels during the personal reign (1661-1715)

employed some thousands of workers and devoted themselves to luxury articles: tapestries, glass, gold brocade, mirrors, etc. In the Grande Galerie of the Louvre the King housed some 30 workshops for especially fine productions, the cabinetmaker Boulle among others. Parisians founded industrial enterprises throughout the provinces. But the problems of the city grew worse. It seemed that the overcrowding of the population had increased. The bourgeoisie bought country houses to escape the crush; the gardens of the rich, of the King, even of the monasteries, were opened to the public (there was much more park land than today). The provisioning of Paris became a national problem. Throughout the kingdom, the orders given by lieutenants de police for food had executive force. When the harvests were bad, scarcity was transformed into famine in wide areas by the city's siphoning. Prohibitions against building were ignored. For a century, the troubled monarchy had evoked "the destiny of the most powerful cities of antiquity, having arrived at an excessive grandeur and containing in themselves the principle of their ruin." In the last attempt to stop the growth of this monster, the royal residence was transferred to Versailles (1680) by the monarchy, aware that its presence was responsible for the size of Paris. The creation of a satellite city was a carefully considered step, though not a total one, since a part of the state mechanism remained at Paris. It was too late. Paris was the intellectual capital of the West. Although the university was in decline, more through financial impoverishment than by intellectual sclerosis (which has been exaggerated), the city became a scientific capital, especially through the creation of the Observatory where Roemer, a Dane, discovered the speed of light in 1676.

1 MAISON DE LIBERAL BRUANT (1685, Bruant). The round niches, the arcades falling on double supports, are more related to the Italian Renaissance (Portico del Té at Mantua) than to the court of Les Invalides.

2 HOTEL LULLI (1671, Daniel Gittard). A city house related to its urban surroundings, rather than a suburban house between court and garden. The lower floor of arcades and colossal pilasters point to the nearby façades of Place des Victoires and Place Louis-le-Grand.

3 HOTEL LE BRUN (1700, Gabriel Boffrand). The house is a simple mass. Its beauty rests in the harmony of mathematically established proportions: the balcony divides the façade horizontally according to the ideal relationship (the golden section) borrowed from Vitruvius and in frequent use at this time.

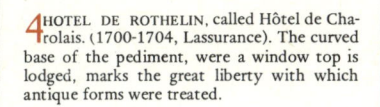

4 HOTEL DE ROTHELIN, called Hôtel de Charolais. (1700-1704, Lassurance). The curved base of the pediment, were a window top is lodged, marks the great liberty with which antique forms were treated.

5 HOTEL DE SOUBISE (1705-1709, Delamair). Behind the beauty of this court of honor with its double-columned porticoes — legacy of the Hôtel du Grand Prieur — the architecture expresses certain social conventions. According to custom the grand display of columns was reserved to royal and, as here, princely residences. In the Marais district, on very expensive land, the vast court is an affirmation of richness and "grand taste": beauty over expense, prestige well before comfort.

6 HOTEL DE ROHAN (1705-10, Delamair). In contrast to the tall, severe façade on the court, the garden façade is covered by windows on one third of its surface. In less than a century, the relief of garden façade had reversed itself: at first it was marked at the ends (pavilions framing a terrace) and accentuated in the middle, while the corner pavilions disappeared completely.

XI The reign of Louis XIV 1643-1715
e / religious monuments

N-D = Notre-Dame
Ct = Convent or monastery
○ Destruction

Not only did Paris dominate the religious life of the diocese (in 1696 seminary training became obligatory for all its priests) and the organization of charity (St Vincent de Paul, d. 1660; Madame de Miramion), but it became a rival of Rome as a center for foreign missions (1659, the foundation of the Société des Missions Etrangères). People came from all over Europe to the seminary of St-Sulpice, only 10 percent of whose seminarians were from the diocese. In 1680, aside from the various gatherings of clergy, 52 bishops passed through Paris. The foundations continued, until there were about 110 monasteries by 1700. In one century 60 communities of women appeared (a phenomenon that has not drawn the attention it deserves). In 1684 Jean-Baptiste de la Salle founded the Frères des Ecoles Chrétiennes to instruct boys. Three new parishes were created: Notre-Dame-de-Bonne-Nouvelle in 1673, St-Jacques-St-Philippe-du-Roule in 1699, and Ste-Marguerite in 1712. Paris was also a center of controversies, such as Jansenism, Gallicanism, and Quietism, which color its traditional image of religious conformity following the great piety under Louis XIII. Protestantism had lost momentum. Social and official pressure, as well as Catholic dynamism, whose proselytizing was pursued by the organized guidance and surveillance of the converted "new Catholics," culminated in the prohibition of Protestantism in 1685. Tolerance was unofficially reestablished after 1690, but most of the rich Protestants had emigrated. It seems that Samuel Bernard, the most important banker of the time, was their agent, a pseudoconvert remaining at home to assure the continuity of business.

1 ABBEY OF VAL-DE-GRACE (1646-67, F. Mansart, then Lemercier, Le Muet, Le Duc). An effort to rival Rome: St-Peter's inspired the dome, the canopy over the altar, the altar itself, by Bernini. The church has two naves, one for the faithful, the other to the side of the choir for the nuns.

1 ABBEY OF VAL-DE-GRACE, cloister (1655, Le Muet?). The austerity of these round-arch openings has suggested that this may have been an adaptation of the buildings from the first convent.

2 ST-ROCH, choir (1653-60, Lemercier). A traditional plan of nave and two aisles which open on a large round Baroque chapel behind the choir (Hardouin-Mansart?).

3 ST-SULPICE, choir (1645-78, Gamard, then Le Vau, then Gittard). Austere French Classicism sought here to rival Notre-Dame, rejecting the Baroque of Borromini.

4 ST-LOUIS-DE-LA-SALPETRIERE (Bruant, 1670). The plan of the church — Greek-cross plan and four chapels converging on the central altar — allowed the separation of the diverse categories of those confined to the hospital.

5 ST-LOUIS-DES-INVALIDES (1679-1708, Hardouin-Mansart). An axial chapel built behind the church of Les Invalides, it amounted to another church. The Greek-cross plan, crowned by a dome, returns to the purest conception of Michelangelo for St-Peter's in Rome. The beauty of the edifice is not entirely classical; effects of indirect lighting produced by the calottes in the dome and the three successive advances of the façade are Baroque. Perhaps the exceptional spring of the dome evokes the challenge of the Gothic churches, whose daring was well appreciated.

XII Louis XV and Louis XVI 1715-1789

a/urbanism

- project for place St-Eustache
- Halle aux farines (flour market)
- Fontaine Maubuée (repairs)
- Fontaine du Trahoir (reconstr.)
- Pont de Neuilly (stone)
- "Grande voirie" (dump) and 2nd Montfaucon gallows
- 2nd porte Maillot
- canalization and covering of sewer
- Etoile de Chaillot (1st grading of the butte)
- Pavillon Perronet
- Pavillon d'Ermenonville
- Fontaine des Haudriettes (reconstr.)
- Chaillot pumping station
- revolving bridge
- dump
- Porte de la Conférence
- court of Louvre cleared
- Grande et Petite-Force (prisons)
- Gros-Caillou pumping station
- Place de Grève (enlarged)
- Place du Palais Bourbon
- Hôtel des Pompes (central fire station)
- laying-out of Champ-de-Mars
- Fontaine « de Necker »
- fair of St-Germain (reconstr.)
- Place St-Sulpice
- Place du Théâtre Français
- Quai du Mail
- Barrière du Trône (customs gate)
- Custom wall (called « mur des Fermiers Généraux »)
- Ivry pumping station
- river port project
- Marché aux chevaux police station
- Place du Pont-St-Michel (1st)
- Pont Notre-Dame and Petit-Pont (houses demolished)
- reafforestation of the bois de Vincennes
- Destruction
- demolition of Petit-Châtelet Place du Petit-Pont
- Place du Palais

In the 18th century Paris experienced a rapid growth. Its population reached about 650,000 in 1789. Parisian life reflected the century's economic evolution, in which a period of rise began about 1733, accelerated after 1763, ebbed from 1770 to 1787, and then recovered with some lapses until 1817. Local factors added to this picture, particularly the temporary abandonment of Versailles in 1715 and the less confining character of court life throughout the century, limiting fewer courtiers to Versailles. The St-Honoré and Gaillon districts developed first; the truck farmers emigrated in the direction of St-Lazare and Les Porcherons; Le Roule was given the status of a suburb in 1722. In 1724 the King again tried vainly to limit the growth of Paris; the city was at a saturation point within the perimeters boulevards and overflowed them, with the impetus especially strong after 1763. Paris branched out toward the neighboring villages across the drained swamp. After 1770 the rich district of the Chaussée d'Antin expanded into the old riverbed, over the covered and canalized sewer trench. In 1778 the Monceau district was begun, and an English-style district moved into Le Roule and the Champs-Elysées. The land between the Cours-la-Reine and the Savonnerie began to be divided up. On the south bank the built-up area reached the Champ-de-Mars, pushing back the lumberyards. The parceling out of the Hôtel de Condé lands re-created a rich center in the declining Luxembourg district, whose poor population moved on to swell the St-Marcel suburb. The rise in population continued along with the price of rents, and the activity of the finance companies paralleled a frenzy of construction (some buildings were built in 2 months, the Opéra in 75 days).

1 FONTAINE DES QUATRE-SAISONS (Fountain of the Four Seasons, 1739-46, Bouchardon). It inadequately supplied the suburb of St-Germain. "Too much stone for too little water" (Voltaire). The ample sobriety of its architecture, its antique purism, and the serenity of its statuary were reactions against the gesticulations and affectations of the Baroque style.

2 PLACE LOUIS XV (1757-72, Jacques-Ange Gabriel). A new type of square, conceived as a palace forecourt. The square was bordered by moats, filled today, with traces preserved by the balustrades. In the center, an equestrian statue of the King by Pigalle. To the north, Gabriel built the palatial town houses of the "ambassadeurs extraordinaires" inspired by the colonnades of the Louvre and the Place Vendôme. One (today the Hôtel Crillon) was rented to various members of the aristocracy, another became a royal furniture repository.

3 4 5 ENCEINTE DES FERMIERS GENERAUX (Customs Wall of the Fermiers Généraux, Barrières of La Villette, Enfer, Chartres; 1784-89, Claude-Nicolas Ledoux). A toll barrier replacing ineffectual fences, the Fermiers' wall extended 14 mi. In the pavilions ("revenue dens transformed into palaces of columns"), Ledoux extended that sometimes peculiar, massive style born in France, England, and Prussia at the end of the 18th century.

6 7 FONTAINE DES INNOCENTS (Innocents' Fountain). Reworked into a square by adding a fourth side, a cupola, and steps, on the site of the Innocents' cemetery destroyed in 1786 (the bones were placed in disaffected quarries, from then on called catacombs).

8 PONT LOUIS XVI (1787-90, Jean-Rodolphe Perronet). Later the Concorde bridge, it attests to the excellence of the Ecole des Ponts et Chaussées (civil-engineering school) created in 1747. For the first time, discontinuous piers formed of two pylons and a vault; the arc is very slight for such a long bridge.

XII Louis XV and Louis XVI 1715-1789

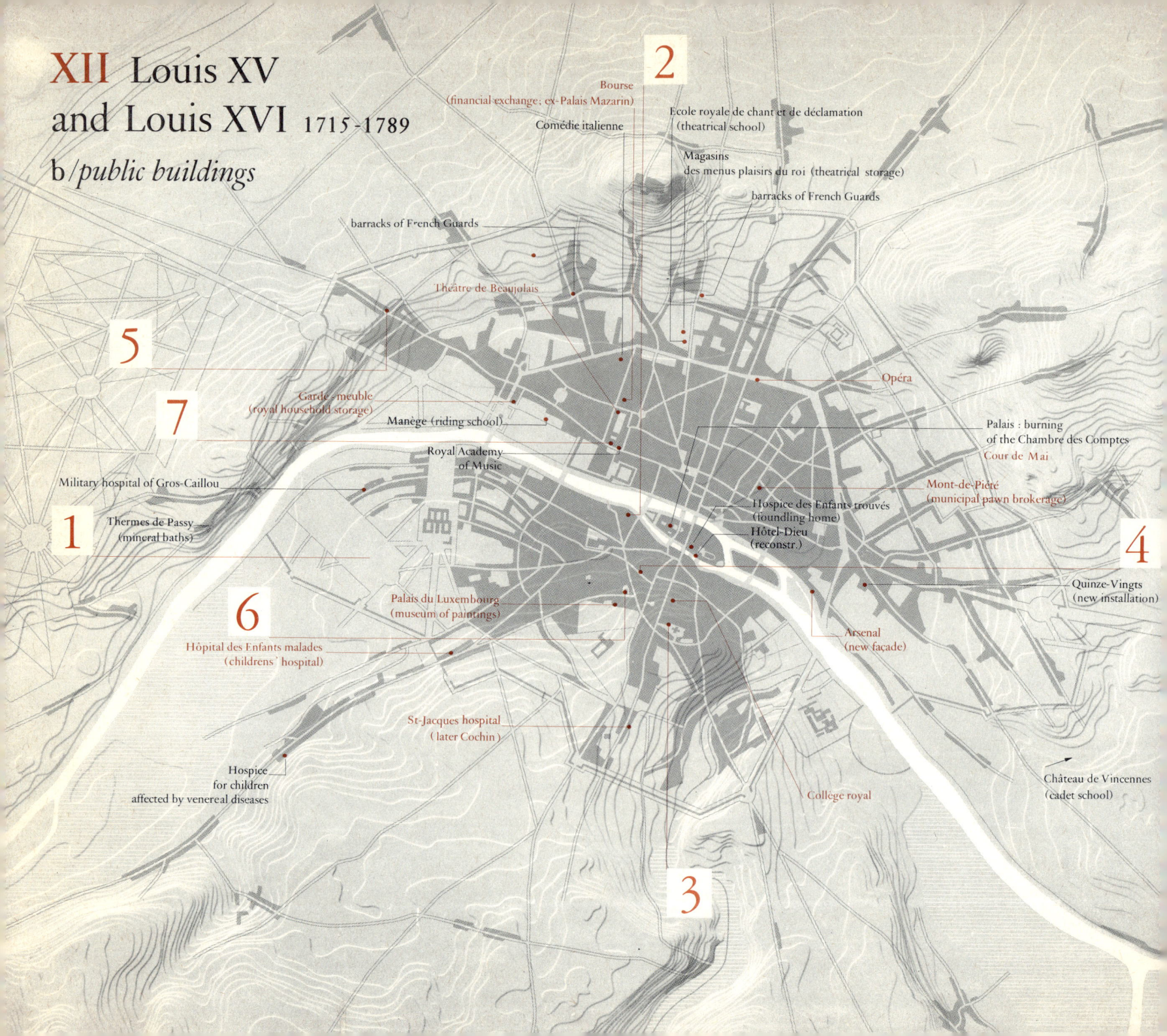

b/ public buildings

- Bourse (financial exchange; ex-Palais Mazarin)
- Comédie italienne
- Ecole royale de chant et de déclamation (theatrical school)
- Magasins des menus plaisirs du roi (theatrical storage)
- barracks of French Guards
- barracks of French Guards
- Théâtre de Beaujolais
- Opéra
- Garde-meuble (royal household storage)
- Manège (riding school)
- Palais : burning of the Chambre des Comptes Cour de Mai
- Royal Academy of Music
- Military hospital of Gros-Caillou
- Mont-de-Piété (municipal pawn brokerage)
- Hospice des Enfants trouvés (foundling home)
- Hôtel-Dieu (reconstr.)
- Thermes de Passy (mineral baths)
- Quinze-Vingts (new installation)
- Palais du Luxembourg (museum of paintings)
- Arsenal (new façade)
- Hôpital des Enfants malades (childrens' hospital)
- St-Jacques hospital (later Cochin)
- Château de Vincennes (cadet school)
- Hospice for children affected by venereal diseases
- Collège royal

Houses reached 10 stories, grouped in vast ensembles often interspersed with greenery or surrounding gardens. The edge of the gardens of the Palais-Royal were parceled out.
In the new districts entire streets were formed by town houses of the aristocracy and bankers.
A series of population shifts began. People of small means were uprooted by rent increases. The rich and their retinues, according to the fate of their fortunes, arrived in or left certain districts; dukes and peers abandoned the Marais for the suburb of St-Germain. The Maîtres des Requêtes left the Marais and St-Germain for the Chaussée d'Antin; the members of the Chambre des Comptes deserted the suburb of St-Germain and the old Ste-Avoye district and arrived in the Marais, where the parceling out of the Temple grounds had revived the northern section. In general, the court nobility was in the suburb of St-Germain, the bankers around the Chaussée d'Antin and Palais-Royal, and the legal profession in the Marais. The center and the St-Michel suburb were overpopulated and unhealthy, and the idea of setting this growth in order became essential. The era abounded with well-conceived urban projects, particularly those by Soufflot and Patte: the Vincennes-Neuilly axis, the destruction of Les Halles, the cleaning up of La Cité, the demolition of the Bastille and of the neighborhood between the Louvre and the Tuileries, the transfer of the Hôtel-Dieu to the country. These great projects would be realized slowly over the next 200 years. In order to plan the works, the first precise map of Paris was made by Verniquet in 1787. The only large-scale operation was the creation of the Place Louis-XV (Concorde), an essential link between the new districts of Paris begun in 1753.

1 ECOLE MILITAIRE (military school, 1752-57, J.-A. Gabriel). Its construction responded to the increasingly technical orientation of the military profession; the cadres and the military doctrines of the Revolution and of the Empire were formed there. Gabriel realized in this building a monumental synthesis of antique (Doric columns), Italian (superimposed porticoes), and French elements (flat-sided dome, reminiscent of the Grand Siècle).

2 HOTEL DES MONNAIES (the mint, 1768-75, Jacques-Denis Antoine). Affirmation of the new style, rejecting pilasters, cantwalls, and ornaments in favor of rectangular mass and a search for proportioned volumes. A return to the palaces of Brunelleschi and Alberti as well as to antiquity.

3 ECOLE DE DROIT (law school, 1770-83, Jacques-Germain Soufflot). The antique purism is accompanied by restraint in the use of columns, which are reserved for the entrance to the building.

4 ECOLE DE MEDECINE (medical school, 1779-86, Gondoin). A court surrounded by an Ionic portico, entered through a triumphal arch before a temple façade. The correctness of antique elements camouflages the freedom in their use.

5 HOPITAL BEAUJON (hospital, 1784, Girardin). Where the austerity proper to the monument lapses into gloominess. Doric building inside.

6 THEATRE FRANÇAIS "Odéon Theater" (1779-82). The new taste for massive forms: a simple geometric volume precedes a Doric portico without a pediment. Nothing expresses the function of the building; the side arcades recall rather the funerary niches on the sides of Alberti's Tempio Malatestiano (S. Francesco in Rimini).

7 THEATRE DES VARIETES AMUSANTES,"Théatre Français" (variety theater, 1786-90, Victor Louis). Louis introduced Paris to the plan of the Grand Theatre of Bordeaux (1773), of which he was the architect.

XII Louis XV and Louis XVI 1715-1789

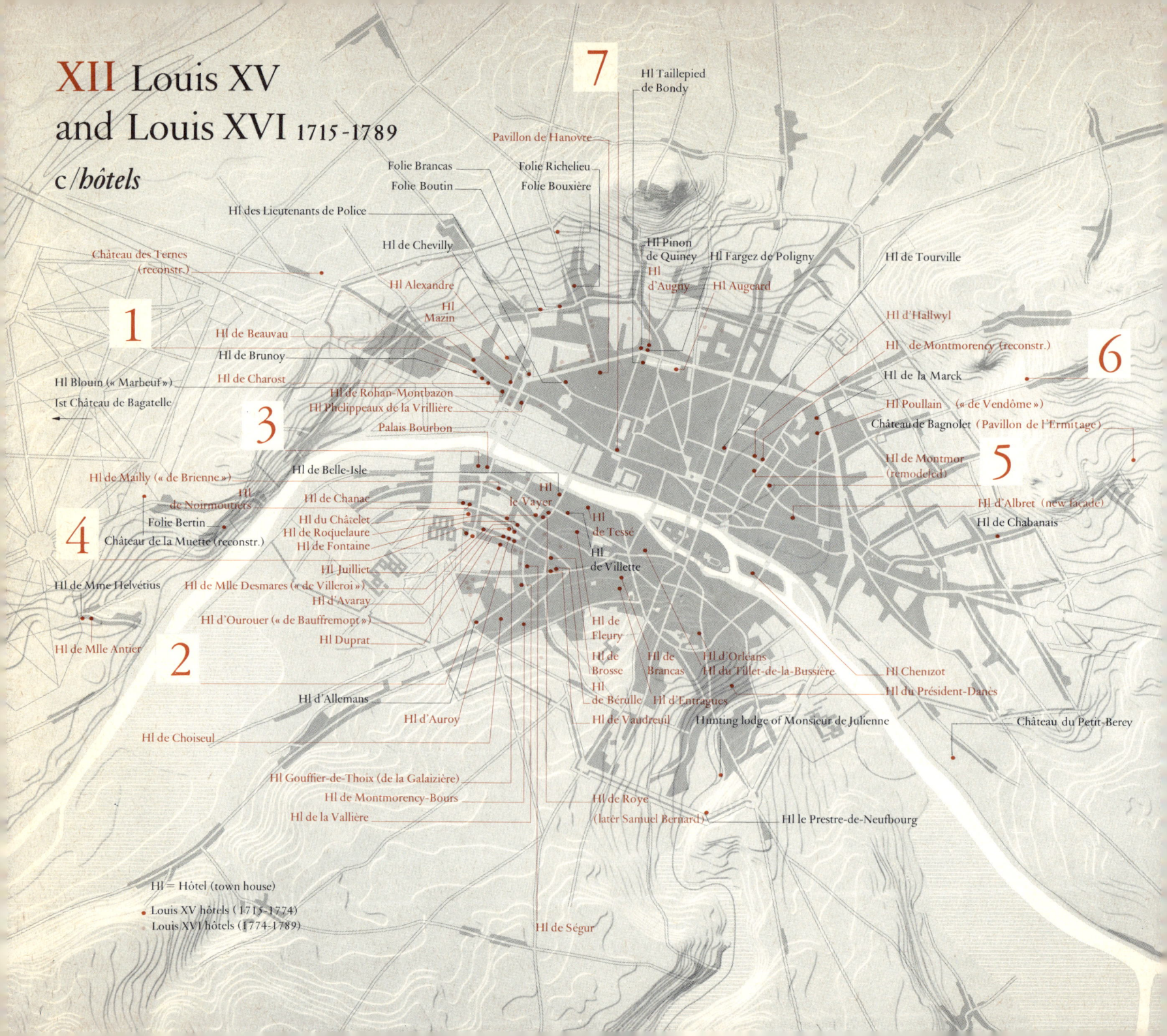

c/hôtels

Château des Ternes (reconstr.)

Folie Brancas
Folie Boutin
Folie Richelieu
Folie Bouxière
Pavillon de Hanovre
Hl Taillepied de Bondy

Hl des Lieutenants de Police
Hl de Chevilly
Hl Pinon de Quiney
Hl Fargez de Poligny
Hl de Tourville
Hl Alexandre
Hl d'Augny
Hl Augeard
Hl Mazin
Hl de Beauvau
Hl d'Hallwyl
Hl de Brunoy
Hl de Montmorency (reconstr.)
Hl Blouin (« Marbeuf »)
Hl de Charost
Hl de la Marck
1st Château de Bagatelle
Hl de Rohan-Montbazon
Hl Poullain (« de Vendôme »)
Hl Phelippeaux de la Vrillière
Château de Bagnolet (Pavillon de l'Ermitage)
Palais Bourbon
Hl de Montmor (remodeled)
Hl de Mailly (« de Brienne »)
Hl de Belle-Isle
Hl le Vayer
Hl de Noirmoutiers
Hl de Chanac
Hl d'Albret (new façade)
Folie Bertin
Hl du Châtelet
Hl de Tessé
Hl de Chabanais
Château de la Muette (reconstr.)
Hl de Roquelaure
Hl de Fontaine
Hl de Villette
Hl de Mme Helvétius
Hl Juilliet
Hl de Mlle Desmares (« de Villeroi »)
Hl d'Avaray
Hl d'Ourouer (« de Bauffremont »)
Hl Duprat
Hl de Fleury
Hl de Mlle Antier
Hl de Brosse
Hl de Brancas
Hl d'Orléans
Hl du Tillet-de-la-Bussière
Hl Chenizot
Hl de Bérulle
Hl d'Entragues
Hl du Président-Danès
Hl d'Allemans
Hl de Vaudreuil
Hunting lodge of Monsieur de Julienne
Château du Petit-Bercy
Hl d'Auroy
Hl de Choiseul
Hl Gouffier-de-Thoix (de la Galaizière)
Hl de Montmorency-Bours
Hl de Roye (later Samuel Bernard)
Hl le Prestre-de-Neufbourg
Hl de la Vallière

Hl = Hôtel (town house)
• Louis XV hôtels (1715-1774)
• Louis XVI hôtels (1774-1789)

Hl de Ségur

This was no longer a closed square, a meeting ground sheltered from traffic. It was a crossroads and a showplace, a grandly conceived complex linked to the Champs-Elysées, to the Etoile de Chaillot, to the bridge at Neuilly. Another bridge led to the growing suburb of St-Germain, while an avenue planned to extend to the Chaussée d'Antin was never built. The banking of the site allowed the piercing of the Tuileries dike fortification and opened the Tuileries to the west. A street running the length of the gardens toward the center was provided for. This masterly conception, a product of mature city planning, hardly foreshadowed the two centuries of decadence that were to follow. In the ancient center of the city the reign of Louis XVI carried out only localized improvements, already showing, with a utilitarian severity heralding the havoc of the next century. The houses on the bridge were razed beginning in 1786, the palace of La Cité completely rebuilt after the fire of 1776; its approaches cleared, the courtyard of the Louvre emptied of the village which had overrun it. Regularized squares were built or planned (St-Sulpice, St-Eustache, and Bastille, which was to be the Place Louis-XVI). A 1783 ruling prohibited the opening of streets less than 33 ft wide and the building of houses more than 66 ft high. The appearance of the streets changed: signs with street names appeared in 1729, oil streetlamps in 1757, and in 1762 shop signs were placed flat on the façades to facilitate night illumination. Shop-front windows became common. Following London's example, sidewalks appeared in 1782 in the Place du Théâtre-Français, the present Place de l'Odéon. The numbering of houses was first instituted in the suburbs in 1728 to prevent new building; it spread through Paris sporadically after 1780.

1 HOTEL D'EVREUX called Elysée Palace (1718, A. C. Mollet). The roof was replaced by a terrace and bordering balustrade, offering a view of the verdant landscape of the Champs-Elysées and the left bank, where Les Invalides still rose out of the open countryside.

2 HOTEL DE MONTMORENCY, later Hôtel de Matignon (1721, Jean Courtonne, then Mazin). Renewal of animated façades with projecting pavilions and fashionable cantwalls.

3 HOTEL DE LASSAY (1722-24, Jean Aubert). Comprising at that time only a ground floor with large round-arch windows under a balustrade decorated with statues, it resembled its neighbor, the Palais Bourbon of 1722.

4 HOTEL PEYRENC DE MORAS, called Hôtel Biron (1728-31, J. Gabriel and Aubert). The only surviving Parisian work of Gabriel, the great architect of the French provinces (Place Royale at Bordeaux and Rennes; Place Bellecour at Lyon). If the projecting pavilions reflect the taste of their time, the façade maintains the nobility of the Grand Siècle, in which Gabriel established his reputation.

6 COUNTRY HOUSE OF CARRE DE BEAUDOIN called Folie Favart (1770). Reduction of Palladio's Villa Emo in the countryside of Ménilmontant. The old word "Folie" is related to "foliate" (leafy), evoking a verdant, rustic place.

7 PALAIS-ROYAL, reconstruction (1764-70, Contant d'Ivry). A fire ravaged a first reconstruction by Cartaud (1752-58). A new campaign was completed by Contant and Moreau on the Court of the Clock, and by Contant and later Louis on the Court of Honor, where the wings of the Cardinal palace survived. Finally, Louis rebuilt the west wing.

5 HOTEL DE SOUBISE, enlarged (1735-45, Boffrand). The oval salon shows all the characteristics of the rococo style: exclusion of the right angle; homogeneous decoration in plaster, stucco, and wood, ignoring the architectural structure; abundance of curves, volutes, and shells.

XII Louis XV and Louis XVI 1715-1789
d/hôtels

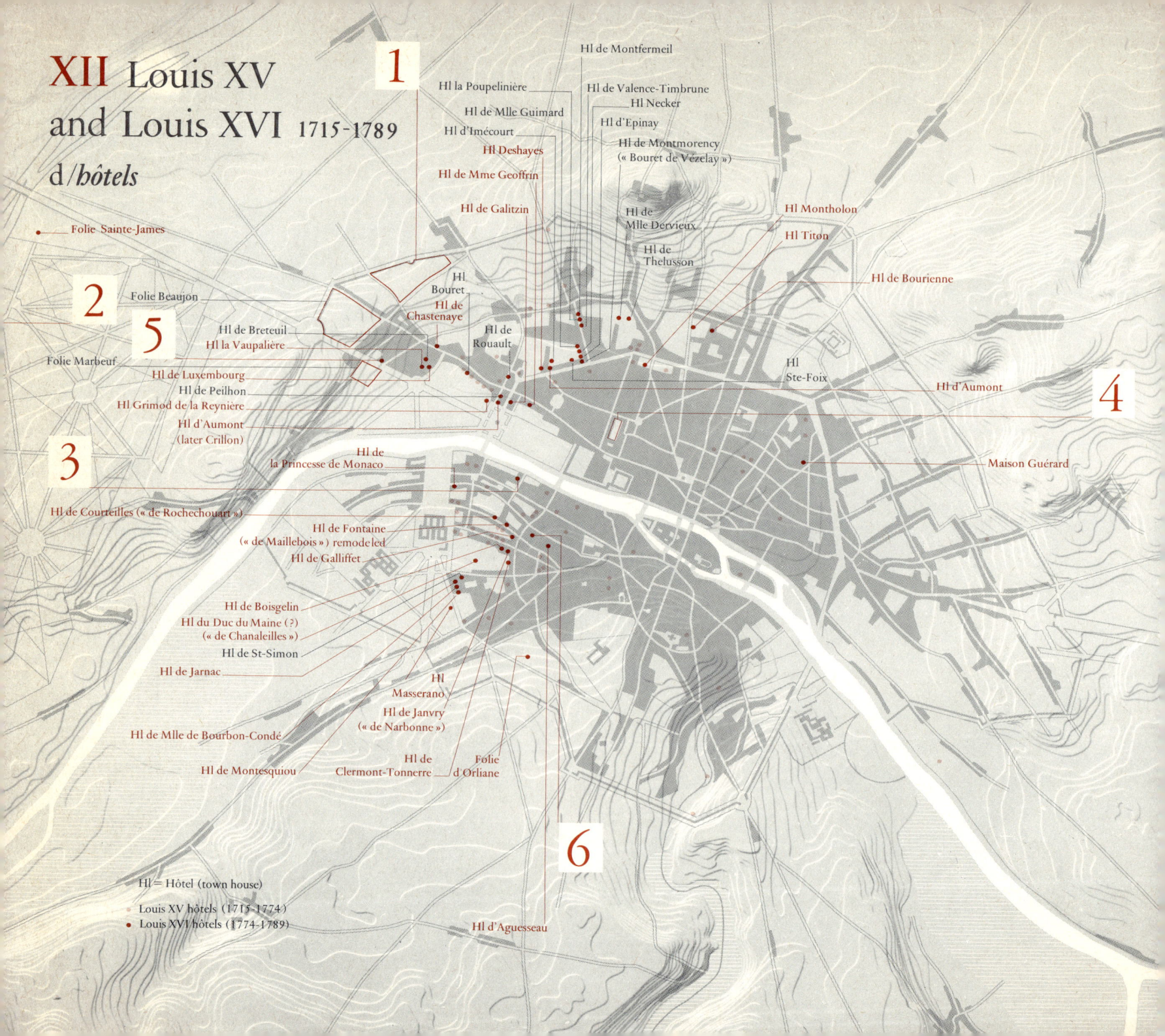

- Folie Sainte-James
- Folie Beaujon
- Folie Marbeuf
- Hl de Breteuil
- Hl la Vaupalière
- Hl de Luxembourg
- Hl de Peilhon
- Hl Grimod de la Reynière
- Hl d'Aumont (later Crillon)
- Hl de Courteilles (« de Rochechouart »)
- Hl de Fontaine (« de Maillebois ») remodeled
- Hl de Galliffet
- Hl de Boisgelin
- Hl du Duc du Maine (?) (« de Chanaleilles »)
- Hl de St-Simon
- Hl de Jarnac
- Hl de Mlle de Bourbon-Condé
- Hl de Montesquiou
- Hl de Clermont-Tonnerre
- Folie d'Orliane
- Hl Masserano
- Hl de Janvry (« de Narbonne »)
- Hl d'Aguesseau
- Hl la Poupelinière
- Hl de Mlle Guimard
- Hl d'Imécourt
- Hl Deshayes
- Hl de Mme Geoffrin
- Hl de Galitzin
- Hl Bouret
- Hl de Chastenaye
- Hl de Rouault
- Hl de la Princesse de Monaco
- Hl de Montfermeil
- Hl de Valence-Timbrune
- Hl Necker
- Hl d'Epinay
- Hl de Montmorency (« Bouret de Vézelay »)
- Hl de Mlle Dervieux
- Hl de Thelusson
- Hl Montholon
- Hl Titon
- Hl de Bourienne
- Hl Ste-Foix
- Hl d'Aumont
- Maison Guérard

Hl = Hôtel (town house)
- Louis XV hôtels (1715-1774)
- Louis XVI hôtels (1774-1789)

The principal sanitation efforts were directed at the cemeteries, particularly the Innocents' whose fumes began to be hazardous. They were all emptied and closed. The sewer was covered, but the Bièvre, polluted after 1788 by the Oberkampf factory at Jouy, contaminated the entire southeast of Paris. Despite the use of three steam pumps, the water supply remained a vulnerable point; two pumps, situated downstream, drew polluted water. Projects to tap the Yvette and to divert the Bièvre toward the Observatory were never completed. The King was driven to these actions as much by fear of this enormous city as by the taste for able administration so typical of the 18th century. The management of Paris was divided among several agencies of the royal administration. The police, under their lieutenant M. de Sartine (1759-74), were a model for Europe. The supplying of Paris became a national problem, dictating policies of public works and road building. Meat came from as far as Auvergne and Brittany, and wood from east and south of the Paris basin, thus killing local industries dependent on wood. Les Halles in Paris was the national marketplace which set prices the provinces had to accept. In the surrounding vicinity the bourgeoisie stepped up its acquisition of land, creating an exodus of small farmers to the city. Another pressure from Paris was its placement of children in foster homes as far away as the Somme, Aube, and Loiret rivers; 200,000 of these children died from 1750 to 1789. The economic life of Paris is unclear. L. Cahen sees all activity limited to provisioning the agglomeration, disallowing even trade, since only 39,000 tons of goods per year moved between Paris and Rouen. Though a certain amount of industrialization did appear in the workers' areas,

1 FOLIE DE CHARTRES, the Naumachie (1778, Carmontelle). The picturesque garden developed from 1720 on, under the twofold influence of England and China, mixed with the archaeological and romantic taste for ruins, creating a "landscape of illusion."

2 FOLIE D'ARTOIS (1777, François-Joseph Belanger), called "Bagatelle." Elegant simple volumes, sober decoration, importance of the garden rotunda. Story added 1860.

3 HÔTEL DE SALM KYBURG (1782, Pierre Rousseau). A remarkable convergence of influences: antiquity, Palladio, and the Ecole de Médecine. Contrast between two façades: the display of the entrance combining a triumphal arch, an Ionic portico, and a temple front in a profusion of columns suggesting a princely residence. On the side of the Seine, an elegant and discrete façade.

4 PALAIS-ROYAL (1781, Louis), residential and commercial ensemble around the gardens. The ordonnance is inspired by the lateral façades of the Grand Theater of Bordeaux, but financial considerations compromised the search for beauty: undersized arcades and weak articulation of the corners to provide for the greatest possible number of apartments.

5 HÔTEL THIROUX DE MONTSAUGE, called Hôtel de Massa (1784, Le Boursier). Now-banished survivor of the Champs-Elysées country houses.

6 HÔTEL DE CHEVREUSE, woodwork (ca 1780), Louvre Museum. Rectilinear antique architectural decoration, clearly articulating the walls. Rejection of the curves of the rococo style.

XII Louis XV and Louis XVI 1715-1789

e/religious monuments

- St-Pierre de Montmartre (façade)
- St-Denis-de-la-Chapelle (façade)
- Chapel of St-Jean-Porte-Latine
- Quinze-Vingts hospice
- N-D des Victoires (portal)
- Capucins
- Congregation of the Oratory (portal)
- Ste-Madeleine (new church)
- Ct des Filles de l'Union chrétienne (reconstr.)
- St-Sauveur
- Ct Ste-Perrine
- St-Martin-des-Champs (new dormitory)
- N-D-de-Bonne-Délivrance (later church of St-Pierre-du-Gros-Caillou)
- St-Louis (replaced collapsed St-Thomas-du-Louvre)
- St-Leu St-Gilles (modified)
- St-Germain-l'Auxerrois (choir altered, windows destroyed)
- St-Barthélemy (renovation and collapse)
- Church of the Carmes-Billettes
- Abbey house of Pentémont (church)
- Chapel of La Charité hospital
- Ste-Catherine-du-Val-des-Écoliers
- Ste-Geneviève-des-Ardents
- Ste-Marie-Madelein (enlarged)
- Seminary of Missions étrangères (Foreign Missions, reconstr.)
- Hôtel-Dieu (1)
- St-Jean-le-Rond
- Collège de Bourgogne
- les Quinze-Vingts (ex-barracks of the Mousquetaires Noirs)
- country house of the St-Sulpice clergy
- Pensionnat de l'Enfant-Jésus
- St-Louis-en-l'Isle (bell tower)
- Notre-Dame (damage to central portal)
- The Petit Séminaire of St-Sulpice, country house
- Monastic hospice of Ste-Trinité (Mathurins) renovation of the church
- Abbey of Ste-Geneviève (cloister)
- Seminary of Trente-Trois, country house
- Collège des Irlandais (2nd site)
- St-Médard (choir altered)
- Seminary of St-Esprit (chapel)
- Ct des Filles de St-Michel

Ct = Convent or monastery
N-D = Notre-Dame

1 Fire, start of reconstruction
○ St-Christophe
● Destruction

and outskirts after 1750, luxury handicrafts remained the most specifically Parisian industry, tied to the rich clientele of court and city and vulnerable to the vicissitudes of their fortunes. Above all, Paris was a great center of finance. With the creation of the Bourse in 1724 and the Caisse d'Escompte (a central banking organization) in 1776, influential people, who came with their fortunes to live there, were attracted from the provinces. Thus Paris emptied the provinces of their talent and their capital. Trade was another source of revenue. In 1785 the state surrounded the city with the so-called Fermiers Généraux wall to control customs. In the intellectual and artistic areas, two characteristics of modern Paris appeared: the proliferation of theaters and of specialized schools (e.g. for civil engineering, mines, military, pharmacy, theater) relieving the declining university. Religious life remained active despite a decrease in construction and in the number of new foundations, and even the closing of certains convents (in 1789 there were 50 monasteries for men, 62 for women, 41 churches, 22 major chapels, 11 seminaries). Among the lower and the lower-middle classes religious faith was still strong. In fact, this period can be seen as the "highest point of religious observance." That it was not simply superficial is demonstrated by the tenacious success of Jansenism among the laity and many Paris priests. Despite the efforts of the monarchy to prevent the growth of the city, by 1789 its administration and maintenance had reached that period's limits, with provisioning dependent on peaceful conditions in the country.

1 ST-SULPICE, façade (1732 and after, Jean-Nicolas Servandoni). Reaction against Baroque façades; curves, decorative wall effects, and pilasters are rejected. Return to antiquity (columns, pediment now missing) and to Palladio (superimposed porticoes). Towers added in 1749 and 1777.

2 ST-ROCH (1735-40, J.-R. de Cotte, designs by Robert de Cotte). Discrete Baroque compared to its contemporaries, the Carmine in Turin and the Vierzehnheiligen of Staffeslstein.

3 ST-EUSTACHE, façade (1754-78, Mansart de Jouy, then Moreau). A heavy and bastardized imitation of the façade of St-Sulpice, combined with that of St-Louis des Invalides.

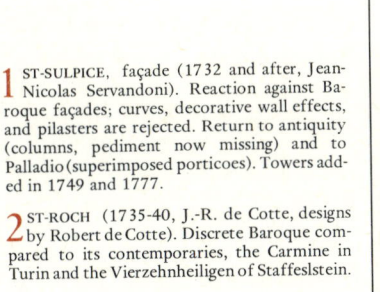

4 ST-PHILIPPE-DU-ROULE (1774-84, Jean-François Chalgrin). In reaction to the Baroque, with its excessive ornamentation, and to plans inherited from the Middle Ages, and buttressed by a more thorough understanding of antiquity, Chalgrin introduced the neoclassical style to Paris. St-Philippe is a basilican church with wooden ceiling and Doric façade.

5 STE-GENEVIEVE (1755-90, Soufflot). Colossal product of the passion for archaeology and of the desire to equal the daring of Gothic architecture with Roman forms, the Pantheon is a fragile tour de force. The grandiose and mathematical space is prodigious.

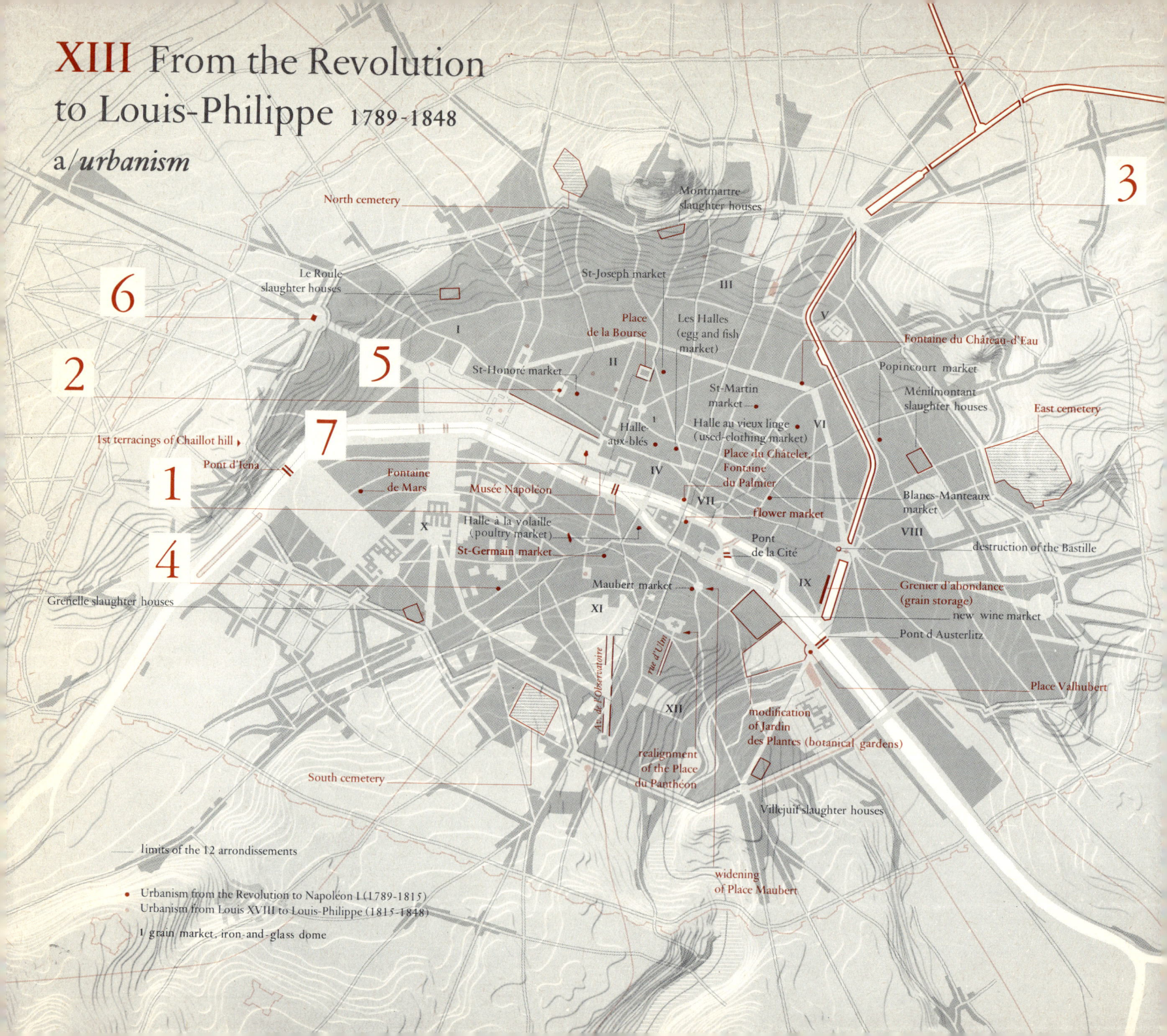

XIII From the Revolution to Louis-Philippe 1789-1848

a/urbanism

- North cemetery
- Montmartre slaughter houses
- Le Roule slaughter houses
- St-Joseph market
- Place de la Bourse
- Les Halles (egg and fish market)
- Fontaine du Château-d'Eau
- St-Honoré market
- Popincourt market
- St-Martin market
- Ménilmontant slaughter houses
- Halle aux blés
- Halle au vieux linge (used-clothing market)
- East cemetery
- 1st terracings of Chaillot hill
- Pont d'Iéna
- Fontaine de Mars
- Musée Napoléon
- Place du Châtelet, Fontaine du Palmier
- Blancs-Manteaux market
- flower market
- Halle à la volaille (poultry market)
- Pont de la Cité
- destruction of the Bastille
- St-Germain market
- Grenelle slaughter houses
- Maubert market
- Grenier d'abondance (grain storage)
- new wine market
- Pont d'Austerlitz
- Place Valhubert
- modification of Jardin des Plantes (botanical gardens)
- realignment of the Place du Panthéon
- South cemetery
- Villejuif slaughter houses
- widening of Place Maubert

limits of the 12 arrondissements

• Urbanism from the Revolution to Napoleon I (1789-1815)
• Urbanism from Louis XVIII to Louis-Philippe (1815-1848)
1 grain market, iron-and-glass dome

The Revolution gravely altered the life of Paris. The disorganization it brought disrupted provisioning, and inflation made all foodstuffs other than bread prohibitive. The riots of the time were caused by the high cost of living, and with the court gone depression set in. Houses were no longer maintained, inflation depreciating rents. The seizure of church property ruined the hospital system; until then 1/4 of church property had been given over to aiding the poor. Parks were threatened as monastery and town-house gardens were overrun by shanties, subdivided by speculators, or closed to the public (under the monarchy all gardens including those of the monasteries had been open to neighboring residents). The sale of property belonging to the church and to émigrés reached 4,400 houses, 1/8 of the city's territory. No one seized this opportunity to build new radial thoroughfares across monastery lands outside the boulevards, a mistake for which Paris still suffers. Instead, the lands were chaotically divided up into small parcels. The departure of frightened citizens, military enlistments, and the Terror —which hit the artisans and lower middle class hardest — caused a decline in Paris. When order was reestablished by the consulate, the first census of the city in 1801 reported 547,756 residents. As heir to the monarchy, the Emperor reinstated the concept of centralization: Paris was to be the capital of Europe. He concentrated all the archives there and wanted to transfer the Holy See to it. He took up royal programs of urbanism again, emptying 16 cemeteries and opening the Rue de Rivoli. Napoleon withdrew all autonomy from Paris and created the Prefect of Police in 1800. He reorganized food distribution with specialized district markets meant to lighten the traffic of the central markets, the slaughterhouses, and the emergency wheat storehouse (grenier d'abondance). To fight unemployment and to indulge his passion for Paris, which he wanted to make "the most beautiful city which could ever exist," Napoleon launched great public-works projects financed by

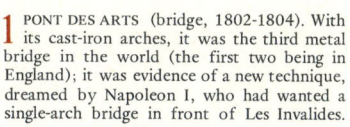

1 PONT DES ARTS (bridge, 1802-1804). With its cast-iron arches, it was the third metal bridge in the world (the first two being in England); it was evidence of a new technique, dreamed by Napoleon I, who had wanted a single-arch bridge in front of Les Invalides.

2 RUE DE RIVOLI (Percier and Fontaine, 1806 and after). Bordered by uniform houses over arcades (after a modest attempt on Rue des Colonnes), it unlocked the Champs-Elysées, linked the boulevards, and served as a rain shelter to the Tuileries gardens.

3 L'OURCQ CANAL. Conceived in 1802 as an aqueduct open to navigation, it was to be, according to the imperial conception, a place of enjoyment, the "Champs-Elysées East."

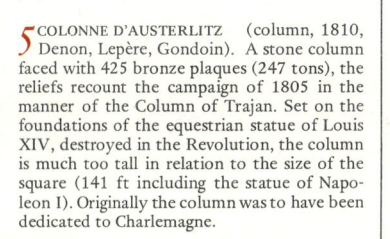

4 FONTAINE DU FELLAH (1806, Bralle). One of fifteen fountains created by the decree of 1806, it expresses the Egyptian mode, but the appearance of the statue remains classical.

5 COLONNE D'AUSTERLITZ (column, 1810, Denon, Lepère, Gondoin). A stone column faced with 425 bronze plaques (247 tons), the reliefs recount the campaign of 1805 in the manner of the Column of Trajan. Set on the foundations of the equestrian statue of Louis XIV, destroyed in the Revolution, the column is much too tall in relation to the size of the square (141 ft including the statue of Napoleon I). Originally the column was to have been dedicated to Charlemagne.

6 THE CHAILLOT ARC DE TRIOMPHE (1806-36). The Emperor wanted "a monument dedicated to the Grand Army, grand, simple, and majestic, without anything borrowed from antique reminiscences"; he had disliked the Carrousel Arch and preferred the Porte St-St-Denis to it. Chalgrin took the hint. Facing a problem of scale which had baffled architects since Colbert (a monument seen from a distance on a hill), he resolved it by raising a simple, powerful, colossal mass (164 by 148 ft).

7 THE CARROUSEL ARC DE TRIOMPHE (1806-1807, Percier and Fontaine). Monumental entrance to the court of the Tuileries palace. Having appeared already at the Hôtel de Salm, this type of entrance reflects Roman inspiration (Arch of Septimius Severus), but revives, in the parades of the Imperial Guard, an authentic function which it could not have had in front of a private residence.

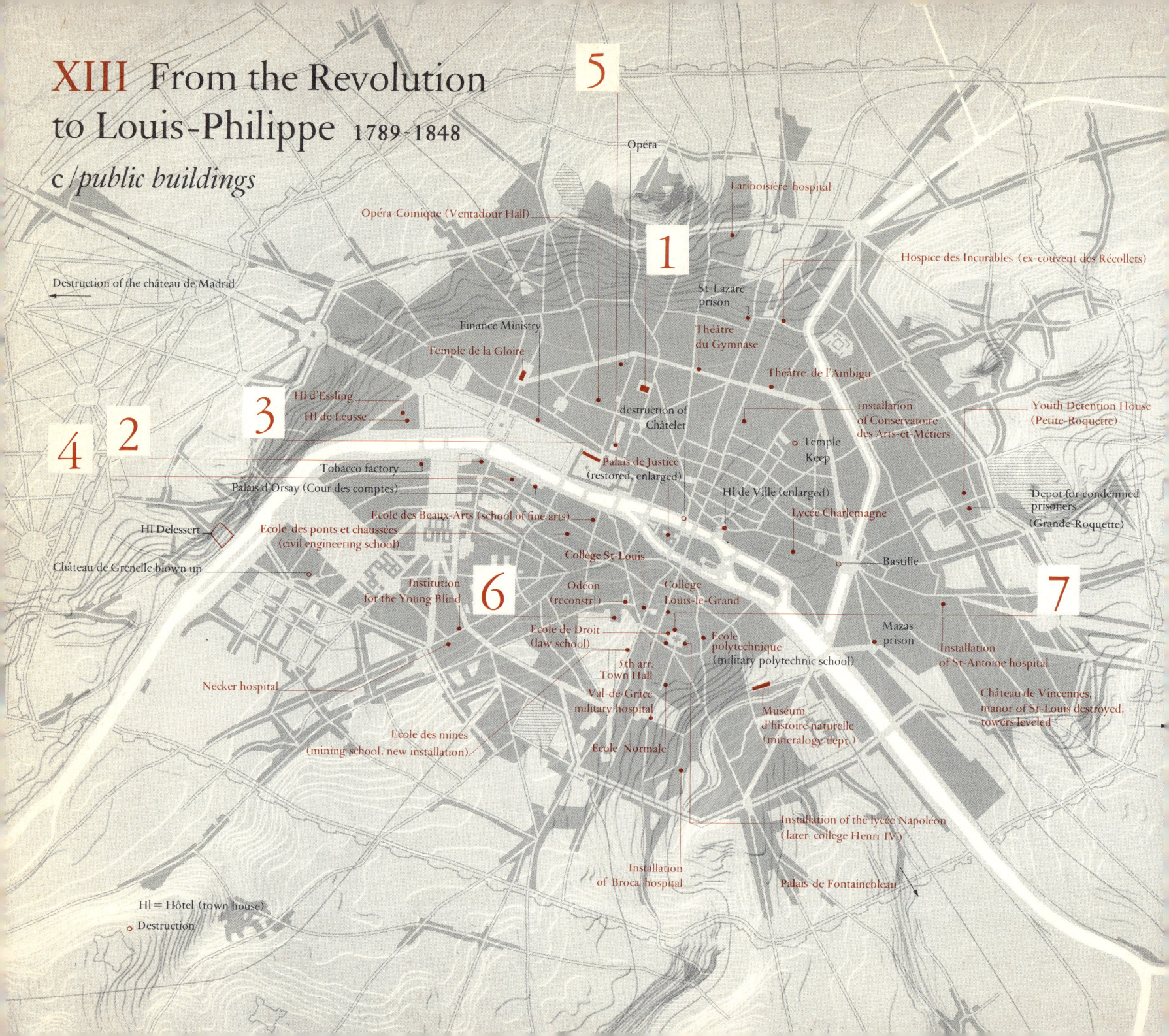

XIII From the Revolution to Louis-Philippe 1789-1848
c / public buildings

Destruction of the château de Madrid

Opéra-Comique (Ventadour Hall)

Opéra

Laribosière hospital

Hospice des Incurables (ex-couvent des Récollets)

St-Lazare prison

Finance Ministry

Théâtre du Gymnase

Temple de la Gloire

Théâtre de l'Ambigu

Hl d'Essling

Hl de Leusse

destruction of Châtelet

installation of Conservatoire des Arts-et-Métiers

Youth Detention House (Petite-Roquette)

Tobacco factory

Palais de Justice (restored, enlarged)

Temple Keep

Palais d'Orsay (Cour des comptes)

Hl de Ville (enlarged)

Depot for condemned prisoners (Grande-Roquette)

Hl Delessert

Ecole des Beaux-Arts (school of fine arts)

Lycée Charlemagne

Ecole des ponts et chaussées (civil engineering school)

Château de Grenelle blown up

Collège St-Louis

Bastille

Institution for the Young Blind

Odéon (reconstr.)

Collège Louis-le-Grand

Ecole de Droit (law school)

Mazas prison

Ecole polytechnique (military polytechnic school)

Installation of St-Antoine hospital

Necker hospital

5th arr. Town Hall

Val-de-Grâce military hospital

Château de Vincennes, manor of St-Louis destroyed, towers leveled

Ecole des mines (mining school, new installation)

Museum d'histoire naturelle (mineralogy dept.)

Ecole Normale

Installation of the lycée Napoléon (later collège Henri IV)

Installation of Broca hospital

Palais de Fontainebleau

Hl = Hôtel (town house)
• Destruction

to 1,053,897 in 1846. The 20 departments had no city of more than 10,000. In 1833 half the Parisians had been born outside Paris, 3/5 of those in the Paris basin. The old city, balanced between middle class and artisan, was submerged by an impoverished proletariat. Construction was active, but " where housing for the middle and lower classes was needed, high-priced apartments were built" (Daubenton). Immigrants overran the furnished lodgings of already overcrowded older districts (the Grève, La Cité, St-Merri). The density in those areas reached 400 per acre as opposed to 125 for the entire city in 1846. The standard of living plunged. The rise in rentals initiated the separation of the middle class from the workers, who had been until then tenants in the same buildings. The demoralization of the workers, driven into slums, began. Violence, prostitution, concubinage, and infanticide characterize the Paris of Balzac. 31 to 39 percent of the children were illegitimate. Abandoned, they formed gangs and became a new criminal force. As in all the large cities of this time, suicide rose because of poverty and isolation: 65 percent of the bodies were unclaimed and unidentified. In 1848, 65 percent of Parisians were so poor that they paid no taxes. From 1824 to 1847, 80 percent of the dead went to a paupers' grave. Sanitary conditions were disastrous. Despite the improved water supply, industrial consumption left only 7 1/2 quarts per person per day. Filled, disjointed, and inaccessible, the sewers were dirty, and covered sidewalks and passages were prevalent. The east of Paris was contaminated by the Bièvre and by the Montfaucon dump; in 1840-44 the former was covered, the latter abandoned. In 1832, after 200 years without plague, a cholera epidemic killed 20,000 people, with the highest mortality in the slums. It was the Paris of "Les Misérables." The pointless revolts in the central districts were born of desperation. These conditions prevailed

1 BOURSE (stock exchange, 1808-26, Brongniart). A return to order: Notre-Dame-des-Victoires, where the Bourse had been installed by the Revolution, was returned to the Church, and the Bourse was housed in a Roman temple.

2 PALAIS-BOURBON (palace), north façade (1806-1807, Poyet). The original low façade was hidden by the Concorde bridge. This new façade echoes that of the Madeleine.

3 LOUVRE, North Gallery (1806-16, Percier and Fontaine). Initiating the complete connection of the Louvre-Tuileries palaces, it symmetrically reproduced the severe ordonnance of the Grande Gallerie, masked since then by a new façade.

4 HOTEL DE BEAUHARNAIS, Egyptian portico (1807, Renard). With the Fellah and Châtelet fountains, it shows the vogue of Pharaonic art even before the publication of the "Description de l'Egypte" in 1809. By its perfection, it also shows the eclecticism and skill of the architects of this era.

5 GALERIE D'ORLEANS, Palais-Royal (1829-31, Fontaine). A double portico separating the palace from its gardens. This harmonious ensemble was glassed-in and filled with shops.

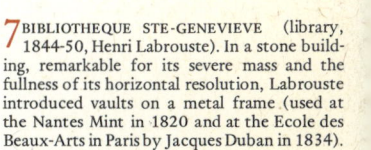

7 BIBLIOTHEQUE STE-GENEVIEVE (library, 1844-50, Henri Labrouste). In a stone building, remarkable for its severe mass and the fullness of its horizontal resolution, Labrouste introduced vaults on a metal frame (used at the Nantes Mint in 1820 and at the Ecole des Beaux-Arts in Paris by Jacques Duban in 1834).

2 PALAIS-BOURBON (palace), meeting hall (de Joly, 1828-32). It replaced that of the Council of the 500 (Gisors, Lecomte). A library and salons were created at the same time.

6 PALAIS DU LUXEMBOURG (palace). Greatly modified for the Senate by Chalgrin in 1804 and by Alphonse de Gisors from 1836 to 1841 to house the Court of Peers. Gisors built a new façade to the south.

XIII From the Revolution to Louis-Philippe 1789-1848
d/religious monuments

- St-Pierre de Montmartre (bell tower)
- St-Jacques – St-Christophe de la Villette
- Ste-Marie des Batignolles
- Chapel of the Martyrs
- Filles Dieu
- Hospice des Enfants Bleus (orphanage)
- St-Jacques hospital
- St-Sépulcre
- N-D de Bonne-Nouvelle (2nd)
- Ste-Madeleine
- Ct des Filles St-Thomas
- St-Jacques-de-la-Boucherie
- Ct des Jacobins
- Ct des Capucins
- Ste-Marie l'Egyptienne
- Temple church
- St-Honoré
- Ct des Feuillants
- Ct des Pères de la Doctrine chrétienne (Doctrinarians)
- St-Germain l'Auxerrois (restoration)
- St-Jean-St-François (ex-church of the Capucins, enlarged)
- Ct des Minimes de Chaillot
- St-Pierre du Gros-Caillou (2nd)
- St-Louis
- Ste-Marie Madeleine
- St-Denys-du-St-Sacrement
- N-D de Grâce de Passy
- Théatins
- Ste-Chapelle (restoration)
- St-Jean-en-Grève
- St-Denis-de-la-Chartre
- Ct des Grands-Augustins
- St-Landry
- Ct des Filles de la Croix
- St-Germain-des-Prés (restoration)
- St-Germain-le-Vieux
- St-Pierre-aux-Bœufs
- St-Paul-des-Champs
- St-Antoine-des-Champs
- Jésuit noviciate
- Ct des Célestins
- St-Jean-Baptiste de Grenelle
- Ct des Bénédictines de l'Adoration perpétuelle du St-Sacrement
- St-Yves
- Ct des Filles de la Trinité
- Notre-Dame (start of restoration)
- Sts-Cosme et-Damien
- Ste Geneviève
- Carmelite monastery
- St-Denis-du-Pas
- Jacobins
- St-Victor (destruction)
- N-D de Bercy
- St-André-des-Arcs
- Collège des Bernardins
- St-Etienne (« des Grés »)
- Collège de Montaigu
- St-Hippolyte
- Collège de Navarre
- St-Hilaire-du-Mont
- Ct = Convent or monastery
- N-D = Notre-Dame
- ○ Destruction
- Carthusian monastery (destruction)
- Ste-Geneviève (Panthéon)
- St-Marcel

throughout the city; only the very rich escaped airless and lightless apartments. Social advance seems to have ceased in the middle bourgeoisie, with property ownership more and more beyond its means. On the other hand, the very rich formed a bourgeois aristocracy. Although expropriation had been defined by law in 1841, the only large-scale works were the completion of the three canals and the fortification of the city, the Fermiers wall still remaining the city limits. Gas lighting (1819 and as early as 1808) permitted the novelty of night life, of which the grand boulevards formed the center. There were other novelties: the cheap newspaper in 1830 and the bus in 1828. The beginning of public transport had already appeared in Bordeaux and Nantes. The era did not lend itself to spiritual life. The slums had succeeded where the Revolution had failed, that is, in the de-Christianization of Paris. Under the Terror, 150 priests continued religious worship in secret, and the expansion of the Church had not stopped (a chapter of the St-Sulpice seminary was founded at Baltimore). After 1799, 62 monasteries were reinstalled in makeshift lodgings. After 1801, churches were returned to religious use, with some now given to Protestants, who, along with the Jews, had renewed their worship openly. The Emperor had made Paris a capital for religious orders and had wanted to supplant Rome in that function. But the ruin of the parishes was fatal to many dilapidated old churches, which were soon torn down. Religious life completely shattered under the Restoration, with the riots beginning in 1822 and the looting of the archbishopric and St-Germain-l'Auxerrois in 1831. Poverty and overpopulated parishes had played as much a role in these events as the royalist politics of the clergy. A reaction took shape in the birth of social Catholicism, the foundation of the Carmelite Friars' school for the higher education of the clergy in 1845, and the intervention of the archbishop, Monsignor Affre, in the battles of 1848 in which he was killed.

1 STE-MARIE-MADELEINE (1806-42, Vignon). Successor to a series of miscarried projects: a domed church, begun in 1764, abandoned in 1777, replaced by another project, razed in 1806. Napoleon wanted a temple of glory dedicated to the Grand Army; but since it duplicated the function of the Arc de Triomphe, it became a church. Vignon created a pastiche of great bearing, an unusual combination of church with pediment or temple with cupolas.

2 EXPIATORY CHAPEL (1815-26, Hippolyte Le Bas and Fontaine) to the memory of Louis XVI, Marie Antoinette, and the 500 dead of the Swiss Guard. Located in the cemetery of La Ville-l'Evêque, where the guillotined of the Terror were buried.

3 NOTRE-DAME-DE-LORETTE (1823-36, Le Bas). As an imitation of Santa Maria Maggiore, it crowned the renaissance of neoclassical architecture begun at St-Philippe-du-Roule. Unvaulted nave and Corinthian portico typical of the archaeological taste of this time.

4 ST-VINCENT-DE-PAUL (1824-44, Lepère, Hittorf). Roman basilica with open timbers, behind a strange façade combining temple and church majestically.

5 TOMB OF NAPOLEON I (1843-61, Visconti). In a crypt at the center of the church of Les Invalides. The Chapel of St-Jerome had sheltered the body of the Emperor from 1840 to 1861.

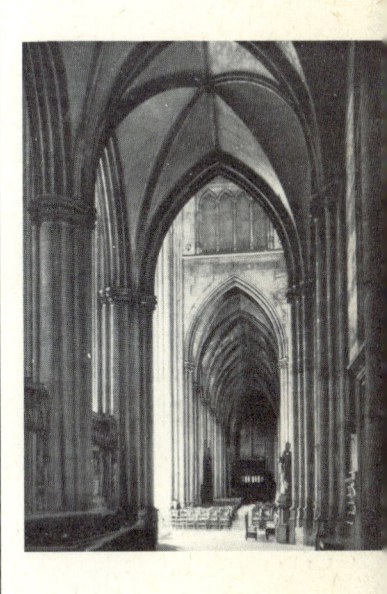

6 STE-CLOTILDE (1846-56, Gau and Théodore Ballu). It represents the reaction of the romantics against the dryness of antiquity as well as basilican churches. But it replaces an often free imitation with a conscientious pastiche, rather successful in the present case. The spires of Ste-Clothilde recall the cathedral of Cologne (Gau's native city), the completion of which had been undertaken in 1842.

XIV The 2nd Republic and Napoléon III 1848-1870

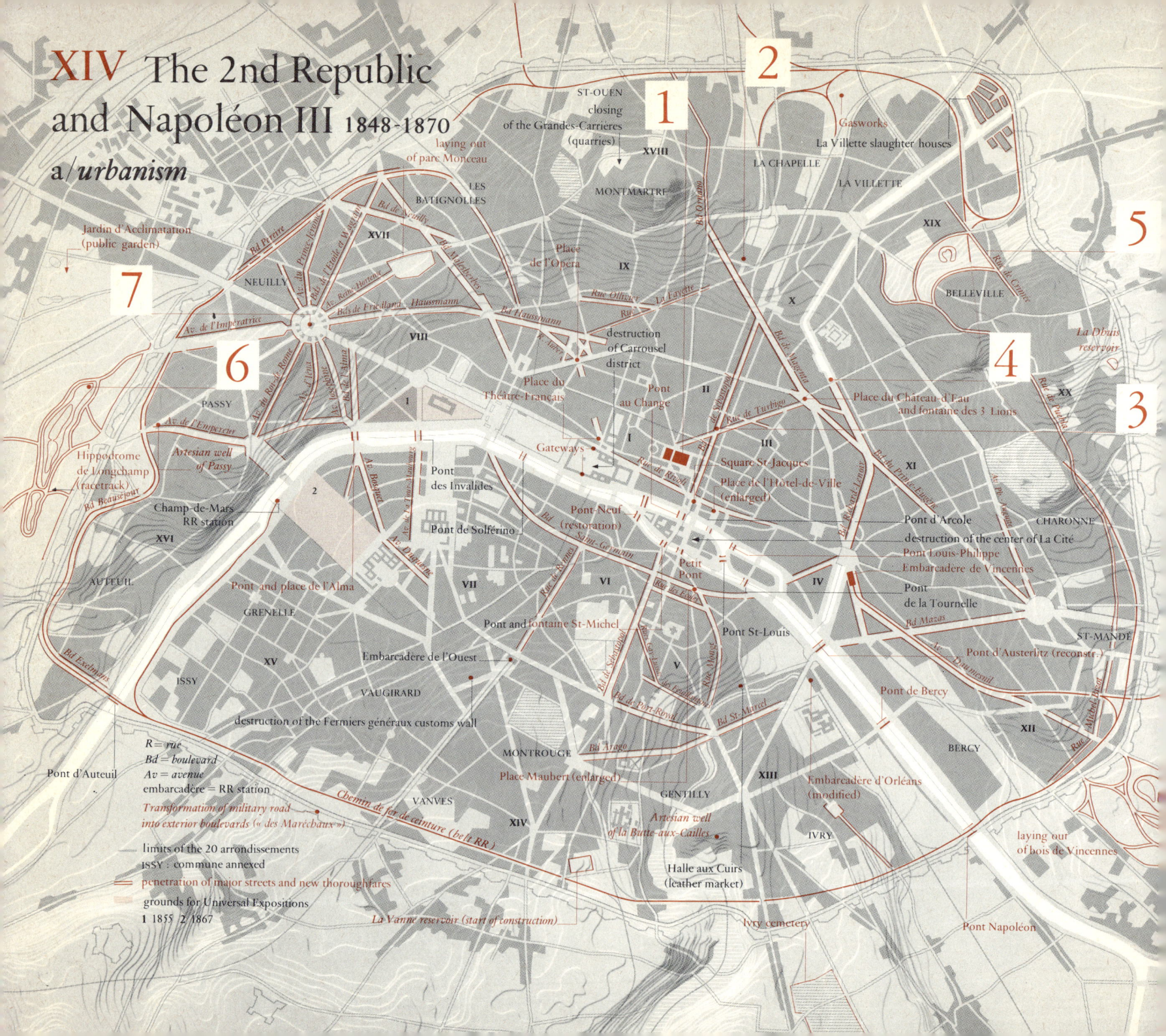

a/ *urbanism*

The radical transformation of Paris under Napoleon III was the response to a catastrophic situation, aggravated by the disorders of 1848 (unemployment, 59,000 premises empty, rents unpaid) and the return of cholera (1848-49, 19,000 dead). The urgency explains the frenetic pace of the work, the brutal determination to move directly to the objective, the lack of diversity, and the otherwise harmless financial contrivances which accompanied the effort. Its momentum and its speed of execution were due largely to the competence of its leaders. The Emperor himself worked alone for 18 months before collaborating with Haussmann, Belgrand, and Alphand. But they also benefited from the economic upsurge of France, in which cast-iron production quadrupled, steam-engine power quintupled as did the length of the railroad, over which transported tonnage decupled. The population grew from 1,053,262 in 1851, with another 234,000 in the suburbs, to 1,825,274 in 1866. By 1870 there were probably 1,970,000. The density in 1856 had been 138 per acre. An impenetrable core of slums formed the center of the city; neither Louis XIV nor Napoleon I had been able to break through it. An old city had never been remodeled intact. Inspired by the example of London's rebuilding, and armed with the expropriation law and the 1850 law against rental of unsanitary housing, the Emperor ordered the overpopulated districts opened up. The new thoroughfares destroyed the slums, aired the population cores. The other major task was to clear the approaches to the railroad stations and to link them. Despite the legend, strategic considerations were secondary. After having drawn up a triangulated plan of the city and, for the first time, surveyed its land forms with precision, they cut through Paris in three campaigns: La Cité was razed, the Rue de Rivoli connected with Rue St-Antoine (the quays had formed the only crosstown artery in Paris), a north-south corridor opened (Blvd. de Strasbourg and Blvd. St-Michel), the circle of grand boulevards completed (Blvd. St-Germain), the radiating circles

1 HALLES CENTRALES (markets, 1852-66, Baltard). The Emperor imposed on Baltard, who had wanted to build in stone, an "umbrella" construction in cast iron and glass, materials used for the first time on a grand scale.

2 GARE DU NORD (R.R. station, Hittorf, 1863). The architect succeeded equally well in both the immense façade with Corinthian pilasters and the glassed metal skeleton, very much admired in their time. The scope of its conception has permitted increasing traffic to be absorbed without modifications.

3 BOULEVARD DE SEBASTOPOL, formerly Blvd du Centre (1855-58). Extending to the Observatory, it produced an infinite perspective. Above all it brutally cleared the way to two stations, linking them to the center of the city. Military imperatives, despite the legend, were secondary.

4 ROOFING OF THE CANAL ST-MARTIN. Depriving the revolutionary districts of a defensive trench and replacing it with gardens, military and humanitarian goals mingled.

5 BUTTES-CHAUMONT (1866-67, Jean Alphand and Barillet). A landscape garden skillfully created at great expense out of old quarries.

6 BOIS DE BOULOGNE (park, 1852-58, Alphand and Barillet). Enlargement (2,157 acres) and transformation of woods and abandoned, dangerous lands into a Parisian Hyde Park.

7 PLACE DE L'ETOILE (1854). On the crest of Chaillot was an intersection of five avenues; Haussmann made it a circle where twelve avenues converged. In 1860 Hittorf constructed twelve identical town houses bordering the circle.

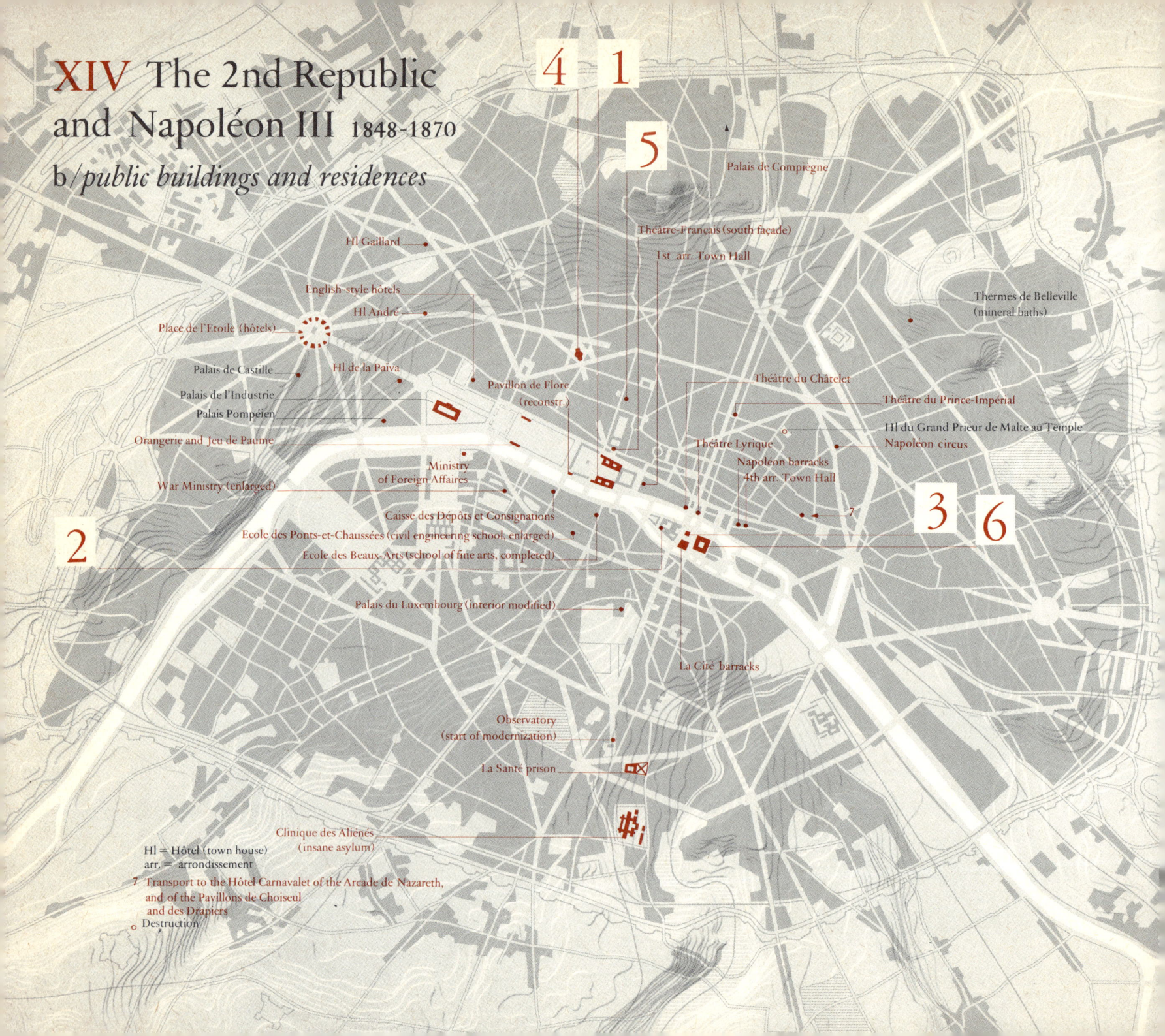

XIV The 2nd Republic and Napoléon III 1848-1870
b/ *public buildings and residences*

Palais de Compiègne

Théâtre-Français (south façade)
1st arr. Town Hall

Hl Gaillard

Thermes de Belleville (mineral baths)

English-style hôtels
Hl André

Place de l'Etoile (hôtels)

Palais de Castille
Hl de la Paiva
Palais de l'Industrie
Pavillon de Flore (reconstr.)
Palais Pompéien
Orangerie and Jeu de Paume

Théâtre du Châtelet
Théâtre du Prince-Impérial
Théâtre Lyrique
Hl du Grand Prieur de Malte au Temple
Napoléon circus
Napoléon barracks
4th arr. Town Hall

War Ministry (enlarged)
Ministry of Foreign Affaires
Caisse des Dépôts et Consignations
Ecole des Ponts-et-Chaussées (civil engineering school, enlarged)
Ecole des Beaux-Arts (school of fine arts, completed)

Palais du Luxembourg (interior modified)

La Cité barracks

Observatory (start of modernization)
La Santé prison

Clinique des Aliénés (insane asylum)

Hl = Hôtel (town house)
arr. = arrondissement
7 Transport to the Hôtel Carnavalet of the Arcade de Nazareth, and of the Pavillons de Choiseul and des Drapiers
o Destruction

of the Place d'Italie, of the Place du Château-d'Eau (République), and of Chaillot (Place de l'Etoile) laid out. Asphalt replaced paving stones, and sidewalks increased from 155 mi in 1842 to 683 in 1870. The cost of 2,500,000,000 francs was paid by the city, state subsidies, loans, and sale of land and materials. Belgrand totally reorganized the water service and introduced a double system with spring water for private use and river water for sanitation. The tapping of the Dhuis in 1863, of the Vanne (completed in 1874), and of the artesian well of Passy doubled the daily water supply to 60 gallons per resident in 1870, before the subtraction of industrial consumption. In 1870 half the houses had water on the ground floor (34,000 versus 6,000 in 1854). A system of entirely new model sewers which would be copied throughout the world was completed in record time (plans done in 1856, main sewers completed in 1868; 93 mi of sewer in 1851, 310 in 1870). The Bièvre was diverted into them. These sewers joined the Seine far downstream from Paris, at Asnières. London's squares and Hyde Park had impressed the Emperor. He wanted to give Paris the parks which it lacked. Although parts of the Luxembourg gardens and the Parc Monceau were appropriated for housing, the installation of narrow squares, parks, and two woods multiplied the city's green area tenfold, to 4,445 acres in 1870. For the paupers' grave Haussmann created the Ivry cemetery in 1853 and envisioned an enormous cemetery at Méry, served by railroad, but opposition put an end to the project. The gas companies merged in 1855 and the number of streetlamps doubled. 1854 saw the first telegraph service. The same year another merger created the bus company, comprising 30 lines and 500 vehicles, but the average Parisian took them only 39 times a year. In 1867 came the omnibus boats. At this date London already had its underground. Paris was surrounded by 18 towns, poorly connected and poorly administered, of 30,000 to 40,000 residents. In 1860 the city limit was extended to the Thiers wall (area: 19,170 acres), annexing these towns. The

1 NEW LOUVRE (1853-57, Visconti, Lefuel). Ending an evolution of 660 years, the Louvre, forming an ensemble with the Tuileries, became the largest palace in the world. After the sobriety of the Louvre of Napoleon, his nephew's addition was distinguished by its overabundance.

2 PALAIS DE JUSTICE, west façade (1857-68, Duc). The sides of the Place Dauphine were opened to disengage this immense façade.

3 TRIBUNAL DE COMMERCE (1865, Ballu). The Italianate dome was constructed to form the focal point of the Boulevard de Sébastopol.

4 THEATRE DE L'OPERA (1862-75, Charles Garnier). A regard for both freedom and logic dictated the combination of masses: loggia for reception, dome over the hall, gable over the stage, enormous volume for the backstage. The profusion of ornament responds to the same regard: Garnier wanted both to proclaim that it was a theater and to create a style in tune with the brilliant Parisian life of the Second Empire.

5 BIBLIOTHEQUE IMPERIALE (library, later Bibliothèque Nationale), reading room (Labrouste, 1868). Perfecting the innovations of the Bibliothèque Ste-Geneviève, Labrouste covered the room with nine iron, faience, and glass cupolas, carried by sixteen cast-iron columns. The walls, detached from the vaults, functioned only to enclose the hall.

6 HOTEL-DIEU (1868-78, Diet). Still Italianate with its arcaded courts. The Hôtel-Dieu should not have been reconstructed on La Cité, for ever since the reign of Louis XV the necessity of relocating it in the outskirts had been recognized.

XIV The 2nd Republic and Napoléon III 1848-1870

c / religious monuments

Synagogue

St-Laurent (new façade)

St-Eugène

Russian church (St-Alexandre-Nevsky)

St-Jean-Baptiste de Belleville

Ct des Filles de la Madeleine (Madelonnettes)

St-Honoré-d'Eylau

St-Joseph

N-D de la Croix de Ménilmonta

Ct des Augustins déchaussés

Ste-Perrine

St-Leu-St-Gilles (new apse)

Ste-Opportune

Ct des Annonciades du St-Esprit

Ct des Récolettes

St-Eloi

Synagogue

Ste-Marine

Monastic hospice of Ste-Trinité

Collège du Cardinal-Lemoine

St-Benoît-le-Bétourné

St-Eloi

N-D des Champs

St-Jean-de-Latran (Hospitallers of St-Jean)

St-Lambert de Vaugirard

St-Marcel

Ct des Filles Anglaises

Chapel of N-D de la Salette

St-Pierre de Montrouge

N-D de la Gare

Ct = Convent or monastery
N-D = Notre-Dame
∘ Destruction

Collège de la Marche

city had outgrown its transportation system. A central station was projected with tracks leading to Les Halles. In the meantime the Belt Railway (19 mi, 27 stations, 3 trains per hour) was in operation between 1862 and 1867 and played an important role in the workers' lives. A steam-run tramway linked Boulogne to the Place de la Concorde in 1854. In addition, the railroad contributed to the development of suburbs such as St-Cloud and Versailles. Despite its upheaval, Paris cut a fine figure. The projects employed 70,000 workers, and raised the price of land (eventually 12 times) and rents. Property was a sure investment. Expropriation compensated well and put both land and capital on the market. The south bank revived as construction flourished. Seven and eight-story buildings provided 215,304 new housing units, versus 117,000 destroyed. They could still not accommodate the wave of immigrants arriving by train. All the activity —the appearance of large department stores, of powerful credit organizations, two world expositions, the brilliance of the court— concealed the workers' problem. At the terminus of canals and railroads, Paris was surrounded by industrial zones. Small and medium-sized enterprises were most prevalent, but a definite concentration of ownership emerged (65,000 employers in 1847, 39,000 in 1866). The annexation of suburban and industrial towns in 1860 brought the proletarian masses of Paris to 416,000 male and 100,000 female workers, many of them foreigners (35,000 Germans, an equal number of Belgians), versus 70,000 artisans. Overtaken by the rise in living costs, high rents drove them back toward the outskirts. There the slums reappeared and drunkenness ran rampant, brought from the countryside but more harmful in the city. Segregation from the bourgeoisie was complete. Traditional restraints broke down; from 1850 to 1900 one out of every two couples living together was unmarried. The Church lost ground, its parishes were crushed by the onslaught (2,500 to 3,000 parishioners per priest), and the revolution of 1848 placed social Catholicism in disfavor.

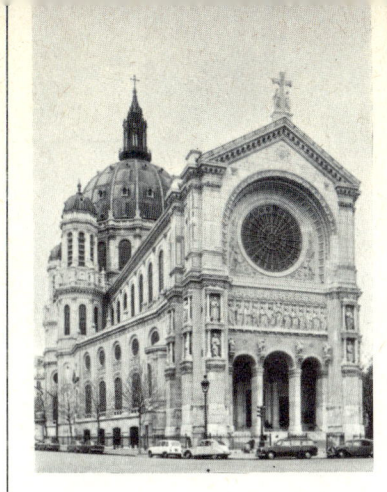

1 ST-AUGUSTIN (1860-71). At first disdaining metallic construction, Baltard was converted after Les Halles. At St-Augustin he built iron vaults on cast-iron piers, enveloped but not disguised by stone walls of Renaissance and Byzantine decoration. The architect thus avoided flying buttresses, which the narrow site prohibited.

2 ST-FRANÇOIS-XAVIER (1861-67, Lusson, Uchard). An uninspired pastiche of neo-Romanesque and pseudo-Renaissance styles.

3 CHURCH OF THE TRINITY (1861-67, Ballu). Attempt at a "style of Napoleon III"; imitative decoration but in its conception a more original façade than many churches of this time.

4 ST-AMBROISE (1863-69, Ballu). A rather successful blend of Romanesque and Gothic, French and Italian. Unlike neoclassical architects, neo-Gothic builders never differentiated their models clearly.

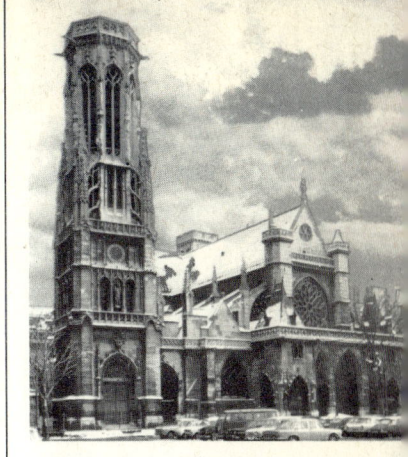

5 BELL TOWER, PLACE DU LOUVRE (1860, Ballu). Pseudo-religious building connecting St-Germain-l'Auxerrois to the neo-Gothic town hall of the 1st arrondissement.

6 NOTRE-DAME, restoration (1844 and after, Viollet-le-Duc). The cathedral was falling into ruin. Despite the success of "Notre-Dame de Paris" by Hugo (1831), the restoration decree did not intervene until 1844. The statuary of the façade is a more or less faithful imitation, the return of certain bays of the nave to their 12th-century state is inexact, but the entire structure of the building was reworked with admirable understanding. The spire, reconstructed in 1860 in cast iron, was a fine success.

XV The Siege of Paris and the Commune
1871

German bombardments

Docks de la Villette (warehouses)

stray shells of the Neuilly batteries

Communard batteries

toppling of Vendôme column
Finance Ministry

Théâtre de la Porte St-Martin

Banque de France

last Communard stronghold

bombardments of the Mont Valérien fort

St-Eustache

Tuileries

Légion d'Honneur
Conseil d'Etat and Cour des Comptes
Caisse des dépôts et consignations

Palais Royal

Théâtre du Châtelet and Théâtre Lyrique

Communard batteries

Hôtel de Ville

Palais de Justice

Préfecture
Notre-Dame

St-Sulpice

Carmelite Friars

Odéon
Sorbonne

Collège de France

Panthéon

Bibliothèque Ste-Geneviève (library)

Ecole Normale

Muséum
Val-de-Grâce
St-Médard

12th arr. Town Hall

Notre-Dame-de-la-Nativité

Observatory

Santé

St-Pierre de Montrouge

Ste-Anne

Gobelins

arr. = arrondissement

burning of the château de Meudon

— Northern limit of German bombardments
— Zone of concentrated German bombardments
• Monuments damaged by German fire
--- Zone bombarded by the Versaillais
--- Zone bombarded by the Communards
→ Advance of the Versaillais
▨ Communard points of appui and zones of most vigorous fighting
• Serious fires of the Commune
○ Destructions anticipated by the Commune

German batteries from Bellevue to Châtillon

The disasters that struck Paris at the end of the Second Empire — the German siege from September 20, 1870, to January 28, 1871, and the revolt of the Commune — were brought on by causes within the city. They climaxed deep unrest which had affected the population and the structure of the city over the preceding 50 years. But some political myths have obscured the facts: Paris was to have been defended by her population, enrolled in the National Guard, but it was betrayed by the "capitulards." In fact, the National Guard hardly fought. Consider the general picture: the garrison at Paris (560,000, of which 110,000 were professional soldiers) lost 5 percent of its total strength, whereas the customary losses during the American Civil War were 25 to 35 percent. The details of losses by category are instructive. The professional army, which totaled 21 percent of its effective strength, or 72.3 percent of total losses. The Garde mobile constituted another 21 percent of the garrison and lost 6 percent of its strength, or 21.3 percent of total losses. The National Guard, forming 58 percent of the garrison, lost .05 percent of its strength, or 6.4 percent of total losses. The defense of Paris had been assured by some units of the professional imperial army, some of which sustained almost 100 percent losses, and by the Mobiles de l'Ouest. The desperate efforts of a handful of trained soldiers entangled in a fleeing mob could not initiate successful sorties. The National Guard, riddled by poverty, ignorance, and alcoholism, which was aggravated during the siege, led by blustering orators, could only impede the army. What is more, the very structure of the city hampered its defenders. Confronted by 110,000 trained soldiers, a force of 236,000 Germans, spread out along 50 miles, was able to block this vast area with little difficulty. Theoretically the defenders would have needed only one day of forced marching, versus two for the enemy, to engage the same troops at two opposite points on the city's perimeter, an advantage which should have forced enemy reserve troops to race from point to point. In fact, the famed "Paris crossroads" obstructed rather than facilitated defensive maneuvers. The lack of wide thoroughfares and of connection between boulevards and outskirts, and the feeble delivery of the Belt Railway slowed the movements of troops. It took two days to send 80,000 men from Neuilly to Vincennes. On the eve of the battle of Buzenval, the congestion of the western quarters was monstrous. Trochu could not think of daily attacks in various directions, which had freed Richmond in 1862 and protected Atlanta in 1864. But the labyrinth of streets was also the principal defense of the city; this maze and the wall, less out of date than has been said, discouraged assaults. German opinion forced Moltke to bombard Paris from January 5 to 28. Some 12,000 shells fell on the left bank, striking 1,400 houses and driving 20,000 people toward the right bank. The statistics: 97 dead, 2,786 wounded, a fiasco more costly in men and materials to the bombarder, under fire from the forts to the south, than to the bombarded. The great stone-and-brick cities would survive bombardment until 1945. Paris was well stocked, with hundreds of thousands of sheep and cows pasturing on the greens, yet all were eaten by November. The faulty system of rationing imposed great shortages on the poor, however, but except for the elderly poor, there was not a true famine. An exceptional cold wave and the lack of heat made poverty that much more punishing. In contrast, alcohol abounded. The siege brought out the adaptability of industry, which produced 300,000 cartridges per day and 400 cannons in 4 months. There were 65 gas balloons, making heavy demands on the short coal supply, which carried 2,500,000 letters and 164 passengers. The first airline, making 2 or 3 departures per week, was extremely lucrative. Peace found the city in a deep malaise. All economic activity had ceased; 100,000 (?) people, primarily the well-to-do, left the city, abandoning it to the poor. The new conservative assembly took provincial revenge on Paris. It ended the moratorium on rents just when the population consisted largely of ruined tenants, and terminated payment of the National Guard, which had acted as an unemployment benefit. The government moved to Versailles. The revolt of the eastern districts on March 18 and the proclamation of the Commune on March 28 produced a new siege and the retaking of Paris by the government army between May 22 and 28. Not more than 40,000 residents fought for the Commune revolution. Neighborhood loyalties, which were strongest among the lower classes, fragmented the defense and left the hostile rich districts unoccupied. The army infiltrated primarily through the outlying gardens, the narrow streets, and the roofs. At times the broad avenues impeded them, since the insurgents had cannons. It was by a series of outflankings, coming from Montmartre, that the Communard positions at the Place de la Concorde finally fell. The Commune set its first fires there to drive back the rooftop snipers. The tally: 3,000 or 4,000 Communards killed in combat, nearly 40,000 prisoners interned at Versailles, about 20,000 executions, 8,700 deported or detained, certain trades decimated (50 percent of plumbers, 35 percent of painters, roofers, cobblers, and cabinetmakers killed, arrested, or in flight), a poisoned social atmosphere (330,000 denunciations), the total rupture between lower middle class and proletariat, until then together at the barricades, a battered city, the Hôtel de Ville destroyed with the archives, entire streets devastated — such was the outcome of the gravest crisis in the history of Paris.

XVI The 3rd Republic 1871-1914

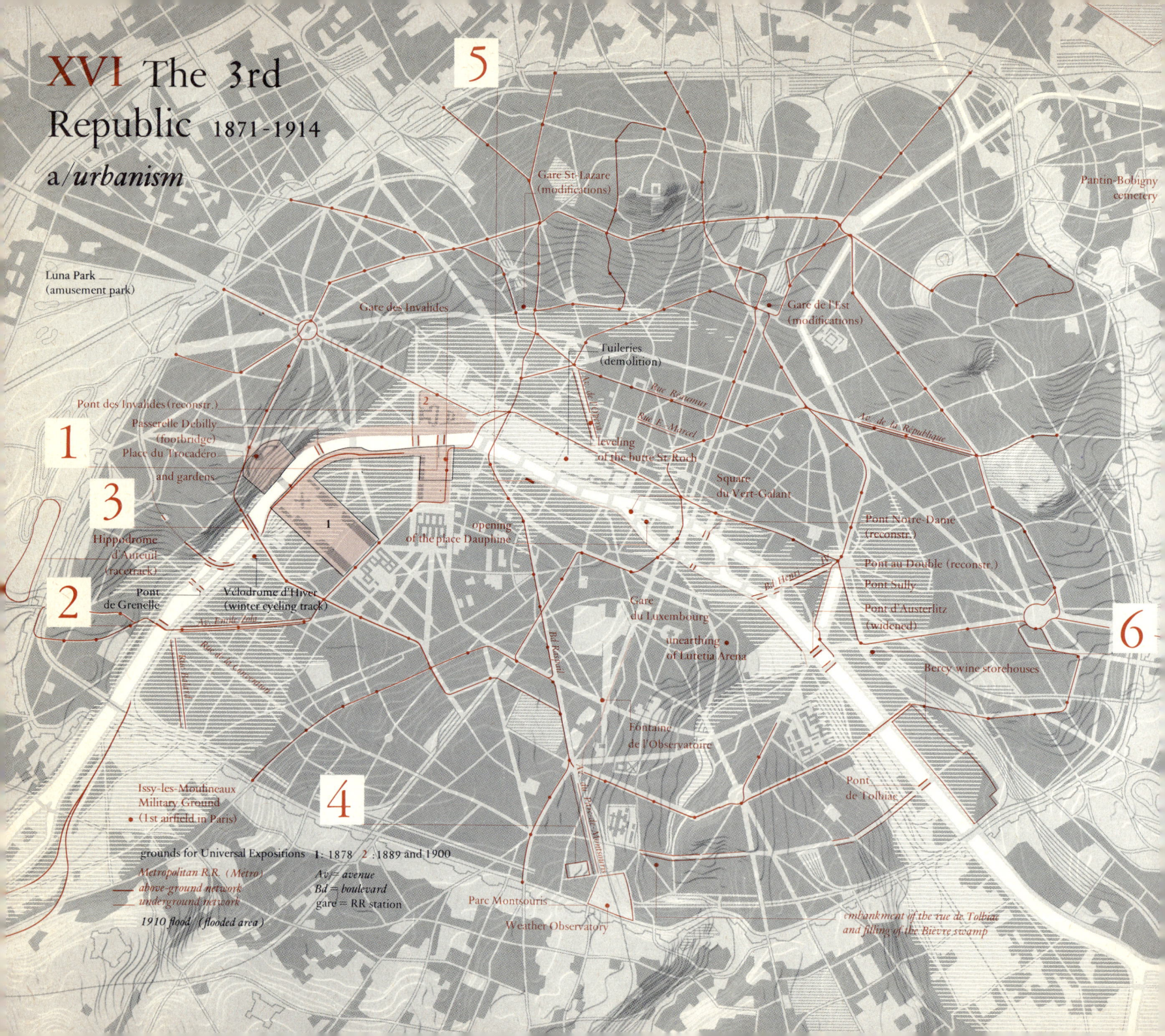

a/*urbanism*

Luna Park (amusement park)

Gare St-Lazare (modifications)

Pantin-Bobigny cemetery

Gare des Invalides

Gare de l'Est (modifications)

Tuileries (demolition)

Rue Réaumur

Rue E. Marcel

Bd de la République

Pont des Invalides (reconstr.)
Passerelle Debilly (footbridge)
Place du Trocadéro and gardens

leveling of the butte St-Roch

Square du Vert-Galant

Pont Notre-Dame (reconstr.)

Hippodrome d'Auteuil (racetrack)

opening of the place Dauphine

Pont au Double (reconstr.)
Pont Sully
Pont d'Austerlitz (widened)

Pont de Grenelle

Vélodrome d'Hiver (winter cycling track)

Gare du Luxembourg

unearthing of Lutetia Arena

Bercy wine storehouses

Bd Raspail

Fontaine de l'Observatoire

Pont de Tolbiac

Issy-les-Moulineaux Military Ground
• (1st airfield in Paris)

Parc Montsouris
Weather Observatory

embankment of the rue de Tolbiac and filling of the Bièvre swamp

grounds for Universal Expositions 1: 1878 2 : 1889 and 1900

Metropolitan R.R. (Metro)
— above-ground network
--- underground network

Av = avenue
Bd = boulevard
gare = RR station

1910 flood (flooded area)

The population of Paris grew from 1,851,792 in 1872 to 2,888,110 in 1911. This increase had slowed and was due primarily to immigration from central France. The birth rate and death rate were almost the same: 25 versus 23 per 1,000. The city reached its saturation point. The density at the core began to decrease around 1890, and the flow back toward the outlying areas was evident. Nevertheless the density, 117 per acre, was relatively low, though it climbed to 402 in the first arrondissement and 421 around Bonne-Nouvelle. A shift of minority groups took place in Paris. Persecutions in central Europe made Paris a stopping place for Jewish emigrants on their way to the U.S. About 30,000 settled in Paris between 1881 and 1914, submerging the Paris Jews. The liquidation of the Commune and recovery were slow. The depression lasted until 1886. Capital was turned to construction only after 1909, with ruins still standing at the turn of the century. The termination of the National Guard and the election of the Municipal Council through universal suffrage were voted immediately but the Assembly did not return to Paris until 1879. In reaction to the foundation of Sacré-Cœur as revenge for the Commune by the conservatives, the Empire was liquidated and amnesty for the Communards, granted in 1880, was sealed by the destruction of the Tuileries palace — still largely intact — in 1882. Depression, the financial burden inherited from Haussmann, absence of authority, red tape, and an obliging attitude toward political fraud marked this era of "inorganic Empire." Some of Haussmann's works were completed, such as the Avenue de l'Opéra, but for the most part disjointed localized operations such as street widening were carried out with complete vandalism. The Expositions of 1878, 1889, and 1900, located in areas that were already developed, resulted in monuments but no extensive city planning. The suburbs expanded chaotically. The primary effort, both

1 PONT ALEXANDRE III (bridge, 1896-1900, Résal and Alby). Typical of both the triumphs and the faltering of late-19th-century architecture: a superb metallic arch (353 ft) to which had to be added garlands, candelabra, and four enormous stone pylons with gilt statues. Before the heights of the Grand Palais, the most striking Baroque vision of Paris.

2 PONT MIRABEAU (1895, Résal). It escaped the over-ornamentation of the late 19th century, at the moment when the point of Vert-Galant Square (see map) had to be embellished with a triumphal bridge, teeming with decorative motifs.

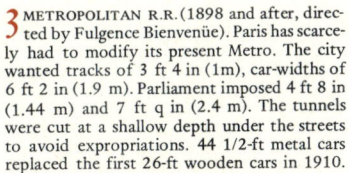

3 METROPOLITAN R.R. (1898 and after, directed by Fulgence Bienvenüe). Paris has scarcely had to modify its present Metro. The city wanted tracks of 3 ft 4 in (1m), car-widths of 6 ft 2 in (1.9 m). Parliament imposed 4 ft 8 in (1.44 m) and 7 ft q in (2.4 m). The tunnels were cut at a shallow depth under the streets to avoid expropriations. 44 1/2-ft metal cars replaced the first 26-ft wooden cars in 1910.

4 MONTSOURIS RESERVOIR (1860-74). Begun in the Second Empire, it received water from the Vanne, Lunain, Voulzie, and Loing rivers, with an 2,925,000 cu ft capacity.

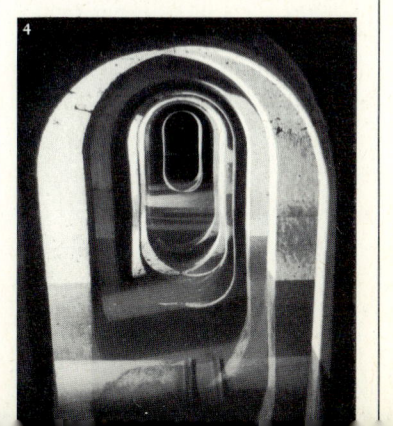

5 GARE D'ORSAY (R.R. station, 1898-1900, Laloux). It was to have been the central station, in the middle of Paris, serving the southwest. Its heavily sculptured colossal façade hid a metallic structure, blending a glass and iron roof with coffered domes, making it the bizarre monument to late-19th-century Baroque.

6 GARE DE LYON (R.R. station, 1899, modified 1927). A clear retreat from the Gare du Nord: illogical façade, flabby sculptures, reminiscences of Big Ben and of the bell tower of Parliament.

XVI The 3rd Republic 1871-1914
b/ *public buildings*

- 18th arr. Town Hall
- Claude-Bernard hospital
- Lycée Jules-Ferry
- Lycée Rollin
- Magasins du Printemps (dept. store)
- Opéra-Comique
- 19th arr. Town Hall
- Rue Bergère telephone exchange
- Cour des Comptes
- 10th arr. Town Hall
- Bourse (stock exchange, enlarged)
- Bourse du travail (labor union headquarters)
- Théâtre Marigny
- Bibliothèque nationale (periodical room)
- Musée Guimet
- Palais-Royal (restoration)
- École Centrale (engineering school)
- Lycée Janson-de-Sailly
- Palais du Trocadéro
- Hôtel des postes (central post office)
- Tenon hospital
- Wings of Louvre (restoration)
- Bourse de Commerce (national business assn.)
- Caisse des dépôts et consignations
- Magasins de la Samaritaine (dept. store)
- installation of musée Carnavalet
- Lycée Molière
- Palais de Justice (tribunal correctionnel enlarged)
- demolition of old Hôtel-Dieu
- Galerie des Machines (exhibition hall)
- École de médecine (medical school, enlarged)
- Célestins barracks
- St-Antoine hospital (reconstr.)
- Magasins du Bon-Marché (dept. store)
- Laënnec hospital
- École pratique de médecine (medical school)
- Institut médico-légal (morgue)
- Lycée Montaigne
- Sorbonne
- Trousseau hospital
- Lycée Buffon
- Lycée Louis-le-Grand (reconstr.)
- Institut Pasteur
- Institut agronomique (agricultural school)
- Muséum (paléontological dept., zoological dept.)
- École de pharmacie
- La Pitié (new hospital)
- 14th arr. Town Hall
- École coloniale (colonial administrative school)
- École nationale des Arts et Métiers (engineering school)
- provisional Broussais hospital
- Institut de paléontologie humaine (institute of human paleontology)
- Faculté de droit (law school, enlarged)
- Institut océanographique
- Lycée St-Louis (enlarged)

arr. = arrondissement

public and private, was made in the area of large facilities: lycées (high schools), hospitals, university buildings, and large professional schools. Technical installations, such as electric lighting (Place de l'Opéra in 1878), which was blocked at first by resistance from the gas companies, signaled the modernization of Paris. Gas consumption rose from 6,177,600,000 cu ft in 1875 to 11,021,200,000 in 1899. The poor areas helped produce this rise, benefiting from a credit sales campaign of gas stoves (120,000 in 4 years). Water-supply projects brought in 75 gallons per resident per day in 1899. In 1881 came the telephone, and in 1905 the Eiffel Tower wireless station. The problem of public transport moved to the forefront. 15,000 cabs, 100 lines of buses, trams (steam, electric, or compressed air), and cable cars (Charonne, Belleville, Montmartre) carried 330,000,000 passengers per year. 106 omnibus boats on the Seine provided transportation to and from the suburbs for 25,000,000 passengers a year. The surface transport system, an incongruous outgrowth of technical trial and error, was inadequate for the expected crowds for the 1900 Exposition. It was doubled by an underground railway, the fourth in the world after London, New York, and Chicago. In defiance of the state, which had wanted to connect the major railway lines beneath Paris, the municipality built its own system, with tunnels purposely too small for standard railroad cars. The first line, Vincennes-Maillot, opened July 19, 1900. Its simplicity and uniform means of access assured it immediate success. Neither the Couronne station disaster in 1903 (84 dead) nor the difficulties of adjustment for a public that was slow-moving unaccustomed to mechanization nor the numerous small accidents diminished the popularity of the Métro. In 1905 the gasoline-driven bus

1 PALAIS DE JUSTICE, Salle des Pas-Perdus (1872-75, Duc and Daumet). Replacing the great hall burned by the Commune, the stone and marble hall, divided by piers and arcades into two tall naves, displays a cold but incontestable grandeur.

2 HOTEL DE VILLE (City Hall, 1874-82, Ballu and Deperthes). Its central section is an imitation of Boccador's Hôtel de Ville, burned in 1871.

3 GRAND PALAIS (1897-1900, H. Deglane, L. Louvet, A. Thomas). Cast-iron exhibition hall, masked by an Ionic façade bristling with sculptures.

4 PETIT PALAIS (1900, Girault). Museum in neo-Ionic style around a semicircular patio.

5 EIFFEL TOWER (1887-89, Eiffel, Koechlin, Nouguier, Sauvestre), 6,900 tons, 984 ft. A stone monument of more than 550 ft was considered impossible; metal construction, first used in England in 1883, solved the problem. A 1,000-ft tower was a dream of the century. The Eiffel Tower realized it, materializing a mathematical formula into an ideal form for wind resistance.

6 THEATRE DES CHAMPS-ELYSEES (1911-13, Auguste and Gustave Perret). First use of reinforced concrete in monumental architecture, and badly criticized as such for its rectilinear resolution during the waning of Art Nouveau. Nevertheless, except for the columns, the concrete is not apparent. A clever use of space permitted the housing of three theaters in one building.

7 GALERIES LAFAYETTE, grand hall (Chanut, 1898). The late-19th-century Baroque style loved rotundas with cupolas and stairways, not limited to department stores (e.g., steamship decoration).

XVI The 3rd Republic 1871-1914

c/residences and offices

- 185, rue Béliard
- 11 to 19, rue de Rochefort
- 36, rue de Tocqueville
- Céramic Hôtel (hôtel)
- Hl Cernuschi
- 14, rue d'Abbeville
- 50, av. Victor-Hugo
- Hl Thiers
- Hl de Sagan (Palais rose)
- Hl de Camondo
- 16, rue d'Abbeville
- Hl de Caillavet
- Hl du Figaro
- 96, av. Poincaré
- Hl d'Ennery
- 104, Champs-Elysées
- 142, rue Montmartre
- 65, rue des Belles-Feuilles
- 39, av. Victor-Hugo
- Restaurant Maxim's
- 11, rue Hamelin
- 30, av. Marceau
- 39, rue Réaumur
- 2, rue de Richelieu
- Syndicat de l'Epicerie (grocers' assn.)
- 7, rue Le Tasse
- 16, rue du Louvre
- 23, av. Rapp
- 9, rue Claude-Chahu
- 29, av. Rapp
- 2, rue de Passy
- 151,
- 134, rue de Grenelle
- 3, square Rapp
- 54, rue de Varenne
- Hl populaire d'Hommes (workmen's residen[ce])
- 18, rue Sédillot
- 195, bd St-Germain
- 96, rue de Charonne
- 33, rue du Champ-de-Mars
- 76-76 bis, rue des Sts-Pères
- Hl Lutetia (hôtel)
- Cercle de la librairie (publishing trade assn.)
- 4, av. de Tourville
- Maison Félix Potin
- Restaurant Vagenende
- 112, av. Mozart
- Hl de la Société de géographie
- 14, av. Perrichont
- Rue La Fontaine
- 24, place Félix-Faure
- 14, rue de l'Abbé-de-l'Epée
- workers' housing, rue de la Saïda

Av = avenue
Hl = Hôtel (town house)

appeared. Controls on public health were institutionalized for the first time: medical examinations in the schools in 1879, housing inspections in 1883, a department of contagious diseases in 1892, records of building sanitation in 1893. The fact that the death rate near St-Merri was 10 times greater than around the Champs-Elysées raised the question of housing. In 1884, 215,000 people lived in furnished apartments. Only 13 percent of families of 6 had more than one room per person. Nevertheless Paris was less overcrowded than Berlin or Vienna, where 50 percent of one-room accomodations had 3 to 5 occupants. In Paris two thirds of such lodgings had single tenants. Already driven out of the center, the workers were now driven from the outlying districts by new high-rent buildings. Workers' rents rose steadily, even though an overabundance of housing resulted in brief interludes of relief for middle-class tenants. Starting in 1880, low-priced housing had been considered and discussed, but the idea did not begin to coalesce until 1896, with the Departmental Committee for Low-Cost Housing (Habitations à Bon Marché). On the other hand, these demands were tempered by such factors as the workers' advance into the middle class, by a decrease in large families, and by the increasing number of single people (31 percent of the population in 1894 versus 6 percent in Berlin). The law of 1884 allowing divorce had swelled this last category. The demand was for smaller units in greater number and, for a large stratum of the population, more comfort. The elevator became common, which permitted uniformly high rents and the same social makeup on all floors. Following the eclecticism of the 70s and 80s in architecture, the Art Nouveau style, concrete, and the revival of the cantilevered floor characterized

1 PALAIS GALLIERA (1878-88, Ginain). Conceived from the beginning as a private museum, this Italian Renaissance imitation is typical of the eclecticism of the 1880s.

2 OFFICE BUILDING, 124, rue Réaumur (1903-1905, Georges Chedanne). A visible metal frame filled in with glass, realizing the house of "iron timbers" envisioned by Viollet-le-Duc. Related in its technique and its bay windows to the great newspaper buildings of London.

3 CASTEL BERANGER, 14, rue La Fontaine (1898, Guimard). A manifesto of Art Nouveau in France, reaction against the dryness of neoclacissism. Guimard balanced the austerity of the façades with a very calculated asymmetrical abundance of decoration limited to precise points, the entrance in particular with its vegetal grill and reliefs of glazed ceramic.

4 PRIVATE TOWN HOUSE, 60, rue La Fontaine (1911). Elegance, severity, and simplicity characterized the end of Guimard's Art Nouveau style. The modeling of the façade is a Baroque legacy.

6 APARTMENTS, 25 bis, rue Franklin (1903, A. Perret). If metal-frame construction was pioneered in the United States, the reinforced concrete building was conceived in Paris in 1878. But it was affirmed with this building of reinforced concrete sheathed in granite.

7 APARTMENTS, 26, rue Vavin (1912, Henri Sauvage). With its successively retreating volumes, covered by white ceramic, this building represents a particular current, different from the early International Style.

5 APARTMENTS, 18, av. du Président-Wilson (1913, Tauzin). Reaction against Art Nouveau: flat surfaces, stylized neoclassical elements, a successful search for elegant simplicity. Beginning of the style of 1925.

XVI The 3rd Republic 1871–1914
d/religious monuments

- Ste-Geneviève-des-Grandes-Carrières
- St-Jean-l'Évangéliste
- St-François-de-Sales
- St-Charles-de-Monceau
- Ct des Filles de l'Union chrétienne
- St-Georges
- N-D de Lourdes
- St-Stéphane (Greek church)
- Armenian church
- St-Thomas-d'Aquin (portal)
- Ct des Hospitalières de Notre-Dame
- demolition of old Hôtel-Dieu
- Collège des Prémontrés
- Ct des Filles de la Croix
- Institut catholique (Catholic University)
- St-Antoine-des-Quinze-Vingts
- Collège de Navarre (library)
- St-Eloi (reconstr.)
- N-D d'Auteuil
- Ste-Pélagie
- St-Jean-Baptiste-de-la-Salle
- Carmel de l'Incarnation
- Seminary of the Trente-Trois country house
- Ste-Anne-de-la-Maison-Blanche
- N-D-du-Rosaire
- St-Hippolyte

N-D = Notre-Dame
Ct = Convent or monastery
○ Destruction

the striking phenomenon of the fine
neighborhoods, the beaux quartiers. Behind
Baroque façades, Art Nouveau architecture
introduced the flexible floor plan; the apartment
was divided up to suit the tenant. The
division between rich and poor is strikingly reflected
in religious life, as witnessed by the ratio of
civil burials. Around 1900, the churchgoing
districts were Auteuil, Chaillot, and the western
part of Les Batignolles, with a north-south
division drawn at about St-Sulpice. 20 percent
of the funerals in the Marais were civil,
33 percent in the 20th arrondissement; there
were 6 times more civil burials at Charonne than at
Passy. Paris had 69 parishes at this time. The
new churches were built outside the old
Fermiers Généraux wall. Innovations alongside
imitations appeared, such as the reinforced
concrete cupola on St-Jean-de-Montmartre, 1897.
More than ever a literary and artistic capital,
Paris was the world center for painting
and was outstanding in the sciences as well (the
wireless and radium, 1898; the Pasteur
Institute; decisive advances in aviation). Three
world expositions met with growing success.
With the development of artificial lighting, night
life grew: cabarets, music halls, and, in
1895, motion pictures with 64 theaters by 1911.
The accompanying proliferation of posters
changed the street scene, of which Paris and
London were the centers. All this created
a brilliant and largely illusory image of Paris and
of the belle époque. The great flood of 1910
recalled to this modernized city the continuing
presence of its millenial problem resulting
from the occupation of the old riverbed. The
war, entailing a moratorium on rents,
neatly ended the growth of construction,
creating a break in the history of Paris.

1 BASILICA OF SACRE-CŒUR DE MONTMARTRE (1876-1919, Abadie). White, enormous, and unfaithful imitation of Romano-Byzantine churches, particularly St-Front de Périgueux; improved by the 308-ft tower built 1905-10 by L. Magne.

2 NOTRE-DAME-DU-TRAVAIL (1899-1901, Jules Astruc). An iron construction like the glass roof of a station or a market hall, awkwardly initiating the adaptations of religious architecture to modern materials and forms.

3 ST-JOSEPH-DES-EPINETTES (ca 1910). Work of an anonymous architect, it is one of the churches where the gropings of a new style were manifest. The thin concrete supports make no attempt to imitate Romanesque piers. The cupola recalls the grand halls of department stores.

4 SYNAGOGUE, rue Pavée (1913-21, Guimard). The convex-concave movement, with the porch roof introducing a contrary direction, transposed with extreme simplification the façades of Borromini or of P. da Cortona, demonstrating the affinity between the Baroque and Art Nouveau.

5 ST-DOMINIQUE (1913-21, Gaudibert) was to religious architecture what the Théâtre des Champs-Elysées had been to civil architecture: the first large building in concrete. The stylistic inspiration, however, remained Byzantine.

XVII The 3rd Republic 1914-1940
a/*urbanism*

- administrative limits
- gare = RR station
- ISSY : commune partially annexed (from 1925 to 1930)
- Metropolitan R R (metro)
  - 1914 network
  - 1940 network
- underground passage

1. grounds for 1925 Exhibition of Decorative Arts
2. 1931 Colonial Exposition grounds
3. 1937 Universal Exposition grounds

Between the two wars, the problems of Paris completely outstripped the means and, even more, the concepts of the controlling powers. Crushing needs accumulated. The general situation must be kept in mind: the declining population in France, the worlwide economic crisis (the first signs appeared in France in 1932, with a depression lasting from 1934 until the war). With 2,829, 753 inhabitants in 1936, or 148 per acre (6 times the density of New York), Paris was now only the dense center of a formless agglomeration of 6,190,457 inhabitants. In the 70 years preceding the crisis, the population had increased by 70 percent, while that of the suburbs had grown 500 percent. Since 1890, centralization, the convergence of railroad lines, and the abundance of manpower had formed the country's largest industrial complex around the capital (1,250,000 workers in 1933). Between 1911 and 1936, 60,000 residents moved back toward the suburbs, while a large foreign population immigrated to the center: 46,000 Russians in 1931, 58,000 Poles, 70,000 Jews, driven out by the disturbances in eastern Europe. Paris was encircled by industrial suburbs, at first developed to the north and west on flat terrain, along the canals and railroad tracks supplying the factories. The towns blessed with a railroad station grew 10 times faster than those without. Between the railroad lines, especially on the plains to the south, farmland still began at the city's gates (in 1840, 88,920 acres cultivated in the Seine department; in 1933, 44,460). As industrial, financial, and commercial capital, hosting the Paris Fair of 1920, and as seat of the head offices of all the large companies and a great river port and air center (Le Bourget airport handled 64,000 passengers in 1932, 105,000 in 1936), Paris had drained all nearby cities and ruled at the center of a broad agricultural region. The city consumed 17,550,000,000 cu ft of gas per year. For electricity, the Massif Central with the Eguzon dam served as reinforcement to the city's steam generators. The area from

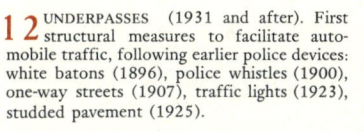

1 2 UNDERPASSES (1931 and after). First structural measures to facilitate automobile traffic, following earlier police devices: white batons (1896), police whistles (1900), one-way streets (1907), traffic lights (1923), studded pavement (1925).

3 PONT DU CARROUSEL (1935-39). Concrete with stone veneer. The preceding bridge (1834), which became inadequate, had not been on axis with the Louvre gateways. Its statues were reused on the new bridge.

4 PORTE DE ST-CLOUD (fountains by Landowski). Several gateways to Paris were installed at this time according to traditional conceptions, more esthetic than practical (Porte Dorée with fountains, Porte de la Muette with statues).

5 BOIS DE VINCENNES ZOO. Opened in 1934, modified in 1935-36. Covering 35 acres, it replaced a 1931 zoo left from a colonial exhibition. These had been preceded by the royal menagerie and the old but lush menagerie of the Jardin des Plantes (botanical gardens).

6 LES TOURELLES SWIMMING POOL STADIUM (1924, Bévière). As at La Butte-aux-Cailles, concrete and the increased conveyance of water allowed pools to be built on the heights, in a common people's district far from the Seine bathing facilities.

7 LA BUTTE-AUX-CAILLES SWIMMING POOL (1922). A nave with clerestory transposed into concrete, it resembles a church more than do many more recent churches.

8 PIERRE-DE-COUBERTIN STADIUM (1935-38, Crevel, Carée, Schlienger). Enclosed, it specialized in indoor sports and tennis. One of the stadiums installed in the "Military Zone."

XVII The 3rd Republic 1914-1940

b/*public buildings*

- Pleyel Hall
- Bichat hospital (reconstr.)
- Bretonneau hospital
- Champerret firemen's barracks
- Claude-Bernard hospital (reconstr.)
- Firemen's barracks: 8, rue Mesnil
- Théâtre de Chaillot
- Aquarium du Trocadéro
- Printemps (new stores)
- Galeries Lafayette (renovation)
- Palais de la Découverte (science museum)
- Bibliothèque nationale (catalogue room)
- St-Lazare
- École, 21 av. de la République (primary school)
- Banque de France (enlarged)
- Palais-Royal (courts cleared)
- Samaritaine (new stores)
- Caisse des Dépôts et Consignations (enlarged)
- PTT Ministry
- Merchant Marine Ministry
- Bon-Marché (new stores)
- Collège de France (laboratories)
- Hôpital des Enfants-malades (children's hospital, enlarged)
- Institut d'optique
- Institut du radium
- 5th arr. Town Hall (reconstr.)
- Maison de la Mutualité (convention hall)
- Lycée Hélène-Boucher
- Institut d'art et d'archéologie
- Curie hospital
- Muséum (wild animal and monkey houses) (botanical gallery)
- Lycée La Fontaine
- Lycée Claude-Bernard
- Lycée Camille-Sée
- 15th arr. Town Hall
- École normale supérieure (enlarged)
- Musée d'Orléans
- De Rotschild hospital
- Bureau central des chèques postaux (postal bank)
- Service technique des constructions navales (shipbuilding institute)
- 15th arr. Town Hall (enlarged)
- Cochin hospital (modernization)
- La Pitié hospital (modernization)
- Manufacture des Gobelins (enlarged)
- École nationale supérieure d'aéronautique (aeronautical engineering school)
- Institut d'hygiène dentaire (dental school)
- Musée de l'Industrie du bois (wood products)
- École, rue des Morillons (primary school)
- Broussais hospital
- École de puériculture (school of child welfare)
- École de la rue Kuss (primary school)
- restoration of the château de Vincennes
- Cité universitaire (university residences)

arr. = arrondissement
PTT = Post, Telephone and Telegraph
Destruction

which Paris drew her provisions spread as far as Poland and Morocco. The administrative framework was still that of the Second Empire, and Paris had special problems which no one was trying very hard to resolve. The west-central area was overrun with offices, losing 35 to 50 percent of its population, while the density reached 433 per acre near St-Gervais. Infant mortality (66.9 per thousand in the department in 1938) was higher than the French average. Mortality from tuberculosis was 3 or 4 times higher in the poor arrondissements (11th, 13th, 19th, 20th) than in the well-to-do 16th. Out of 17 housing blocks declared unsanitary in 1923, only 2 were destroyed. The problem of housing and of parks became urgent. The failure of authority in these areas was especially disastrous. The only political solution was to destroy parks. There was talk of transforming the site of the old fortifications, razed 1920-24 (law of April 19, 1919), and the military zone, annexed 1925-30, into a belt of park. But the project miscarried under the maneuvering of political opposition and pressures from various interests. The area did receive some sports installations and the Cité Universitaire (student residential complex) but all in all, it was covered with mediocre buildings which soon became neighborhood afflictions, e.g. the Habitations à Bon Marché (low-income housing, called HBM) and Habitations à Loyer Modéré (middle-income housing, called HLM). The administrative measure of annexing the Bois de Vincennes and the Bois de Boulogne changed nothing, though the surface of Paris now increased from 19,266 acres to 26,024. The politics of housing were worse. To avoid aggravating the inflation, rents had been frozen at very low rates. The law of 1918 made permanent the 1914 moratorium on rents and prohibited rents from going above their level of August 1914. Economic crises quickly canceled out the small revisions of 1922 and 1925. In 1935 a decree reduced all rents by 10 percent. Construction was carried on only in the rich areas. To modernize or even maintain the old buildings in modest neighborhoods became impossible for owners. The property ownership of Paris was mortally

1 MUSEE DES COLONIES (museum, 1931, Laprade, Jaussel). Its peristyle and bas-relief inaugurated the neoclassicism of the 1930s, condemned by the partisans of glass cubes. Their works have deprived their protests of much weight.

2 MOBILIER NATIONAL (state furniture repository, 1935). Perret was much closer to the classicists than was thought at the time: three-part plan, peristyle, mathematical division of the façades.

3 MUSEE DES TRAVAUX PUBLICS (Museum of Public Works, 1937-38, A. Perret). First modern museum in Paris, it remained unfinished until 1956, when it was given another use.

4 PALAIS D'ART MODERNE (Museum of Modern Art, 1935-37, Dondel, Aubert, Viard, Dastugue). The two museum buildings, linked by a portico, form a harmonious ensemble utilizing the slope of the land but are badly adapted to their function.

5 ECOLE PRATIQUE DE MEDECINE (medical school, 1937-53, Madeleine and Walter). Dwarfing its venerable neighborhood, this catastrophe would serve as a warning and not a model for the future Paris.

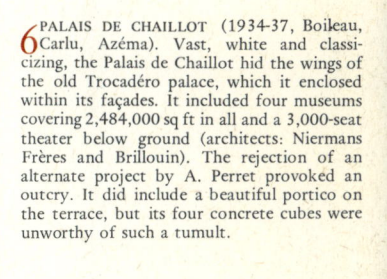

6 PALAIS DE CHAILLOT (1934-37, Boileau, Carlu, Azéma). Vast, white and classicizing, the Palais de Chaillot hid the wings of the old Trocadéro palace, which it enclosed within its façades. It included four museums covering 2,484,000 sq ft in all and a 3,000-seat theater below ground (architects: Niermans Frères and Brillouin). The rejection of an alternate project by A. Perret provoked an outcry. It did include a beautiful portico on the terrace, but its four concrete cubes were unworthy of such a tumult.

XVII The 3rd Republic 1914-1940
c/residences and offices

13, rue des Amiraux

168-172, Faubourg St-Honoré
Cercle militaire (officers' club)

3 131-133, av. Malakoff

Ford Building

Hôtel Prince-de-Galles
Hôtel George-V
Garage Marbeuf

33, av. Montaigne

115, av. Henri-Martin

1, av. Paul-Doumer

2

8, rue du Renard
Vert-Galant Building **6**

5, rue du Dr-Blanche
89, quai d'Orsay
51-55, rue Raynouard
10, square du Dr-Blanche
3, quai Conti
41, rue Raffet

1

42, av. de Versailles
25, av. de Versailles

137, bd Raspail

126, bd du Montparnasse
Transfer of Hôtel de Massa

5　　　　　　　　　　　　　　　　　　　　　　　　　　　　**7**

Cité Seurat
Maison Ozenfant **4**

Av = avenue
Bd = boulevard

Fondation Deutsch-de-la-Meurthe
Fondation Internationale

wounded. The urban deterioration of Paris became perhaps irremediable in other ways. Some projects of Haussmann were completed, but new public buildings were built too small. One could speak calmly of gutting the Marais and the St-Germain-des-Prés area, which had been blighted by the new medical school. The suspicious inaction of the administration abandoned Paris to the insidious vandalism of speculators. "The historic areas fell into disrepair, the new areas were below the level of mediocrity" (A. Chastel). A significant development, with striking consequences today, was that the opposition, the "progressive" theoreticians, pressed for further rigidity, destruction, and impersonality. Le Corbusier wanted to raze the center of Paris, to dwarf La Cité, the Marais, and the Louvre under 18 identical giant towers. On the subject of this Voisin Plan (1925), the great American historian Lewis Mumford wrote: "Unfortunately, Le Corbusier's imagination, deeply in harmony with the negative tendencies at work in contemporary society, has for a whole generation been the most powerful single influence over architecture and city planning." Traffic, regulated by a 1925 ordinance, began to be a problem. By 1938 there were 1,000,000 vehicles, 320,000 of them automobiles. The encircling "Boulevards des Maréchaux" were modified to accommodate them. The automobile played a part in the shift of activity from the boulevards to the Champs-Elysées, where the breadth and circles re-created the effect of the former carriage promenade of the Cours-la-Reine. The biggest projects, such as the successful 1937 Exhibition and the extension of the Métro into bordering communities (approved in 1927, completed in 1937), were conceived to employ the idle during the economic crisis. In 1933, before the depression, trams (with routes covering 683 mi), buses (373 mi), and the Métro (89 mi) carried 1,030,145,000 passengers. But the problems of the suburbs were even greater than those of Paris, where public authority was even weaker. While the state crushed property

1 APARTMENTS, 14, rue Guynemer (1928, Roux-Spitz). Search for simplicity, elegance, light. Façade in smooth stone, disguising the concrete structure.

2 RUE MALLET-STEVENS (1927, Robert Mallet-Stevens). Bare surfaces, cubic and cylindrical volumes fit together: the first obvious example in Paris of the International Style.

3 LE POSTE PARISIEN BUILDING, 116 bis, Champs-Elysées (broadcasting center, 1929, Debouis). Bay windows dominated and modeled the façade. First commercial broadcasts in France began in 1921, television in 1932.

4 FONDATION SUISSE, Cité Universitaire (Swiss students' center, 1930, Le Corbusier and Pierre Jeanneret). First major achievement by Le Corbusier in Paris: pilotis, obvious structure, glass walls, opposition of volumes, distinction of functions.

5 COLLEGE NEERLANDAIS, Cité Universitaire (Dutch students' center, 1927, W. Dudok). As a Neoplasticist, Dudok employed large juxtaposed volumes which were his characteristic but not his usual deep-set windows. He tended to International Cubism.

6 CLINIC-RESIDENCE OF DR. D'ALSACE, "Maison de Verre" (1931, Pierre Chareau). The new material of glass brick appeared at the same time as concrete. Guimard had already used it in Castel Béranger; in 1914, Bruno Taut combined it with a steel frame (Glass House, Cologne). Reverting to this technique, together with innovations in the organization of interior space, Chareau created a monument which remains unequaled.

7 REFUGE DE L'ARMEE DU SALUT (Salvation Army, 1932, Le Corbusier). An imperfect realization of his theories: he was unable to control the proliferation of windows or to oppose additional supports for the masses.

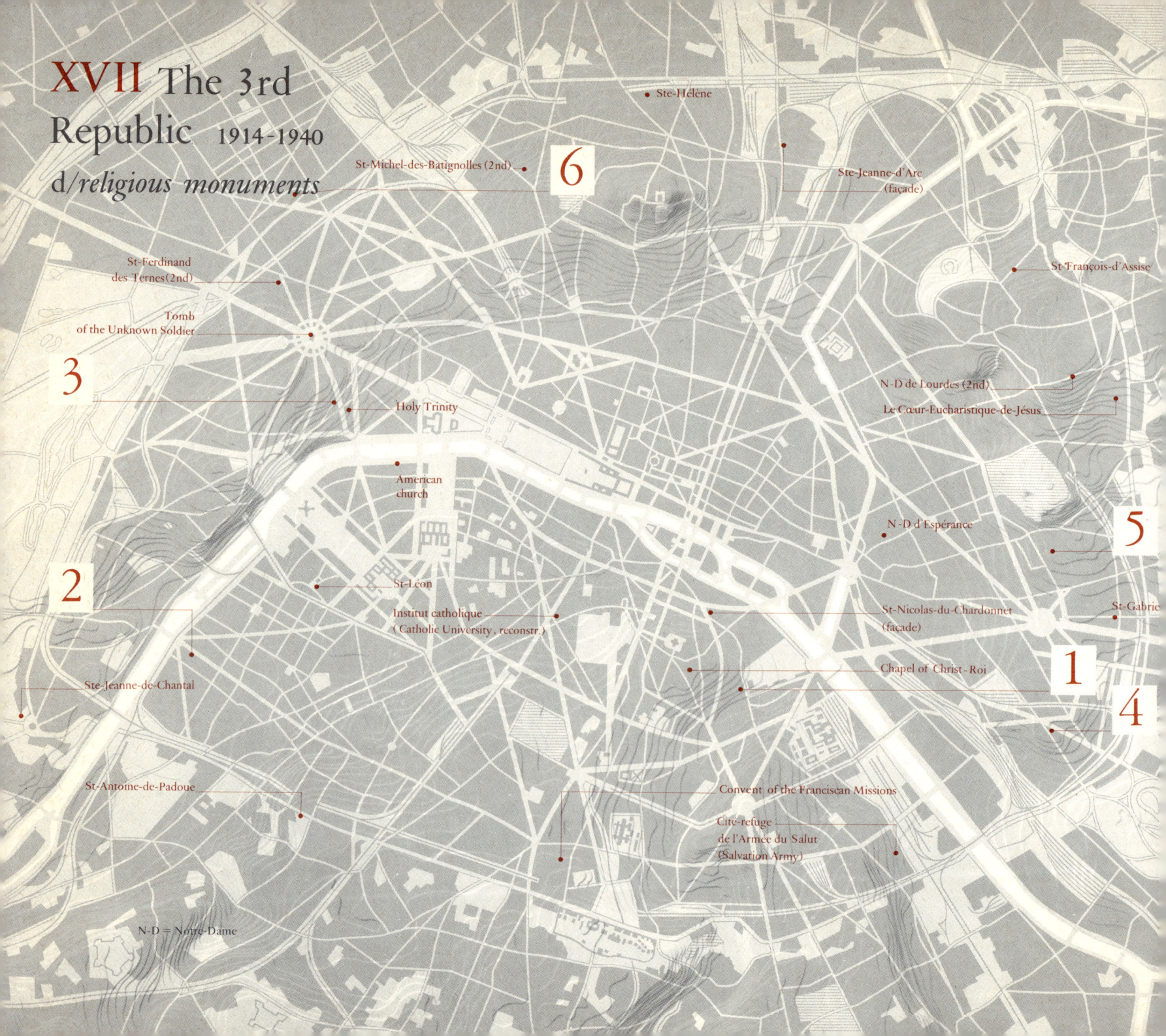

XVII The 3rd Republic 1914-1940
d/*religious monuments*

- Ste-Hélène
- St-Michel-des-Batignolles (2nd)
- Ste-Jeanne-d'Arc (façade)
- St-Ferdinand des Ternes (2nd)
- St-François-d'Assise
- Tomb of the Unknown Soldier
- N-D de Lourdes (2nd)
- Holy Trinity
- Le Cœur-Eucharistique-de-Jésus
- American church
- N-D d'Espérance
- St-Léon
- St-Nicolas-du-Chardonnet (façade)
- St-Gabriel
- Institut catholique (Catholic University, reconstr.)
- Ste-Jeanne-de-Chantal
- Chapel of Christ-Roi
- St-Antoine-de-Padoue
- Convent of the Franciscan Missions
- Cité-refuge de l'Armée du Salut (Salvation Army)

N-D = Notre-Dame

ownership in Paris, it gave incentive to
individual construction in the suburbs (the
Loucheur law of 1928) without making any
provision for its organization. Thousands of acres
were covered with dwellings lacking sanitary
facilities, sometimes a 45-minute walk from
a station. The daily journey for workers often
reached an exhausting two hours, which
overwhelmed public services and choked the
Paris stations and their approaches. A vicious circle
resulted: the new, purely residential agglomerations
("sleeping communities") had limited revenues
and could not improve the function of their
services. The failure was total when in 1939 a
worker's family, the supposed beneficiary of the
Loucheur law, could not afford to build
a small cottage. Once recognized, the problem was
buried in a High-Level Committee for the
Organization and Expansion of the Paris Region
(1928), which took until 1934 to draw up
a regional urban plan, and until 1939 to approve it.
The social structure of the agglomeration,
the deplorable conditions of life, and the depression
were reflected in the deep malaise of the 30s.
The suburbs moved toward a more and more
extreme left, first socialist, then communist.
37 to 45 percent of the electorate in the Seine
department outside Paris supported the
far left in 1928 and 1932, 45 to 52.5 percent in
1936, as a result of the depression and the
Front populaire. Paris, meanwhile, moved to the
political right and saw itself surrounded by
what was called the red belt. As early as 1924,
P. Vaillant-Couturier could write: "Paris
has its faubourgs (working-class districts) again."
There were furious and bloody riots in
January and February of 1934. In this atmosphere
the rejection of the Church could only increase,
despite a vigorous effort in construction outside
the city (e.g., the building projects of
Cardinal Verdier in 1932 and after). Yet
formalities remained strong: 80 percent of infants
in the surburbs were baptized versus 72
percent in Paris. But the number of civil weddings
increased over those in the Church.

1 MOSQUE (1922-26, Huebès, Fournez, Mantout). Religious, intellectual, and commercial center, a pleasant imitation of Hispano-Moroccan style.

2 ST-CHRISTOPHE-DE-JAVEL (1926-34, Ch. Besnard). A blend of bastardized, old-looking forms with modern elements lacking great style. The principal interest of the building is its having been the first to be constructed from prefabicated elements of reinforced concrete.

3 ST-PIERRE-DE-CHAILLOT (1933-37, E. Bois). A perfect example of Romanesque-Byzantine-Cubist combinations, showing the difficulties of architects at this time to create church façades. The interior is somewhat more successful than the exterior.

4 CHURCH OF THE HOLY SPIRIT (1928-35, Tournon). Inspired by Hagia Sophia in Constantinople. Reinforced concrete allowed the architect to attempt the vast interior space of Byzantine churches and to rediscover their majesty.

5 ST-JEAN-BOSCO (1933-37, Rotter). Using reinforced concrete, Rotter did not try to imitate the curves of stone vaults. The decoration of the panels just below the ceiling is typical of the 1925 style and recalls the salons and bedrooms of this period.

6 STE-ODILE (1934-38, Barge). Reinforced Concrete covered on the exterior by pink brick, it again invokes Byzantine influence in its ceiling with three segmental cupolas.

XVIII The War, the 4th and 5th Republics

a/*urbanism*

If defeat and war left Paris largely undamaged (.8 percent destruction versus 7 percent for the others French cities), they aggravated the deterioration in housing and facilities. Stripped of 1,000 vehicles, the bus service took 20 years to regain its 1939 level. The overtaxed Métro became run-down. Rents were frozen in 1940. With the increases of 1945 and 1947 canceled out by inflation, 1948 rents represented 4 or 5 percent of their 1914 value. The net revenue of properties was zero, while the cost of construction had increased 40 percent since 1914. Protected from eviction, tenants became de facto owners, subletting at prohibitive prices. Construction did not resume. Despite the war and temporary exodus and annihilation of the Jews, cornered at last by their persecutors, the population did not decline. A terrible housing crisis developed, yet entire districts were emptied of tenants and overrun by offices and shops, which were still profitable because of less tightly regulated rents. Recovery was initiated with the law of September 1, 1948, which began to free rentals, which multiplied 6 times between 1948 and 1956, while the cost of living doubled. Construction started up again, but it was so far behind that it could not hope to catch up in a city that continued to grow (population 2,295,000 in 1941; 3,035,000 in 1960). The completely urbanized area had more than 6,600,000 residents, Greater Paris about 8,000,000. This was a normal phenomenon, with some 15 cities in the world boasting more than 4,000,000 residents. Giant cities had become a characteristic of contemporary civilization. In France itself, other cities grew faster than Paris, but Paris was abnormal in its density:

1 LEFT BANK EXPRESSWAY. Installed at low cost on the banks of the Seine, it doubled the traffic of the quays. Elsewhere the banks became parking lots.

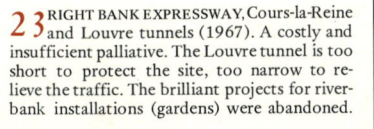

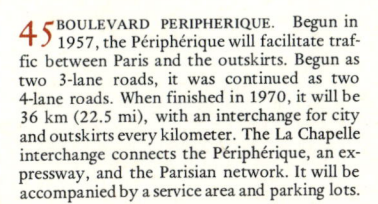

2 3 RIGHT BANK EXPRESSWAY, Cours-la-Reine and Louvre tunnels (1967). A costly and insufficient palliative. The Louvre tunnel is too short to protect the site, too narrow to relieve the traffic. The brilliant projects for riverbank installations (gardens) were abandoned.

4 5 BOULEVARD PERIPHERIQUE. Begun in 1957, the Périphérique will facilitate traffic between Paris and the outskirts. Begun as two 3-lane roads, it was continued as two 4-lane roads. When finished in 1970, it will be 36 km (22.5 mi), with an interchange for city and outskirts every kilometer. The La Chapelle interchange connects the Périphérique, an expressway, and the Parisian network. It will be accompanied by a service area and parking lots.

7 MAINE-MONTPARNASSE ENSEMBLE (Lopez, Beaudoin, de Marien). Business complex concentrating 21,000 people on one station, in an already congested area, without easy access to the city. The architecture is of questionable quality, a disfiguration of Paris.

8 REGIONAL EXPRESS SYSTEM (1961 and after). Traversing Paris, connected to the Métro, it will offer commuters on certain axes highly efficient rapid transit with specific exits which bypass the rush-hour crowds of the railroad stations.

9 PONT DU GARIGLIANO (1967). Forms the closing of the ring of exterior boulevards.

6 UNDERGROUND PARKING GARAGE (1963), the first in Paris (720 places) to free the Les Invalides esplanade, overrun by cars.

XVIII The War, the 4th and 5th Republics

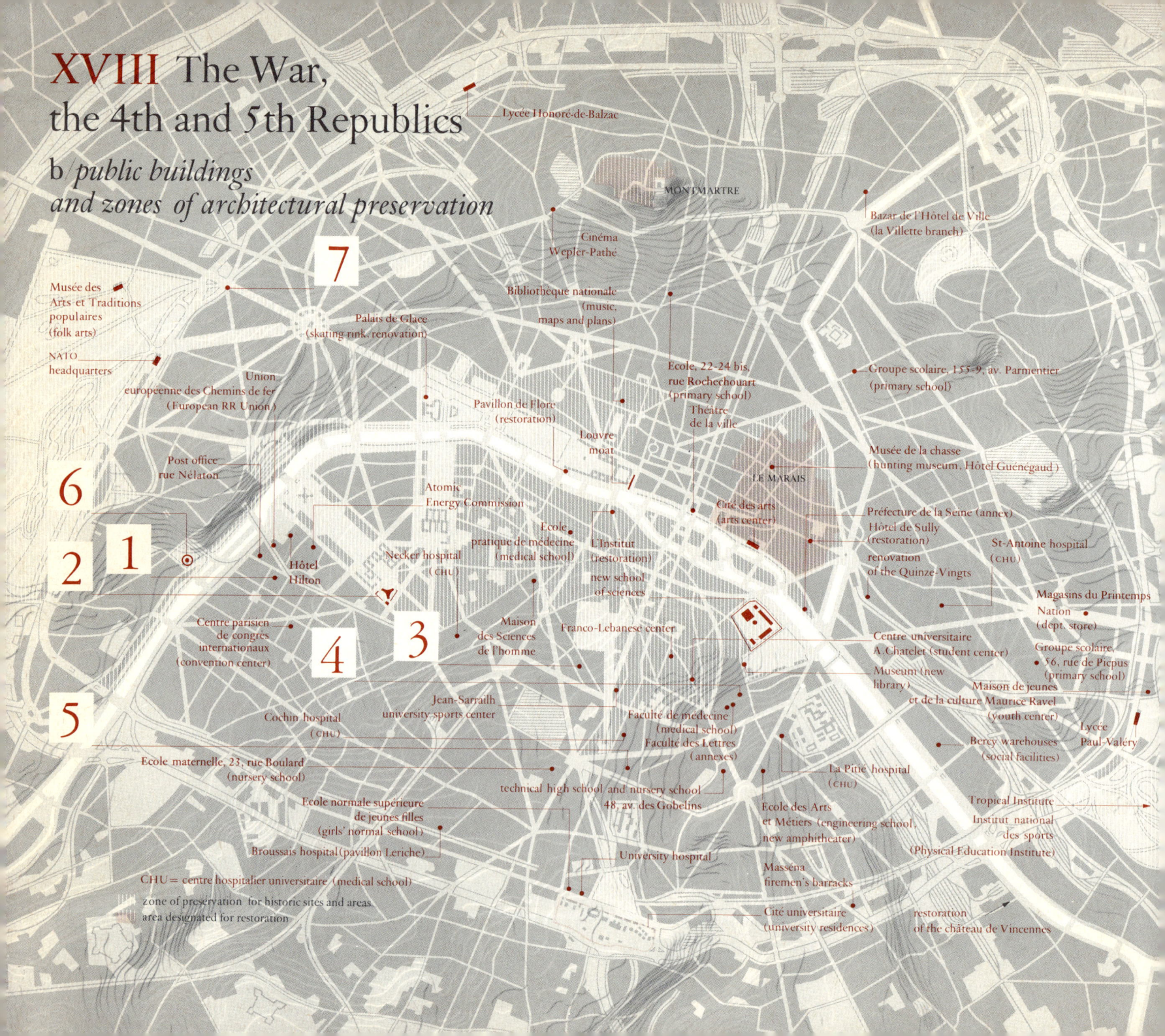

b/ *public buildings and zones of architectural preservation*

Lycée Honoré-de-Balzac

MONTMARTRE

Cinéma Wepler-Pathé

Bazar de l'Hôtel de Ville (la Villette branch)

Musée des Arts et Traditions populaires (folk arts)

Palais de Glace (skating rink, renovation)

Bibliothèque nationale (music, maps and plans)

NATO headquarters

Union européenne des Chemins de fer (European RR Union)

Pavillon de Flore (restoration)

Ecole, 22-24 bis, rue Rochechouart (primary school)

Groupe scolaire, 155-9, av. Parmentier (primary school)

Théatre de la ville

Louvre moat

Cité des arts (arts center)

Musée de la chasse (hunting museum, Hôtel Guénégaud)

LE MARAIS

Post office rue Nélaton

Atomic Energy Commission

Ecole pratique de médecine (medical school)

L'Institut (restoration) new school of sciences

Préfecture de la Seine (annex) Hôtel de Sully (restoration) renovation of the Quinze-Vingts

Hôtel Hilton

Necker hospital (CHU)

St-Antoine hospital (CHU)

Centre parisien de congrès internationaux (convention center)

Maison des Sciences de l'homme

Franco-Lebanese center

Magasins du Printemps Nation (dept. store)

Centre universitaire A. Chatelet (student center)

Groupe scolaire, 56, rue de Picpus (primary school)

Museum (new library)

Maison de jeunes et de la culture Maurice Ravel (youth center)

Cochin hospital (CHU)

Jean-Sarrailh university sports center

Faculté de médecine (medical school) Faculté des Lettres (annexes)

La Pitié hospital (CHU)

Bercy warehouses (social facilities)

Lycée Paul-Valéry

Ecole maternelle, 23, rue Boulard (nursery school)

technical high school and nursery school 48, av. des Gobelins

Ecole des Arts et Métiers (engineering school, new amphitheater)

Tropical Institute

Ecole normale supérieure de jeunes filles (girls' normal school)

Institut national des sports (Physical Education Institute)

Broussais hospital (pavillon Leriche)

University hospital

Massena firemen's barracks

CHU = centre hospitalier universitaire (medical school)
zone of preservation for historic sites and areas
area designated for restoration

Cité universitaire (university residences)

restoration of the château de Vincennes

up to 142 per acre and much higher in localized areas. London, with a population of 8,200,000, reached only 53 per acre. Paris was too small, but with 463 to 560 sq mi versus London's 834 sq mi. Nine tenths of this agglomeration was suburbs, where 60 percent of the population lived, only 40 percent worked, and where immigrants were relegated. More than 1,000,000 came from the provinces between 1945 and 1960. While the inner suburbs counted births as half their population increase, the distant suburbs counted immigration as two thirds of theirs. In all, 46 percent of the agglomeration residents in 1960 had been born in the provinces, and one in ten was not French (North African, Spanish, Portuguese). French immigration came as much from the west and central country as from the east and southwest cities. The average age was 20 to 25 years, and 56 percent were female. This influx of labor and management, constantly replenished, reflects and maintains the economic supremacy of Greater Paris and reinforces the accusation that Paris is turning the rest of the country into a desert. 17 percent of the French population, 25 percent of the workers, 27.5 percent of the employed, 21 percent of industrial installations, 38 percent of higher management, and 50 percent of business conducted by industrial and commercial companies is located on 2 percent of the country's territory. Paris is at the same time the seat of government and the center of business management. It has seen the size of the commercial and service sector sextuple between 1862 and 1962, while the industrial sector, still made up of small units, has only tripled. In this enormous

1 CAISSE D'ALLOCATIONS FAMILIALES rue Viala (public welfare, 1960, Lopez, Reby). Polyester curtain walls, with colored panels.

2 UNESCO HOUSE (1955-58, Marcel Breuer, Pier Luigi Nervi, Bernard Zehrfuss). The principal building, the Secretariat, is 7 stories on piers. Its concave façade, result of the Y-plan, harmonizes the building with its environment (Place de Fontenoy). In fact, it is too tall for the latter and too low for its function, an error in trying to place more modern architecture next to the older.

3 FACULTE DE DROIT ET DES SCIENCES ECONOMIQUES. (law and economics school, 1951-62, Lenormand). Overcrowded, the university splintered into modern or, as in the Middle Ages, existing annexes.

4 CENSIER UNIVERSITY RESTAURANT (1965, H. Pottier, J. Tessier). Its high glass façade marks the only architectural success in the new expansion of the Latin Quarter.

6 MAISON DE L'O.R.T.F. (broadcasting center, 1964, H. Bernard). A double crown of buildings encircles a tower whose actual height (246 ft) is unfortunately less than the 328 ft planned. A fine architectural success.

7 INSTALLATION OF LA PORTE MAILLOT (G. Gallet). Monumental gateway to Paris and reception complex. 1,000-room hotel, 3,000-seat convention center which is inadequate. Placed to the side, the hotel tower (460 ft) takes into consideration the view of Etoile, a regard that is exceptional among many disquieting projects.

5 MINISTRY OF NATIONAL EDUCATION project (J. Faugeron). A 520-ft tower, one of the few beautiful forms among the projects threatening Paris. Situated within the vista of the Champ-de-Mars, it would disfigure it less than Montparnasse tower, but the latter will hide it.

XVIII The War, the 4th and 5th Republics

c/residences, offices, and zones of renovation

4 — Porte Pouchet, RIQUET, FLANDRE TANGER, OURCQ

1 — SECTEUR 9, 85, rue Jouffroy, 27, place St-Ferdinand, 7-9, rue La Pérouse, 23, av. Marceau, Centre Boussois (documentation center for the glass industry), PLACE DES FÊTES, HAUTS DE BELLEVILLE, ÎLOT 7, ÎLOT 11, MARAIS, ST-BLAISE

5 — Square Mozart, 19, rue du Dr-Blanche, 3, rue Henri Heine, 54, av. de Versailles, FRONT DE SEINE, 54, bd de Grenelle, Mutuelle du Bâtiment et des Travaux publics (public works contractors assn.), 96, bd Raspail, Tour Érard, ST-ÉLOI

6 — LECOURBE CROIX-NIVERT, 53-9, av. du Maine, 5,15, rue Maturin-Régnier, ALLERAY PROCUIÈRE, VANDAMME

7 — PLAISANCE, MARINIERS, BERCY, ÎLOT 13, BIÈVRE, DEUX MOULINS, ITALIE, LA HIRE CLISSON

2 3 — Maison de l'Italie, Maison du Mexique, Maison du Liban, (students' centers) Maison du Cambodge

Bd = boulevard
Av = avenue
Zone of renovation

city the situation remained critical until the end of the 50s. Needs were such that, despite an immense effort, a solution is no closer.
In the winter the hospitals were short 2,000 beds. Out of 52,500 hotel rooms only 15,000 had modern comforts. The suburbs were underequipped, with one lycée per 44 sq mi versus one per 6 sq mi in Paris, 58 to 87 gallons of Seine water per inhabitant versus 95 to 119 gallons of so-called pure water for Parisians (Rome 143, Chicago 265 gallons per person). The need for water was just barely satisfied in dry seasons. Out of 63,180,000 cu ft of waste water, 35,100,000 had to be poured back into the Seine without treatment. A third of the garbage was burned, 20 percent used as fertilizer, and no one knew what to do with the rest. There were 6.28 sq yds of park area per Parisian (Rome 11, Vienna 42), 1.2 sq yds of children's park per 15 children! The Parisian house was older, smaller and more poorly equipped than those of the large provincial cities. 30 percent of the buildings were more than 100 years old, another 35 percent more than 50 years old, Out of 3,000,000 dwellings, 500,000 had no water, 1,400,00 had no private toilet, 2 out of 3 had no bath or shower (if they had them, water rationing would have prevented their use). The construction of 427,374 housing units from 1944 to 1960 did not ease the crisis, which also slowed the destruction of slum dwellings (412,000 counted, housing 1,060,000 people). In 1959 more than 400,000 people lived in furnished rooms and shanties. New housing was on the average too small, often badly constructed (1/4 of these "new slums" should be destroyed), and always too expensive. Because

1 CAISSE D'ASSURANCES, 37, rue de la Victoire (insurance building, 1959, Balladur, Lebeigle, Tostivin). A beautiful steel and glass form, a stranger to its older surroundings.

2 MAISON DU BRESIL, Cité Universitaire (Brazilian students' center, 1957, Le Corbusier and Lucio Costa). After the Unité d'Habitation in Marseille and the realization of Ahmedabad and Chandigarh, Le Corbusier reverted to the formula of the Fondation Suisse with a system of sun-shielding loggias.

3 APARTMENTS 67, rue Barrault (Auger and Pulcinelli). A humorous transformation of a pile of bottle cases, one housing unit per case.

4 ANNEX OF THE BAZAR DE L'HOTEL-DE-VILLE 119, rue de Flandre (1962, Anger). Commercial and residential ensemble, built by a department store, of interesting prismatic forms. It relates to redevelopment plans for declining districts.

5 SEINE FRONT (R. Lopez, H. Pottier). One of the areas of renovation of the 15th arrondissement. It will include sixteen 115-ft towers over 5 stories of concrete slabs separating traffic, parking, and green areas into special levels.

6 OPERATION BERCY (Zehrfuss). On the site of the partially preserved wine warehouses; 3,240,000 sq ft of offices; 4,000 residences; commercial, social, and sports facilities.

7 PLACE D'ITALIE DISTRICT (Ascher, Holley, Braunsarda, Micol, Solotareff). Restructuring and balancing of functions: services on the avenue, housing away from it.

XVIII The War, the 4th and 5th Republics

d/*religious buildings and commemorative monuments*

of this, in 1966 from 15,000 to 30,000 new dwellings were vacant, unsold despite the persistent crisis. The sale of apartments as condominiums became widespread from 1950 to 1960, driving out the tenant of moderate means and locking the well-to-do elderly retired in the center of the city, where work and schools were nevertheless concentrated. Such were the results of rental policies from 1914 to 1948, and of unchecked speculation which, from 1900 to 1963, multiplied the price of land 200, 500, and even 1,000 times (e.g., the Champs-Elysées), bringing about excessive exploitation. Private houses, gardens, and buildings in perfect repair were destroyed and replaced by modern blocks with the complicity of the state (the law of January 24, 1956, permitted the destruction of parkland because of their "insufficient" use). At the same time, the irresponsible choice of automobiles over adequate housing aggravated these evils and created new ones. In 1949 parking was allowed on public thoroughfares in violation of public law which strictly prohibited it. As a result, in 1963 there were more than 1,700,000 cars for 330,000 parking spaces. The sidewalks were overrun, the streets permanently choked, cleaning operations paralyzed, public transport, fire engines, ambulances, delivery trucks, and police vehicles obstructed by the permanent congestion. The most essential services were sacrificed to the big-money interests and vanity of a minority, for in Paris the automobile is a social symbol more than a means of transport. Aside from the din, the enormous loss of work hours, and the resultant irritation, the exhaust fumes (also from

1 STE-JEANNE-DE-CHANTAL (1936 and after, Barbier). Built of rubble, finished after World War II, it shows the segmental cupola and porch-façade typical of certain churches since St-Dominique. The façade is flanked by a detached bell-tower as at Marie-Médiatrice.

2 STE-MARIE-MEDIATRICE (1950-54, H. Vidal) essentially conforms to the traditional church type, but combines modern techniques (concrete framework) with modified older elements (segmental vault in brick) and archaisms (lantern tower, detached baptistry to the right of the façade).

3 BASILICA OF ST. JOAN OF ARC. To a heavy neomedieval façade (1932) was grafted a new nave spanning independent concrete ribs. It supplanted a magnificent project by Perret, a church in the form of a tower with projecting concrete ribs and recessed glass walls rising 660 ft.

4 MONUMENT TO THE UNKNOWN JEWISH MARTYR (1956, Goldberg, Persitz, Arretche). Combining in one austere complex a memorial crypt and a documentation center.

5 MEMORIAL TO THE MARTYRS OF THE DEPORTATION (1962, H. Pingusson). A crypt with cells and a gallery on an open moat; an enclosed court with high white walls.

XVIII The Greater Paris Agglomeration
e/transportation

zones of urbanization

autoroutes and arterial highways
— completed before 1940
— completed since 1945 or under construction
     projected

— existing railway system
— regional express railway system (to be created or integrated with present system)

Scale: 1/250,000

domestic oil heat) have polluted the atmosphere. In 10 years the death rate from lung cancer has doubled and chronic bronchitis increased by 20 percent. With the failure of public transport, more than half the population travels more than an hour per day. The sudden discharge of hundreds of thousands of suburbanites by some stations paralyzes certain districts. Yet the Parisian pays a high price for these inferior conditions, 42 percent more than the average Frenchman, 26 percent more than the average town dweller. These living conditions have succeeded in changing religious activity. Although the Church reacted earlier than the state, it has not been able to correct the situation despite an enormous effort. A 1942 study showed that church attendance hardly existed except in well-to-do areas (22 percent at St-Pierre de Neuilly, 6 percent at St-Hippolyte). The 1953 investigation confirmed the link between religious observance and housing conditions: up to 3 percent observance among people living in a single room. 2 percent observance can be average in certain suburban areas, where it has been learned that a church cannot attract from more than half a mile around. In all, the Church needs 4.5 times more priests, 3 times more places of worship, 4 times more parishes. Facing such a disastrous situation — a congested city, underequipped suburbs, and an agglomeration unprepared to cope with daily traffic, epidemics, prolonged drought, a major fire, much less a war (50 people could be treated for radioactive burns), the Fifth Republic undertook an immense program of correction and reorganization. In 1958 the Urban District of the Paris Region was created, redefined in the law of August 2, 1961. This was accompanied by the Plan for Arrangement and General Organization of the Paris Region (PADOG, decreed August 6, 1960) and the Quadrennial Installations Program (1962-65), which corrected the preceding program and resumed certain 1955 projects such as the express Métro and radiating thoroughfares. The aims of the programs were to make broad projections and to abandon decentralization. In accepting the devouring threat of the city, the hope was to guide it methodically to the scale of a European metropolis, in a country of 70,000,000 inhabitants with 5 times their present buying power. In the year 2000 the city will have to house 12,000,000 to 16,000,000 residents and 5,000,000 automobiles. The number of apartments will have to double, the number of rooms triple, allowing 1,100, rather than 375, sq ft per person for housing, parking, and parks. It will be necessary to enlarge the overcrowded agglomeration, accelerate transport, provide more outlets for commuters, preserve and renovate the historic center of Paris, remodel its outskirts — built with very indifferent standards over the past 100 years — and make the urban environment more human than it is today. Having ruled against the present formless suburbs and having rejected the idea both of a "parallel Paris" (i.e., a new city located at a distance) and of satellite cities, which would wind up merging again, the master plan is calculated to avoid a radiating

1 AUTOROUTE SOUTH (1962). Already too narrow to carry normal traffic as well as that of Orly Airport, which is not serviced by rail, and the new Les Halles at Rungis, it is in the process of enlargement (1968).

2 ORLY AIRPORT (1956-60, Vicariot, Becker). Much enlarged, equipped with an enormous terminal (2,000 ft of façade on the runways), Orly can now handle an expected traffic of 6,000,000 passengers per year.

3 DEFENSE ENSEMBLE. Underground traffic exchange combined with the regional express system tunnels, meant to free the surface completely of dense traffic.

XVIII The Greater Paris Agglomeration

f / *public facilities*

PONTOISE-CERGY
Préfecture du Val-d'Oise
MONTMORENCY FOREST
95
BEAUCHAMP
Achères purification plant
ST-GERMAIN FOREST
Faculté de Villetaneuse (university)
Faculté de Nanterre (university)
93
André Malraux Cultural Center
Tour Schöffer
Préfecture de la Seine-St-Denis
Lac de Jablines
LA DÉFENSE

2 1

MANTES
new slaughter houses of La Villette
MARLY FOREST
92
75
BRY-SUR-MARNE
NOISY-LE-GRAND
Cité de la télévision (television center)
incineration plant of Issy-les-Moulineaux
pleasure park at Tremblay
MEUDON WOODS

3

TRAPPES
Préfecture du Val-de-Marne
Ecole des Hautes Etudes commerciales de Jouy-en-Josas (business school)
78
Ecole centrale (engineering school)
94
Saclay Atomic Research Center

Ecole polytechnique (engineering school)
Faculté d'Orsay (university)
Draveil marina
Viry-Châtillon marina
SÉNART FOREST

Préfecture = district administration
limits of new départements
zones of urbanization
Préfecture de l'Essonne
Prison
TIGERY LIEUSAINT
EVRY

concentric development by stretching an urban gauze over 3 or 4 axes (the Seine to Rouen, the Marne, and the Oise) served by ample means of transportation. Along these axes complete urban centers will be created or remodeled to contain their own economic life. Expressways will have to penetrate and traverse the nucleus of Paris. Forests, which are still abundant in the area, will be preserved between the urbanized axes. The entire Paris basin around the agglomeration, an underused agrarian countryside now, will have to be more efficiently employed, with large provincial cities at its edges, according to the projections. With the largest number of works projects since the time of Napoleon III, these plans have begun to be put into effect. The Métro has been in the process of modernization since 1956; suburban transportation lines are being electrified; the Boulevard Périphérique being constructed; the river banks turned into thoroughfares; a purification plant built at Achères along with new steam generators; the central markets (Les Halles) moved to La Villette and Rungis; the water, gas, and electricity distribution systems completely revised; new reservoirs and dams created on the Seine and the Marne rivers; underground garages dug; the entire city gradually scrubbed clean; the railroad stations modernized; new university buildings constructed; and so on. Administratively, 5 new departments were created July 10, 1964. The Church, too, created 5 dioceses for which it intends to build 150 churches from now until 1985. Paris has been convulsed by an enormous effort of unquestionable necessity after a long preceding period of incompetence.

● But behind all the projects, what are the real workings of the program? What is the direction of this evolution? Will there be continuity of direction and finance over the long period which the plan requires? A more serious problem: the plan assumes the growth of Paris to be throttled, with immigration reduced from 80,000 to 20,000 or even 10,000 people per year. Can one hope to stabilize a city of 15,000,000 when it could not be done at 500,000? The plan also assumes a miracle in water supply. The part played by the automobile can only create concentric suburbs on a radiating system, further choking the center. To avoid an increase of concentric and radiating growth, the city would have to ban private vehicles and give public transportation an absolute monopoly. To make the development along axes work would require the relentness enforcement of building restrictions. But because of weak enforcement, more than 70,000 dwellings have already been built in "restricted" sections. Parks will someday be protected; meanwhile they are being cut away to make room for cars. Superhighways run through forests, trees are uprooted in the city. Monuments will someday be protected. But in fact, the authorities have neither the power nor the stamina needed to combat the tenacious maneuvering of business sharks. Despite the fine talk, the destruction of the center of Paris is being prepared for by the enormous buildings which smother it through sheer proximity (e.g., Maine-Montparnasse complex, the Faculté des Sciences, the Morland Tower, etc.) or simply by being planned there (projects for Les Halles, Orsay, Alma?). While speaking

1 DEFENSE ENSEMBLE (Auzelle, Camelot, de Mailly, Herbé, Zehrfuss). One of six centers in the restructuring of the near suburbs, it will include the Hauts-de-Seine prefecture (administration), university buildings, a museum, and exhibition grounds. On the axis of La Defense-Nanterre, a prolongation of the Avenue de la Grande-Armée.

2 HAUTS-DE-SEINE PREFECTURE, Nanterre (1967 and after, André Wogensky). Administrative center of a new department which will have 1,800,000 inhabitants by 1970, enlivened by a university and by the enlargement of the Port de Gennevillers as well as by new major station.

3 RUNGIS NATIONAL MARKET. With the market of La Villette, it will replace Les Halles, which choked the center of Paris. At Rungis a road station will serve as terminal for large trucks, even those carrying nonfood products. The redistribution to the city will be carried out by lighter vehicles, better adapted to difficult traffic.

of humanizing the city, the
authorities ignore the imaginative
projects which have been
proposed for the banks of the Seine
and the St-Martin canal.
While pretending to return
the city dweller to clear sun and
air, they condemn him to the Métro
every Sunday by canceling bus
service. The sonorous phrases, such
as "reconquer" and "take up
our century," hide outworn concepts,
legacies from the utopians and
architects of the 1920s and even
of the 19th century. The image
of a city of towers crammed with
machines whizzing along the
surface and in the air is simply a
whitened, chromed version of the
urban hell prophesied by Wells and
Robida. The repetition of
demonstrated errors is applauded:
superhighways penetrating the city,
tearing the urban frabic; the street,
essential to social life,
abolished and replaced by tunnels
and by unintelligible spacing
of towers on concrete deserts; the
university, a center of life,
enclosed in the campus system
just when the United States is
harvesting that system's bitter fruit.
Even under good direction, today's
efforts run into problems which
were encountered as early
as the ancien régime: the costs of
the city are growing much faster
than its economy and revenues. The
costs are increased by, among
other things, air pollution, causing a
general corrosion, and paralyzed
traffic, squandering time and fuel.
One kilometer (.6 mi) of the

Boulevard Périphérique costs the
equivalent of 1,000 housing units
or 1,800 hospital beds. And
underground garages, so costly for so
few places, will never satisfy
the demand, for by 1975 the space
required for parking will be
greater than that required for
streets. As in all the large cities,
certain mechanisms (of degeneration)
are appearing and just beginning
to be studied — for example, the
abandonment of slowly
accumulated progress: Paris is losing
its sidewalks and its address
numbering system (illegally covered
by signs) along the large
thoroughfares; property ownership
is less well known now than in
1914; the police admit to being less
and less well informed. The major
services operate badly, laws have
become only principles, filled with
loopholes and so on. Parkinson has
drawn attention to the process
by which bureaucracies see their
power increase while their
effectiveness decreases despite
crushing labor. Lewis Mumford has
shown how the ruinous efforts by giant
cities have at the very best only
slowed their deterioration
and how an economy based on
consumption and waste ceaselessly
builds, destroys, and rebuilds
"consumable" cities in its own
image, lacking value, past, and
character. Paris stands at the
beginning of this phenomenon. Its
problems — scarcity of water,
increasing crime, the gap between
violent recourse and judicial
indulgence, slums — can be seen at

worse stages, in New York for instance.
To tell the truth, they carry no
plausible human solution.
This apparent absurdity leads one to
suspect a perfectly logical
but inhuman mechanism. Until
about 1900 Paris, as a center of
immigration with high mortality, was
above all a regulator of population
equal to famine and epidemic.
It concentrated population surpluses
from the far-reaching regions of
France and killed them. In Europe
famine and epidemic have
disappeared. War has replaced them.
The same phenomenon must be at
work in the city, an agglomeration
ever more colossal, its population
stacked in tall, narrow glass
buildings intensifying the problems
of evacuation and fire control.
These seeming aberrations
in fact adapt the target to atomic
weapons and prepare it for
maximum effectiveness in its passage
"from Metropolis to Necropolis,"
to quote Lewis Mumford. This
image of finality reveals a process
already well under way. Those
economists, sociologists, and
architects who call for even greater
crowding, judging it inevitable
and therefore desirable, and extolling
even more vulnerable structures
are part of the phenomenon.
are part of the logic of the phenomenon.
Thus, despite their show of lucidity,
they are really blind tools.
If, unfortunately, it is
impossible for the city planner
to hope for much before he
embarks, it is imperative that he know
where he is going before he proceeds.

index

The location of the monument is indicated either by a precise address or by the name of the building which now stands on the original site. The present building sometimes greatly exceeds them area of the earlier monument. For example: " Vézelay, Hl of the abbots of. Bibliothèque Ste-Geneviève" means that the site of this hôtel is now occupied by the library, but the latter covers a much larger area. In this case, as in that of monuments once situated where there are now streets or squares, the format of this book does not allow a more precise plotting.

Hôtel

Before acquiring the meaning, as in English, of an establishment housing travelers, hôtel designated, before the end of the nineteenth century in France, a town house of rich and monumental character, belonging to a high-ranking aristocrat or a merchant living on an aristocratic level. These hôtels were designated by the name of their owner or occupant (they were often rented): Hôtel de Condé, Hôtel de Nesmond, Hôtel de la Païva, and so on.

A

Abattoirs (slaughterhouses), see Grenelle, Ménilmontant, Montmartre, Roule (le), Villejuif, Villette (La).

Abbé-de-l'Epée, 14 rue de l' Building, 1909 by Le Roy. XVIc

Abbeville, 14 rue d'. Building, ca. 1900. XVIc

Abbeville, 16 rue d'. Building, 1902, XVIc

Académie royale de musique, see Royal Academy of Music.

Achères Purification Plant (Station d'épuration d'). By Utudjan. Achères I, 1937-40. Achères II, 1965. Achères III, 1970 (?). XVIIIf

Adjacet, Hl d', see Châteauvilain, Hl de.

Aguesseau, Hl d'. 28 rue St-Guillaume. 1789. Now Institute for Latin-American Advanced Studies (Institut des hautes études de l'Amérique latine). XIId

Albiac, Hl d'. 34 rue de la Montagne-Ste-Geneviève. 16th c. Destroyed 18th c., at that time Collège des Trente-Trois. IXa

Albret, Hl d', see Blois, Hl de.

Albret, Hl d', see Montmorency, Hl de.

Alemans, Hl d'. 86 rue de Sèvres. 1750. Destroyed 1908. XIIc

Alençon, Hl d', see Alphonse de Poitiers, Hl d'.

Alexandre, Hl, called Suchet, rue de la Ville-l'Evêque. ca. 1750 by Boullée. XIIc

Alexandre-III, Pont. 1896-1900 by Résal and Alby. XVIa

Aligre, Hl d', see Chenizot, Hl.

Allée des Cygnes. 1825. Planted with trees 1878. XIIIb

Alma, Place de l'. 1858. Underground expressway 1956 XIVa, XVIIIa

Alma, Pont de l'. 1854-56. XIVa, XVIIIa

Alméras, Hl d'. 30 rue des Francs-Bourgeois. 1598. Xb

Alphonse de Poitiers, Hl d', called d'Alençon. Place du Louvre. 13th c. Reconstructed beginning 16th c. Destroyed 17th-18th c. VI

Ambassadeurs de Hollande, Hl des, see Amelot de Chaillou, Hl.

Ambassadeurs extraordinaires (ambassadors extraordinary), Hl des. Place de la Concorde. Now Ministry of the Navy and Hl Crillon. See Aumont, Hl d', called Crillon; Garde-meuble royal. XIIa

Ambigu, Théâtre de l'. 2 ter blvd St-Martin. 1829. Destroyed, façade extant. XIIIc

Amelot de Bisseuil, Hl, see Amelot de Chaillou, Hl.

Amelot de Chaillou, Hl, later Amelot de Bisseuil, called des Ambassadeurs de Hollande. 47 rue Vieille-du-Temple. Begun 1638, again in 1655, by P. Cottard. Xb, XIc

Amelot de Chaillou, Hl, called de Tallard. 78 rue des Archives. 1640 by Bullet, then Le Muet. Xb

Amiraux, 13 rue des. Building. 1925 by Sauvage. XVIIc

André, Hl. 158 blvd Haussmann. Second Empire, by Parent. Now Musée Jacquemart-André. XIVb

André-Malraux Cultural Center (Ensemble culturel). Nanterre. Project by Wogensky. XVIIIf

Angoulême, Hl d', called Lamoignon. 24 rue Pavée. 1584-86 by J. Thiriot. IXa

Arc de triomphe, see Carrousel, Chaillot, Porte St-Antoine.

Archbishopric. South side of Notre-Dame. Bishopric 6th c. rebuilt 12th as Archbishopric.

Rebuilt 1697, restored 1809, destroyed 1831. XId

Archevêché, Palais de l', see Archbishopric.

Archevêché, Pont de l'. 1827. XIIIb

Arcole, Pont d', earlier "de la Grève." 1828. Rebuilt 1854, rebuilt 1888. XIIIb, XIVa

Arènes de Lutèce, see Lutetia Arena.

Annonciades Célestes, convent, see Anville, Hl d'.

Annonciades du St-Esprit, convent. 2 rue de la Folie-Méricourt. 1654. Destroyed 1781-1864. XIe, XIVc

Antier, Hl de Mademoiselle. 43-47 rue d'Auteuil. 1715. XIIc

Antoine Chevalier, Hl d'. 33 rue du Fbg-St-Honoré. 1774. Destroyed. XId

Antoine Crozat, Hl d'. 19 Place Vendôme. 1700 by Bullet. XIIa

Anville, Hl d'. 25-27 rue de Sévigné. 16th c. Later convent of Annonciades Célestes (1626). IXa

Aquarium du Trocadéro. Palace of Chaillot gardens. Rebuilt 1937. XVIIb

Arc de triomphe de Chaillot, see Chaillot, Arc de triomphe.

Arc de triomphe de la Porte St-Antoine, see Porte St-Antoine, Arc de triomphe.

Arc de triomphe du Carrousel, see Carrousel Arc de triomphe.

Archives nationales, see Soubise, Hl de.

Armagnac, Hl d', see Chastel, Hl du.

Armagnac, Hl d'. Rue du Fer à Moulin. 14th c. Destroyed. VIIa

Armée du Salut, Cité-refuge de l' (Salvation Army). Rue du Chevaleret. 1932 by Le Corbusier. XVIIc

Armenian church (église arménienne). 15 rue Jean-Goujon. 1903 by Guilbert. XVId

Arsenal, Grand. 3 rue de l'Arsenal. Was municipal arsenal

(q.v.), then royal (from 1551). Part blown up 1538, rebuilt 1594 (by Ph. Delorme), remodeled 1723 ff. (by Boffrand). Xa, XIIb

Arsenal Municipal, see Municipal arsenal.

Arsenal, Petit. North part of blvd Bourdon. ca. 1540. Blown up 1563 and rebuilt. Destroyed IXa, Xa

Arsenal, Petit, called Salpêtrière. 47 blvd de l'Hôpital. 1634: Vestiges. Xa

Artois, Hl d', later de Bourgogne. 20 rue Etienne-Marcel. 1270.Tower ca. 1400. All but tower destroyed 1543. VIIa, VIIIa

Arts, Cité des. Quai de l'Hôtel-de-Ville. 1965 by Tournon and Cacoub. XVIIIb

Arts-et-Métiers, see Ecole nationale des arts et métiers.

Arts et Métiers, Conservatoire des. 292 rue St-Martin. Was abbey of St-Martin-des-Champs.

Arts, Pont des. 1802-1804. XIIIa

Assumption, Church of the, see Dames de l'Assomption.

"Astry," Hl d'. 18 quai de Béthune. 1643. XIc

Atomic Energy Commission (Commissariat à l'Energie atomique). 29 rue de la Fédération. 1964 by Dufau. XVIIIb

Aubert de Fontenay, Hl, called Salé, de Juigné. 5 rue de Thorigny. 1656 by J. Boullier. XIc

Aubray, Hl. 12 rue Charles-V. Before 1666. XIc

Augeard, Hl. 11 blvd Poissonnière. ca. 1750. Destroyed 20th c. XIIc

Augny, Hl d'. 6 rue Drouot. 1750 by Briseux. Now 9th arrondissement town hall. XIIc

Augustines de Nanterre, convent, later called (1742) convent of Ste-Perrine de Chaillot. 1-19, rue Quentin-Bauchard. 1659. Destroyed 1860-65. XIe, XIIe, XIVc

Augustins déchaussés, monastery, "Petits Pères." Place des

Petits-Pères. 1628. Destroyed 1850. Chapel survives: see Notre - Dame - des - Victoires. Xc, XIVc

Augustins, Grands, see Grands-Augustins.

Augustins, Petits, see Petits-Augustins.

Augustins, Pont des, see Pont-Neuf.

Aumônerie de la Croix de la Reine, see Trinité (La) hospital.

Aumont, Hl. Called Crillon, Place de la Concorde, west palace. 1760-75 by Gabriel. XIId

Aumont, Hl d', see Scarron, Hl.

Aumont, Hl d'. 4 rue St-Paul. Before 1386. Destroyed. VIIIa

Aumont, Hl d' 2-2 bis, rue Caumartin to 30, blvd des Capucines. 1780 by Aubert. XIId

Auroy, Hl d'. 58 rue de Varenne. 1750. XIIc

Austerlitz column, called Vendôme column.Place Vendôme. 1810 by Denon, Gondoin, Lepère. XIIIa, XV

Austerlitz, Pont d'. 1802-1807, rebuilt 1855, widened 1884-86. XIIIa, XIVa, XVIa

Auteuil, Hippodrome d' (racetrack).Bois de Boulogne. XVIa

Auteuil, Pont d'. 1886 by Bassompierre. Destroyed 1964. XIVa, XVIIIa

Autoroute east. Work begun 1964. XVIIIa, XVIIIe

Autoroute north. Opened 1966. XVIIIa, XVIIIe

Autoroute south. Opened 1962. XVIIIa, XVIIIe

Autoroute west.1935-39. Tunnel opened 1946. XVIIa, XVIIIa, XVIIIe

Autun, Hl of the bishops of, called de Savoie. 2 rue des Haudriettes. Before 1350. Destroyed. VIIa

Auvergne, Hl d'. 28 rue St-Dominique. 1710 by Le Camus des Touches. Now Maison de la Chimie. XId

Auxerre, Hl of the bishops of. South of blvd St-Michel-rue

de Vaugirard intersection.13th c. Destroyed 16th c. VIIa

Avaray, Hl d'. 85 rue de Grenelle. 1718 by J.-B. Leroux. XIIc

Avaux, Hl d', later de St-Aignan. 71 rue du Temple. 1645-50 by Le Muet. XIc

Aycelins, Collège des, see Montaigne, Collège de.

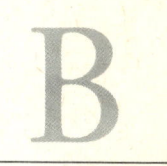

B

Bagatelle, Château de, later Folie d'Artois. 1720. Razed. Rebuilt 1777 by Bellanger. XIIc, XIId

Bagnolet, Château de. 148 rue de Bagnolet. Begun 1719, destroyed 1769 ff. Pavillon de l'Ermitage, 1734 by Serin, survives. XIIc

Bailliage, Hl du. Palais de Justice. 1485. Destroyed. VIIIa

Banque de France. 39 rue Croix des Petits Champs. HI de la Vrillière (q.v.) and annexes. 1924-50. XV, XVIIIb

Bar, Hl of the counts of. Impasse Clopin- rue A. Comu. 13th c. Destroyed. VIIa

Barbette, Hl, see Mauregard, HI de.

Barbier, Pont, also called Pont-Rouge. Axis of rue de Beaune. 1632. Finally destroyed 1684. Xa

Barrault, 67 rue. Building. 1962 by Auger and Pulcinelli. XVIIIc

Barres, Hl des. 2-10 rue des Barres. 14th c. Destroyed. VIIIa

Barrés, Monastery, Carmes, monastery.

Barrière (customs house) de Chartres, d'Enfer, de la Villette, du Trône, see Fermiers Généraux customs wall. XIIa

Bastille (La), first called Château St-Antoine, Place de la

Bastille. 1370-82. Destroyed 1790-92. VIIa, XIIIa, XIIIc

Batignolles Tunnel. 1835-37. Destroyed 1922. XIIIb, XVIIa

Baudoyer, Porte. In the 11th-c. walls. Place Baudoyer. IV

Bauffremont, HI de, see Ourouër, HI d'.

Bautru de Serrant, HI. 2-2 bis rue Vivienne. ca. 1650. Destroyed. XIc

Bazar de l'Hôtel-de-Ville, annex. 119 rue de Flandre. 1962 by Auger. XVIIIc

Beauharnais, HI de, see Boffrand, HI.

Beaujolais, Théâtre de, later Montansier. 19 rue de Valois. 1784. Modified 1831. Now Théâtre du Palais-Royal. XIIb

Beaujon hospital. 208 rue du Fbg-St-Honoré. 1784 by Girardin. XIIb

Beauvais, Collège de, or de Dormans. 9 bis rue Jean-de-Beauvais. Begun 1370. The chapel (by Raymond du Temple) survives, much altered. VIIb

Beauvais, HI de. 68 rue François Miron. 1655 by A. Lepautre. XIc

Beauvau, HI de, now Ministry of the interior. 96 rue du Fbg-St-Honoré. 1770 by Le Camus de Mézières. XIIc

Beaux-Arts, Ecole des (school of fine arts). 14 rue Bonaparte. 1820-62 by Debret, then Duban. XIIIc, XIVb

Bec-Hellouin, HI of the abbots of. Sorbonne. Rue St-Jacques facing No 123. 1410. Destroyed 1632-20th c. VIIIa

Béguines, convent. Rue Charlemagne-rue de l'Ave Maria. 1264. Replaced 1480 by nuns of the Ave Maria. Destroyed. VI

Belgiojoso, HI, see Orliane, Folie d'.

Béliard, 185 rue. Building, 1913 by Deneux. XVIc

Belle Isle, HI de. 56 rue de Lille. 1721 by Bruant. Destroyed 1858. XIIc

Belles-Feuilles, 65 rue des. Building, 1904 by L. Sorel. XVIc

Belleville, Thermes de (mineral baths). 6 ter rue de l'Atlas. 1868. XIVb

Bénédictines anglaises, convent. Rue des Tanneries-rue Léon-Maurice-Nordmann. 1664. Destroyed 1799 ff. XIe

Bénédictines de l'Adoration perpétuelle du St-Sacrement, convent. First 11 rue Férou (1654), destroyed, then 12-16 rue Cassette (1669). Destroyed. XIe, XIIId

Bénédictines de la Ville-l'Evêque, priory, called Notre-Dame-de-Grâce. 2 rue de l'Arcade. 1613. Destroyed 1790. Xc

Bénédictines de Montmartre, convent. Top of the butte. Calvary garden, reservoirs, rue Azaïs, square Nadar. 1133. Reinstalled around Place des Abbesses in 1686. All but church of St-Pierre-de-Montmartre (q.v.) destroyed 1794. IV

Bénédictines du Cherche-Midi, convent, called Notre-Dame-de-la-Consolation. 23 rue du Cherche-Midi. 1669. Destroyed 1796 ff. XIe

Bénédictins anglais, monastery. 268-269 bis rue St-Jacques. 1640. Chapel 1674. Xc, XIe

Bercy, Château de. Rue de Paris-route du Château-rue du Petit-Château (Charenton). Known since 1316. Rebuilt 1658 by Le Vau. Destroyed 1861. XIc

Bercy, Château du Petit. Rue de Pommard. 18th c. Destroyed 1819 ff. XIIc

Bercy, Pont de. 1864. XIVa

Bercy wine storehouses (Entrepôts des vins). Quai de Bercy. 1877-85, plans by Viollet-le-Duc. Renovation planned by Zehrfuss. XVIa, XVIIa, XVIIIa

Bergère téléphone excnange, central téléphonique Bergère). rue Bergère, rue du Fbg-Poissonnière. 1911-12 by F. Le Cœur. XVIb

Beringhen, HI de, see Roquelaure, HI de.

Beringhen, HI de. 8 rue de Tournon. Ca. 1600. Destroyed 1712. Xb

Bernardins, see St-Bernard, chapel and collège.

Berthier de Sauvigny, HI, see La Marck, HI de.

Bérulle, HI de. 15 rue de Grenelle. 1766 by Brongniart. XIIc

Bibliothèque nationale (National Library). 58 rue de Richelieu. See Mazarin palace; Duret de Chevry, HI. Reading Room (Salle des Imprimés): 1868 by Labrouste. Periodicals Room (Périodiques), 1900 by Pascal and Recouva. Catalogue Room, Maps and Plans: (cartes et plans): 1942-54 by Roux-Spitz. Prints (Estampes): 1946 by Roux-Spitz. Musique, square Louvois: 1963 by Chatelin and Large. XIVa, XVIb, XVIIb, XVIIIb

Bicêtre, Château de. Site of present Hospice. End 14th c. Destroyed. VIIIa

Bicêtre, Commanderie de St-Louis = Hospice des Soldats Invalides (Hospice for disabled soldiers):1634. Important remains in the present Hospice de Bicêtre. Xb

Bichat hospital. 170 blvd Ney. Rebuilt 1928. C.H.U. project by Marchand, Séac, Fantelli. XVIIb

Birague, HI du chancelier de, see Meudon, HI du cardinal de.

Biron, HI, see Peyrenc de Moras, HI.

Bizet, HI du Président. Square Paul-Painlevé. 15th c. Destroyed. VIIIa

Blancs-Manteaux, Marché des (market). 46 rue Vieille-du-Temple. 1813-1819. XIIIa

Blancs-Manteaux, monastery. 16 rue des Blancs-Manteaux. 1258. Rebuilt 17th c. Partly destroyed 19th c. Church survives, see Notre-Dame-des-Blancs-Manteaux. VI, XIe

Blois, HI de, later d'Albret. 1 rue Valette. 15th c. Destroyed. VIIIa

Blomet, 17 rue. Swimming pool (piscine), 1960 by Dupuis and Jabouille. XVIIIa

Blouin, HI, called Marbeuf. 31 rue du Fbg-St-Honoré. 1718 by Lassurance. Destroyed 1887 ff. XIIc

Bon Marché (Le), department store. Square Boucicaut. 1869-89 by L.-A. Boileau and Eiffel. 1924 by L.-C. Boileau. XVIb, XVIIb

Boncourt, Collège de. 21 rue Descartes. 1353. Absorbed by Collège de Navarre (q.v.) 1638. VIIb

Boffrand, HI, "de Beauharnais." 78 rue de Lille. 1714 by Boffrand. Egyptian portico 1807 by Renard. Now German embassy. XId, XIIIc

Bois de Boulogne, see Boulogne, Bois de

Bois de Vincennes Zoo, see Vincennes Zoo, Bois de.

Boisgelin, HI de. 47 rue de Varenne. 1787 by Parent. XIId

Bonneval, HI de. 73 rue de Richelieu. 1684. XId

Bons-Enfants, Collège des. Rue des Bons-Enfants. 1208. Destroyed end 18th c. V

Bons-Enfants d'Arras, Collège des. 8 impasse Chartrière. 13th c. Rebuilt 15th c. Destroyed 1909. VI

Bonshommes de Chaillot, see Minimes de Chaillot.

Borghèse, HI, see Vaudreuil, HI de.

Boucher d'Orsay, HI, see Seissac, HI de.

Boucherat, HI, called du Grand-Veneur or d'Ecquevilly. 60 rue de Turenne. 1686. XId

Boucicaut, Square. XVIIIa

Boulard, 23 rue. Ecole maternelle (nursery school). 1954 by Maillard. XVIIIb

destroyed 19th c. Church survives, see Notre-Dame-des-Blancs-Manteaux. VI, XIe

Boulevard périphérique (circular expressway). Begun 1957.

Boulogne, Bois de (woods). Enclosed 16th c., laid out 1852 by Alphand, Varé, Barillet. IXa, XIVa

Boulogne, HI de. Rue du Fer-à-Moulin. 13th-14th c. Destroyed. VIIa

Bourbon, HI de. Place du Louvre, south of colonnade. ca. 1310. Destroyed 1527-1758. XIIc

Bourbon-Condé, HI de Mademoiselle de. 12 rue Monsieur. 1786 by Brongniart. XIId

Bouret de Vézelay, HI, see Montmorency, HI de.

Bouret, HI. Rue de l'Elysée, rue du Fbg-St-Honoré. 1777. Destroyed 1851 ff. XIId

Bourg St-Marcel, see St-Marcel (Bourg) walls.

Bourget Airport (Le). 1914. Commercial airport 1919. XVIIa

Bourgogne, Collège de. Faculté de médecine, 12 rue de l'Ecole-de-Médecine. 1331. Destroyed 1763. XIIe

Bourgogne, HI des ducs de, see Artois, HI d'.

Bourgogne, HI des ducs de. Rue Valette, facing rue Laplace. 13th c. Destroyed 1418. VIIIa

Bourienne, HI de (called). 58 rue d'Hauteville. 1787. XIId

Bourse (financial exchange). Rue Vivienne. Installed in Mazarin palace 1724-93. XIIb

Bourse (stock exchange). Place de la Bourse. 1808-26 by Brongniart, then Labarre. Enlarged 1903. XIIIc, XVIb

Bourse de Commerce (natl. business assn.). Rue de Viarmes. 1889 by Blondel. XVIb

Bourse du Travail (labor union hq). Place de la République. 1890 by Bouvard. XVIb

Bourse, Place de la. 1808. Parking garage, 1967. XVIIa, XVIIIa

Boussois, Centre (documentation center for glass industry).

22 blvd Malesherbes. By Anger and Thual. XVIIIc

Bragelongne, HI de, called de Villette. 27 quai Voltaire. 1712. XId

Brancas, HI de. 6 rue de Tournon. 1719. XIIc

Brésil, Maison du (Brazilian students' center). Cité Universitaire. 1959 by Le Corbusier and L. Costa. XVIIIc

Bretagne, see Brittany.

Breteuil, HI, called de Fersen. 17 rue Matignon. 1778. Destroyed 1921. XIId

Bretonneau hospital. 5-7 rue Carpeaux. XVIIb

Bretonvilliers, HI de. 3,5,7,9 rue St-Louis-en-l'Ile. 1637-43 by J. Androuet du Cerceau. Destroyed 1840-66. XIe

Brienne, HI de, see Duret, HI du Président.

Brittany, HI of the dukes of. Former rue St-Nicaise, Cour du Carrousel. Louvre. 14th c. Destroyed. VIIa

Brittany, Manor of the dukes of. Rues Beethoven, Le Nôtre, blvd Delessert. 13th c. Given to Minimes in 1493 (q.v.). VIIa

Broca hospital. First De Lourcine hospital. 43 blvd Arago. 1834-36, De Lourcine hospital. 1892, Broca hospital. XIIIc

Broglie, HI de, see Revel, HI de.

Brosse, HI de.1 rue de la Chaise. XIIc

Broussais hospital. 96 rue Didot. 1883, provisional. Built 1928-38. Enlarged after 1945. XVIIb

Brunoy, HI de. 47 rue du Fbg-St-Honoré. ca. 1760 by Boullée. Destroyed. XIIc

Buffon, Lycée (high school). 16 Blvd Pasteur-rue de Vaugirard. 1887. XVIb

Bureau central des Chèques postaux (postal bank). 19-21 rue d'Alleray. 1936 by Roux-Spitz. XVIIb

Bureau de la Rivière, HI. 58-60 rue des Francs-Bourgeois. 14th c. Destroyed. VIIIa

Butte-aux-Cailles, Piscine de la (swimming pool). 1922 by L. Bonnier. XVIIb

Butte-aux-Cailles, Puits artésien de la (artesian well). Place Paul-Verlaine. 1864-68. XIVa

Butte - du - Chapeau - Rouge, Square de la. 1939. XVIIa

Buttes-Chaumont, Parc des. 1866-67 by Alphand and Barillet. XIVa

C

Caillavet, HI de. 12 av. Hoche. 1878. XVIc

Caisse des Dépots et Consignations.1-3 quai Anatole-France. 1857. Destroyed 1871, reconstructed after 1871, enlarged 1934. XIVb, XV, XVIb, XVIIb

Calvaire, convent of Religieuses du. 19 rue de Vaugirard. 1622. Destroyed 1848. Cloister and chapel survive. Xc

Cambodge, Maison du (Cambodian students' center). Cité Universitaire.1957 by Andoul. XVIIIc

Camille-See, Lycée (high school). Square St-Lambert. 1934 by F. Le Cœur. XVIIb

Camondo, HI de. 63 rue Monceau. 1910 by Sergent. XVIc

Capucines, convent, see Filles de la Passion.

Capucins du Marais, monastery. 6 rue Charlot. 1623. Destroyed 1790, except for chapel (1715), now St-Jean-St-François (q.v.). Xc

Capucins, monastery. 237-239 rue St-Honoré. 1576. Church 1603-10. Destroyed 1790. IXb

Capucins, monastery. 65 rue Caumartin. Begun 1779 by Brongniart. Now Lycée Condorcet and St-Louis-d'Antin. XIIc

Capucins St-Jacques, novitiate. 111 blvd de Port-Royal. 1613-1779. Part survives in Cochin hospital. Xc

Cardinal Palace (Palais Cardinal). Place du Palais-Royal. 1624-45 by Lemercier. Destroyed 18th c. except for gallery of prows. See Palais-Royal. Xb

Cardinal-Lemoine, Collège du. 20 rue d'Arras. 1302. Destroyed ca. 1870. VIIb, XIVc

Carmel, convent. 62 rue Beaubourg. 1619. Destroyed 1796. Xc

Carmel de l'Incarnation, convent. 284 rue St-Jacques and 25 rue du Val-de-Grâce. 1603. Partially destroyed 1797, re-established 1802, destroyed again 1908. Xc, XVId

Carmes (Carmelite Friars), monastery, called Grands-Carmes or Barrés. 1st: 2-8 rue du Petit-Musc, 1256-1309. VI. 2nd: Place Maubert, Marché des Carmes, 1309. Church 1349-53. Destroyed 1813. VIIb XIIId

Carmes déchaussés, monastery. 70 rue de Vaugirard. 1611. Church 1613 (see St-Josephdes-Carmes). Now Institut catholique. Xc, XV

Carmes Billettes, monastery. 22 rue des Archives. Succeeded Frères de la Charité-Notre-Dame (q.v.) 1633. Church 1756. Now Lutheran church. XIIe

Carnavalet, HI. 23 rue de Sévigné. Was HI de Ligneris (q.v.). Remodeled 1602-32 by Jacques Androuet du Cerceau. Remodeled 1655-61 by F. Mansart. Now Musée Carnavalet. Xb, XIc, XIVb, XVIb

Carnot, Piscine du Blvd (swimming pool). 1967 by Dondel and Taillibert. XVIIIa

Carré de Beaudoin, country house, now called Folie Favart. 119 rue de Ménilmontant. 1770 by Moreau-Desproux. XIIc

Carrousel Arc de triomphe, Place du Carrousel. 1806-1807 by Percier and Fontaine. XIIa

Carrousel, Pont du. 1834, rebuilt downstream 1935-39. XIIIb, XVIIa

Castel Béranger. Building. 14 rue La Fontaine. 1898 by Guimard. XVIc

Castille, Palais de. 19 av. Kléber. 1868. Destroyed. XIVb

Castries, HI de, see Dufour, HI de.

Catherine de Médicis, country house of. Palace of Chaillot. 16th c. Destroyed. IXa

Catinat, HI du Maréchal. Square Paul-Painlevé. 2nd half 17th c. XId

Caumont, HI de, see Guénégaud, Petit HI.

Cavoye, HI de, see Creil, HI de.

Célestins, Caserne des (barracks). 12 blvd Henri IV. 1895 by J. Hermant. XVIb

Célestins, monastery. 2-8 rue du Petit-Musc. 1352. Church begun 1365. Enlarged end 14th c. 1482, Chapel of 10,000 Martyrs. Cloister 1539. Suppressed 1779, destroyed 1795 ff. VIIb, VIIIb, IXb, XIIId

Cemetery, East (Cimetière de l'Est, called du Père-Lachaise). Was Jesuit estate (Mont-Louis). 1803-1804 by Brongniart. XIIIa

Cemetery, North (Cimetière du Nord, called Montmartre). 1795. Enlarged 1798, 1806. XIIIa

Cemetery, Protestant (Cimetière protestant). Square, corner rue des Sts-Pères and blvd St-Germain. 1598-1604. Xc

Cemetery, South (Cimetière du Sud, called Montparnasse). 1824. XIIIa

Cent-Filles, Les, see Notre-Dame de la Miséricorde hospital.

Central téléphonique Bergère, see Bergère téléphone exchange, rue.

Centre parisien de congrès internationaux (convention

center). 114 av. Emile Zola. 1966 by Pottier and Leroy. XVIIIb

Centre sportif universitaire Jean-Sarrailh (university sports center). 39 av. de l'Observatoire. 1958-62 by A. Lacoste. XVIIIb

Centre tropical, see Tropical Institute.

Centre universitaire Albert-Châtelet (student center). 8 rue Calvin. 1965. XVIIIb

Centres hospitaliers universitaires (C.H.U., university hospital centers), see Bichat, Cochin, Necker, Pitié-Salpêtrière, St-Antoine hospitals.

Céramic Hôtel. 3 av. de Wagram. 1904 by Lavirotte. XVIc

Cercle de la Librairie (Publishing trade assn.) 117 blvd St-Germain. 1879 by Garnier. XVIc

Cercle militaire. Place St-Augustin. 1927. XVIIc

Cernuschi, HI. 7 av. Velasquez. 1895 by Bouvins. XVIc

Chaalis, HI of the abbots of. 12-14 rue de Jouy. 13th-15th c. All but cellars destroyed. VIIa

Chabannais, HI de. 163 rue de Charonne. ca.1725. Destroyed 1956. XIIc

Chaillot Arc de triomphe. Place de l'Etoile. 1806-36 by Chalgrin. XIIIa

Chaillot culvert (ponceau). Place de l'Alma, on bypassed branch of Seine. Known 1222. Still existed 17th c. V

Chaillot pumping station. Rue des Frères-Périer. 1778-81. Destroyed 1902. XIIa

Chanaleilles, HI de, see Maine, HI du duc de.

Chancellerie, HI de la, first HI Luillier. 11-13 Place Vendôme. 1702. Now Ministry of Justice. XId

Chaillot, Palace and gardens of. 1934-37 by Carlu, Boileau, Azéma. Gardens 1938 by R. Lardat. Palace encompassed Trocadéro palace (q.v.). XVIIb

Chaillot, Théâtre de. Palace of Chaillot. 1934-37 by Niermans frères, Brillouin. XVIIb

Châlon, HI de. 4 rue Valette. 14th c. Destroyed 1553. VIIa

Châlons-Luxembourg, HI, see Le-Fèvre-de-la-Boderie, HI.

Chambre des Comptes. Palais de Justice. 1508 by Fra Giocondo. Destroyed 1737. VIIIa, XIIb

Chamillart, HI. 34 rue Gaillon. 1705-1707 by Levé. Destroyed 1839. XId

Champ de Mars. Laid out 1765, enlarged 1773. XIIa

Champ-de-Mars, Gare du (RR station). 1867. XIVa

Champ-de-Mars, 33 rue du. Building. 1900 by Lavirotte. XVIc

Champeaux, Marché des (market). Site of Les Halles (q.v.). IV

Champerret, Caserne, Quartier central des Sapeurs-Pompiers (firemen's barracks). Place Jules-Renard. 1938. XVIIb

Champs-Elysées, Av. des, formerly Grand Cours. 1667-70 by Le Nôtre (up to the circle), 1724 (up to Neuilly). Altered 72 (up to Neuilly). Altered 1828 ff. XIa, XIIa, XVIIIa

Champs-Elysées, Rond-Point, see Rond-Point des Champs-Elysées.

Champs-Elysées, Théâtre des. 13-15 av. Montaigne. 1911-13 by A. Perret. XVIb

Champs-Elysées, 104 av. des. Building. 1895 by A. Durville. XVIc

Champs-Elysées, 116 bis av. des, see Poste Parisien building, Le.

Chanac de Pompadour, HI. 142 rue de Grenelle. ca. 1750. XIIc

Change, Pont au, first "Grand Pont" (q.v.). 12th c. Rebuilt 1637-47 by J. Androuet du Cerceau. Rebuilt 1858. Xa, XIVa

Chastenay, HI de. 120 rue du Fbg-St-Honoré. 1776. XIId

Château d'Eau, Place du. Later (1879) Place de la République. 1854-62 by Davioud. XIVa

Chapelle expiatoire, see Expiatory chapel.

Chardonnet enclosure (Clos du Chardonnet). Vineyards between rues des Bernardins, St-Victor, des Ecoles, Jussieu, Linné, and la Seine. IV

Charité chrétienne, Maison de la, see Christian charity, House of.

Charité (La) hospital. 39-45 rue des Saints-Pères. 1608. Chapel 18th c. Destroyed 1935-37. Xa, Xc, XIIe

Charlemagne, Lycée (high school). 101 rue St-Antoine. Was House of ordained Jesuits (see Jesuits). 1804. XIIIc

Charles V, wall of. 1356-83. Partial modernizations (bastions) during 16th c. NW front demolished 1633-34. General demolition 1670-1705. VIIa, Xa, XIa

Charny, HI de. 22 rue Beautreillis. 1676. XId

Charolais, HI de, see Rothelin, HI de.

Charonne, Château de. 109 rue de Bagnolet-rue des Pyrénées. ca. 1600. Destroyed 1789-1857. Xb

Charost, HI de. 39 rue du Fbg-St-Honoré. 1723 by Mazin. Now English embassy. XIIc

Chartres, Barrière de (customs house), see Fermiers Généraux customs wall.

Chartres, HI of the bishops of. 1-5 rue Git-le-Cœur. 1300. Destroyed VIIa

Chartreux (Carthusian monastery). South of Luxembourg gardens-av. de l'Observatoire. 1257 in the Château Vauvert. Church and cloister 1276-1325. Reconstructed 17th c. Destroyed 1798. VI, VIIb, XIe, XIIId

Chastel, HI du, called d'Armagnac. 1-5 rue des Bons-Enfants. 1347. Destroyed 17th c. VIIa

Châteauneuf, HI de. 215-219 bis Blvd St-Germain. 1708 by Lassurance. Destroyed 19th c. XId

Châteauvilain, HI de, or d'Adjacet, later d'O. Marché des Blancs-Manteaux. 16th c. Destroyed. IXa

Châtelet, Grand. Place du Châtelet. 1130. Rebuilt often, enlarged 1684. Destroyed 1802-10. IV, V, XIb, XIIIc

Châtelet, HI du. 127 rue de Grenelle. 1770 by Cherpitel. XIIc

Châtelet, Petit. Place du Petit-Pont. 9th c. Rebuilt many times, particularly end 12th c. and 1369. Destroyed 1782. IV, V, XIIa

Châtelet, Place du. 1802. Enlarged 1855-58. XIIIa

Châtelet, Théâtre du. Place du Châtelet. 1862 by Davioud. XIVb, XV

Chaulnes, HI de. 9 Place des Vosges. 1606. Xb

Chenizot, HI, formerly d'Aligre. 51 rue St-Louis-en-l'Ile. 1730. XIIc

"Cheval de bronze" (Bronze Horse). Statue of Henri IV. Installed 1614. By Giovanni da Bologna (Jean de Bologne). 1st statue on a public thoroughfare in Paris. No rider until 1635. Destroyed 1792. Xa

Chevilly, HI de. Church of the Madeleine. 1728. Destroyed 1764. XIIc

Chevreuse, HI de, later de Luynes. Rue de Luynes. 1660-61, by Le Muet. Destroyed 1900. XId, XIId

Children affected by venereal diseases, Hospice, see Hospice.

Chirurgiens, Amphithéâtre des, see Surgeons' Amphitheater.

Choiseul-Praslin, HI de. 4-8 rue St-Romain. 1732 by Gaubier. Now Musée Postal and caisse d'Epargne. XIIc

Choisy, Square de. 1936-37. XVIIa

Christ-Roi, chapel of. Convent of Bénédictines du St-Sacrement. 16 rue Tournefort. 1935-40 by Astruc. XVIId

Christian charity, House of (Maison de la Charité chrétienne), called Apothecaries' Garden (Jardin des apothicaires). 3-17 rue Broca. Garden: 9-21 rue de l'Arbalète. 1578 was in the Lourcine hospital (q.v.). Destroyed 1774, 1859-67. IXa

C.H.U., see Centres hospitaliers universitaires.

Cimetière, see Cemetery.

Cimetière de Pantin-Bobigny, see Pantin-Bobigny cemetery.

Cirque d'Hiver, see Napoleon Circus.

Cité barracks, La (Caserne de la Cité). Parvis Notre-Dame. 1865. Now Préfecture de Police. XIVb

Cité, Caserne de la, see Cité barracks, La

Cité, palace of the, see Palace of the Cité.

Cité, Pont de la, see St-Louis, Pont.

Cité Universitaire (university residences). Blvd Jourdan. 1921 ff. XVIIb, XVIIc, XVIIIb, XVIIIc

Cité Universitaire, see Brésil, Cambodge, Deutsch-de-la-Meurthe, Fondation internationale, Italie, Liban, Mexique, Néerlandais, Suisse.

Claude-Bernard hospital. Blvd MacDonald. 1904. Reconstructed 1930. XVIb, XVIIb

Claude-Bernard, Lycée (high school). 1 av. du Parc-des-Princes. 1938 by Umbdenstock. XVIIb

Claude Chahu, 9 rue. 1903 by Klein. XVIc

Clérambault, HI, see La Monnoye, HI de.

Clermont, Collège de. Site of Lycée Louis-le-Grand. 1562. Destroyed beginning 19th c. See Louis-le-Grand, Collège. IXb

Clermont-Tonnerre, HI de. 118-120 rue du Bac. 1789. XIId

Clignancourt, Manor of the lords of. 101 rue Girardon. End 16th c. Destroyed. IXa

Clinique des Aliénés (insane asylum), Ste-Anne hospital. 1 rue Cabanis. 1861-76 by Questel. XVb

Clisson, HI de. 58 rue des Archives. 1371. All but entrance destroyed. VIIa

Cluny, HI of the abbots of. 6 Place Paul-Painlevé. 1845-98. Now Musée de Cluny. VIIIa, VIIIb

Cluny, Thermes de (baths), see Thermae (baths), Gallo-Roman.

Cochin hospital, first St-Jacques. 1780. Modernized 20th c. C.H.U. 1968 by Nicolas. XVIIb, XVIIIb

Cœur-eucharistique-de-Jésus, church. 22 rue du Lieutenant Chauré. 1938 by Venner. XVIId

Colbert de Villacerf, HI. 23 rue de Turenne. 1650. XIc

"Colbert," HI. 5 rue du Mail. 1666. XId

Colisée (Le) banquet hall. Rue du Colisée. 1771-74 by Le Camus de Mézières. Destroyed 1780. XIIa

Colonies, Museum of the. Av. Daumesnil. 1931 by Laprade and Jaussely. XVIIb

Comédie-Française, see Variétés amusantes, Théatre des.

Comédie-Française, Théâtre de la. Place Boïeldieu. 1781-83. Destroyed 1838. XIIb

Comédie-Française, Théâtre de la. 14 rue de l'Ancienne-Comédie. 1689 by d'Orbay. XIb

Commissariat à l'Energie atomique, see Atomic Energy Commission.

Concini, HI. 10 rue de Tournon. 1607 by Bordoni. Completely altered. Xb

Concorde, Place de la, see Louis-XV, place

Concorde, Pont de la, see Louis-XVI, Pont.

Condé, HI de. 9-15 rue de Condé. 1612. Destroyed 1773. Xb

Conférence, Porte de la. Quai des Tuileries, east of Orangerie. 1633 by Pidoux. Destroyed 1730. Xa, XIIa

Constantine, Pont de. Quai de la Tournelle - Ile - St - Louis. Reign of Louis-Philippe. Destroyed 1874. XIIIb

Constantinople, Collège de. Impasse Maubert. 1206. Destroyed 1422.

Contagieux, Hôpital provisoire des, see Contagious disease hospital, provisional.

Contagious disease hospital, provisional (Hôpital provisoire des contagieux). Bourg St-Marcel. Reign of Henri IV. Xa

Conti, 3 quai. Building. 1932 by J. Marrast. XVIIc

Convalescent hospital (Hôpital des convalescents). 106 rue du Bac. 1652. Destroyed 1812. XIb

Coq, Château du, see Pocherons, HI des.

Coq, Château du. 63-73 rue d'Auteuil. 17th c. Destroyed 19th c. IXd

Coqueret, Collège. 11 impasse Chartière. 1418. Destroyed 1643. VIIIb

Corbie, HI de. 9-15 rue de Condé. 16th c. Destroyed 1612. VIIIa

Cordélières, convent. Broca hospital. 1289. Destroyed 1796-1836. VIIb

Cordeliers, monastery. 15-21 rue de l'Ecole-de-Médecine. 1230. Refectory, dormitories, 15th c. Burned, restored 1580-1602. Cloister rebuilt 1673-83. All but refectory destroyed 1804. VI, VIIb, IXb, XIe

Coulanges, HI de. 1 bis Place des Vosges. 1606. Xb

Coupeaux, HI des. 2-24 rue du Fer-à-Moulin. 1423. Destroyed. VIIIa

Cour de Mai. Palais de Justice. 1783-86 by Demaisons and Antoine. XIIb

Cour des Comptes (civil-service governing board). 13 rue Cambon.1899-1901 by C. Moyaux. XVIb

Cours (grands boulevards). 1670-1705. XIa

Cours, Grand, see Champs-Elysées, Av. des.

Cours-la-Reine. Now Cours-la-Reine and Cours Albert-I. 1616. Xa

Courteilles, HI de, called de Rochechouart. 110 rue de Grenelle. 1778 by Cherpitel. XIId

Courtille-Barbette. Rue des Filles-du-Calvaire, blvd du Temple, rue du Pont-aux-Choux. Beginning 13th c. Destroyed. VI

Creil, HI de, called de Cavoye. 52 rue des Sts-Pères. 1643 by Girard. Xb

Créqui, HI de. Rue St-Guillaume, See Talon, HI.

Créqui, HI du maréchal de. Former rue St-Nicaise. Cour du Carrousel. 1657. Destroyed 1838. XIc

Croulebarbe, 33 rue. Building. 1959 by E. Albert. XVIIIc

Culdoe, HI, later d'Etampes. 17 rue St-Antoine. Before 1399. Destroyed. VIIIa

Curie hospital. 14 rue Lhomond. Ca. 1933. XVIIb

D

Dalsace, Dr., residence-clinic, 31 rue St-Guillaume. 1931 by P. Chareau. XVIIc

Dames de l'Assomption, convent. 263 rue St-Honoré-place Maurice-Barrès.Convent 1622, destroyed 19th c. Church 1670-76 by Errard. XIe

Damiette, Pont de. Quai Henri-IV, Ile St-Louis. Reign of Louis-Philippe. Destroyed 1874. XIIb

Danès, HI du Président. 25 rue de la Clef. 1747. XIIc

Dauphin, HI. 14-16 rue de Seine. Ca. 1586. Destroyed 1825. IXa

Dauphine, Place. Begun 1607. Xa, XVIa

Debilly, Passerelle (footbridge). Quais Branly and de New-York. 1900. XVIa

Défense, Ensemble de la. Begun 1958 by Auzelle, Camelot, de Mailly, Herbé, Zehrfuss. XVIIIf

Delessert, HI. 21-29 rue Raynouard. 1800. Destroyed 20th c. XIIIc

Delisle-Mansart, HI. 22 rue St-Gilles. Beginning 18th c. by Delisle-Mansart. XId

Dépôt des Condamnés, see Depot for condemned prisoners.

Dépôt for condemned prisoners (Dépôt des Condamnés), called Grande Roquette (prison). Rues de la Roquette, Vacquerie, Gerbier. 1837. Destroyed 1899. XIIIc

Dervieux, HI de Mlle. 44 rue de la Victoire. 1774 by Brongniart. XIId

Deshayes, HI, later Radix de Sainte-Foy. 1-3 rue Caumartin. 1779 by Aubert. XIId

Desmares, HI de Mlle, called de Villeroy. 78 rue de Varenne. 1724 by Aubry. XIIc

Deutsch-de-la-Meurthe, Fondation. Cité Universitaire. 1921 by L. Bechmann. XVIIc

Dhuis reservoir,La. Rue Darcy. 1864 by Belgrand. XIVa

Dix-Huit, Collège des. South of the Sorbonne. 1529. Destroyed 1639. IXb

Docteur-Blanche, 5 rue du. Building. 1928 by Patout. XVIIc

Docteur-Blanche, 19 rue du. Building. 1956 by Ginsberg and Ilinski. XVIIIc

Docteur-Blanche, 10 Square du. 1923 by Le Corbusier. XVIIc

Dominicans, General Novitiate. Intersection rue du Bac,

blvd St-Germain, rue de Gribeauval, Place St-Thomas d'Aquin. 1632. Chapel 1683 by P. Bullet. Façade 1787 by R.-P. Claude. Now church of St-Thomas d'Aquin. Xc, XIe

Dominicans or "Jacobins," monastery. Rue Cujas, west of rue St-Jacques-rue Soufflot. Church and cloister begun 1221. Rebuilt 16th c., destroyed 1800-66. V, XIIId

Dominicans, monastery, called Jacobins. Rue du Marché-St-Honoré. 1611. Destroyed 1794-1810. Xc, XIIId

Dormans, Collège de, see Beauvais, Collège de.

Dormans, HI de. Rue Garancière. 1360. Destroyed 15th c. VIIa

Double, Pont au. 1626-34. Rebuilt 1881-85. Xa, XVIa

Draveil marina (boat dock). By Vigor. XVIIIf

Droit, Ecole de (law school). Place du Panthéon. 1770-83 by Soufflot. Ended 1823. Enlarged 1908. Remodeled 1967. XIIb, XIIIc, XVIb

Droit et des sciences économiques, Faculté de (school of law and economics). Rue d'Assas. 1959-62 by Lenormand. XVIIb

Dufour, HI de, called de Castries. 72 rue de Varenne. 1700 XId

Du Guesclin, HI. 17 rue du Temple. 1372-80. Destroyed. VIIa

Duprat, HI de. 60 rue de Varenne. 1728. XIIc

Duprat, HI, see Maine, HI du duc du.

Duras, HI de. 68 rue du Fbg-St-Honoré. Beginning 18th c. by Boffrand. Destroyed 1928. XId

Duret de Chevry, HI, called Tubeuf. 8 rue des Petits-Champs. 1635-42 by J. Thiriot. Xb

Duret, HI du Président. 67 rue de Lille. 1706 by Predot. XId

Duret, HI du Président, called de Brienne. 16 rue St-Dominique. 1714 by Aubry. XId

Duret, HI du Président, called de Maisons, de Soyecourt. 51 rue de l'Université. 1707 by Lassurance. XId

E

Ecole centrale de Châtenay-Malabry (engineering school). By Demaret, Fayeton, Drouin, Vital. XVIIIf

Ecole centrale des arts et manufactures. Rue Vaucanson. 1878-85 by Demimuid and Denfer. XVIb

Ecole coloniale (colonial administrative school). 2 av. de l'Observatoire. 1896 by Yvon. XVIb

Ecole de chirurgie (school of surgery), later Faculté de Médecine (school of medicine). 12 rue de l'Ecole-de-Médecine. 1769-86 by Gondoin. Enlarged (Blvd St-Germain) 1878-1900 by Ginain. XIIb, XVIb

Ecole de Médecine (medical school). 12 rue de l'Ecole-de-Médecine. 1769-86 by Gondoin. Enlarged 1878-1900. Now Faculté de Médecine. XIIb

Ecole de pharmacie. 4-6 av. de l'Observatoire. 1876-85 by Laisné. XVIb

Ecole de puériculture (school of child welfare). 20 blvd Brune. 1933 by Duval, Gonse, Dresse, Houdon. XVIIb

Ecole des hautes études commerciales (business school). Jouy-en-Josas. 1961-65 by Coulon. XVIIIf

Ecole des mines, see Estrées, HI d', called de Vendôme.

Ecole des Ponts et Chaussées (civil-engineering school). 28 rue des Sts-Pères. Installed

1829 in Hôtel deFleury (q.v.) Enlarged 1868 ff. XIIc, XIVb

Ecole maternelle (nursery school), see Boulard.

Ecole militaire (military school). Place de Fontenoy-Champ-de-Mars. 1752-57 by J.-A. Gabriel. XIIb

Ecole nationale des arts et métiers (engineering school). 151 blvd de l'Hôpital. 1919 by Roussi. Amphitheater,1960 by J.-M. Hereng. XVIb, XVIIIb

Ecole nationale supérieure d'aéronautique (aeronautical engineering). 30 blvd Victor. 1932 by L. Tissier. XVIIb

Ecole normale supérieure (school of education). 45 rue d'Ulm. 1846. Enlarged 1933-37. By A. and J. Guilbert. XIIIc, XV, XVIIb

Ecole normale supérieure de jeunes filles (school of education for girls). Blvd Jourdan-rue de la Tombe-Issoire. 1950 by Crevel. XVIIIa

Ecole polytechnique (engineering school). Plateau de Saclay. Begun 1967 by Henri Pottier. XVIIIf

Ecole polytechnique (military polytechnic school). 5 rue Descartes. 1805. Enlarged several times. XIIIc

Ecole pratique de médecine (medical school). 17, 21 rue de l'Ecole de Médecine. 1877-1900. XVIb

Ecole pratique de médecine (medical school). 45 rue des Sts-Pères. 1937-53 by Madeleine and Walter. XVIIb, XVIIIb

Ecole royale de chant et de déclamation (theatrical school). 12 rue Bergère-rue Pères de la doctrine chrétienne. 1772 became Couvent des Pères de la doctrine chrétienne. IXb, XIIIb

Ecossais, Collège des. 65 rue du Cardinal-Lemoine. 1662. (Formerly rue des Amandiers. 1326 ff.) XIe

Ecquevilly, HI d', see Boucherat, HI.

Effiat, HI d'. 26 rue Vieille-du-Temple. ca. 1620. Destroyed 1882. Xb

Eiffel Tower. 1887-89 by Eiffel, Koechlin, Nouguier, Sauvestre. XVIb

Embarcadère de l'Ouest (right bank), later Gare St-Lazare, see St-Lazare, Gare.

Embarcadère de Lyon, later Gare de Lyon, see Lyon, Gare de.

Embarcadère de Strasbourg, later Gare de l'Est, see Est, Gare de l'.

Embarcadère de Vincennes (RR station). Place de la Bastille. 1859 by Berthelin. XIVa

Embarcadère d'Orléans, later Gare d'Austerlitz, see Orléans-Austerlitz, Gare d'.

Embarcadère d'Orsay (RR station). Place Denfert-Rochereau. 1846 by Dulong. Destroyed 1895. XIIIb

Embarcadère du Nord, later Gare du Nord, see Nord, Gare du.

Enfant-Jésus, Pensionnat de l'. 149 rue de Sèvres. 1724. Now Enfants-Malades hospital(q.v.). XIIe

Enfants atteints de maladies vénériennes, Hospice des, see Hospice for children affected by venereal diseases.

Enfants bleus, see Trinité (La), hospital.

Enfants-Malades, Hôpital des (children's hospital), first called Hôpital de l'Enfant-Jésus. 149 rue de Sèvres. 1724. Enlarged 1939. XIIb, XVIIb

Enfants-Rouges, Hôpital des (orphanage). 90 rue des Archives. 1534. Destroyed 1808. 1772 became Couvent des Pères de la doctrine chrétienne. IXb, XIIIb

Enfants-Trouvés, Hospice des (foundling home). 118 rue du Fbg-St-Antoine-square Trousseau. 1674. Destroyed 1902. XIb

Enfants-Trouvés, Hospice des (foundling home). Parvis de

Notre-Dame. 1746 by Boffrand. Destroyed 1877. XIIb

Enfer, Barrière d' (customs house), see Fermiers Généraux customs wall.

English Seminary (Séminaire des Anglais). 26 rue Lhomond. 1687. XIe

Ennery, HI d'. 59 av. Foch. 1870s. XVIc

Entragues, HI d'. 12 rue de Tournon. 1735. XIIc

Epernon, HI d'. 102.rue Vieille-du-Temple. 1605. Altered later. Xb

Epinay, HI d'. 5 rue de la Chaussée-d'Antin. 1775 by Brongniart. Destroyed 1862. XIId

Erard, Tour. Building. Rue Erard. 1965 by Anger. XVIIIc

Ermitage, Pavillon de l', see Bagnolet, Château de.

Ermites de St-Augustin, see Grands-Augustins, monastery.

Essling, HI d'. 8 rue Jean-Goujon, now Maison des Centraux. XIIIc

Essone, Préfecture de l'. Evry. By Lagneau, Weill, Dimitrijevic, Coulomb, Cordiolani, Sieffert, Gennet. XVIIIf

Est, Gare de l' (RR station). First "Embarcadère de Strasbourg." 1st site: rue d'Aubervilliers, blvd de la Chapelle (1848). 2nd site: place du 11 Novembre-1918 (1850). By Duquesnoy. Enlarged 1895-99 and 1924-31. XIIIb, XVIa, XVIIa

Estrées, HI d'. 69 rue des Gravilliers. After 1550. Vestiges. IXa

Estrées, HI d'. 8 rue Barbette. Before 1645. Destroyed. Xb

Estrées, HI d', called de Fürstenberg. 75 rue de Grenelle. 1713 by R. de Cotte. XId

Estrées, HI d', called de Vendôme. 60 bis blvd St-Michel. Ecole des Mines since 1815. 1707 by Courtonne and Le Blond. XId, XIIIc

Estrées, HI de la duchesse d', or Grand Hôtel d'Estrées. 79

rue de Grenelle. 1713 by R. de Cotte. Now Russian embassy.

Etampes, HI d'. North Cour carrée (Square Court) of Louvre. 14th c. Destroyed. VIIa

Etampes, HI d'. 1-5 rue Git-le-Cœur. 1st half 16th c. Destroyed 1671. IXa

Etampes, HI d'. 65 rue de Varenne. 1699. Destroyed. XId

Etampes, HI d'. Rue St-Antoine. See Culdoe, HI.

Etoile, Carrefour, later place de l'. Intersection laid out in 1774, again in 1854 ff. (Haussmann). XIIa, XIVa, XVb

Eu, HI of the counts of. 40 rue St-André-des-Arts. 1300. Destroyed 1536. VIIa

Evreux, HI d'. 55-57 rue du Fbg-St-Honoré. 1718 by A.C. Mollet. Now Elysée palace. XIIc

Expiatory chapel (Chapelle expiatoire). Square Louis-XVI. 1815-26 by Le Bas and Fontaine. XIIId

Expressway, left bank (Voie express rive gauche). 1956-61. XVIIIa

Expressway, right bank (Voie express rive droite). 1961-67. XVIIIa

F

Faculté de Médecine,see Ecole de Médecine.

Faculté de Médecine. 13 rue de la Bûcherie. 1472. Rebuilt in 1744 by Barbier de Bléguière. VIIIa

Faculté de Médecine. Annex. Rue Monge-Rue du Fer-à-Moulin. Project. XVIIIb

Faculté des sciences. Site of the Halle-aux-vins (q.v.). 1962 ff. by Cassan and Albert. XVIIIb

Fargez de Polighy, HI. 2 rue Drouot.1728. Destroyed. XIIc

Faubourg St-Honoré, 168-170 rue du. Building. ca. 1930 by Plousey and Cassan. XVIIc

Fécamp, Hl of the abbots of. 5 rue Hautefeuille. 1292. Rebuilt 16th c. VIIa, IXa

Fédération du bâtiment (office building). 7-9 rue Lapérouse. 1953 by R. Gravereaux R. Lopez. Enlarged 1960 by Badani, Kandjian, Roux-Dorlut. XVIIIc

Félix-Faure, 24 Place. Building. 1900-10, anonymous. XVIc

Félix Potin, Maison. 140 bis rue de Rennes. 1904 by Auscher. XVIc

Fermiers Généraux customs wall. 1784-89 by C.-N. Ledoux. Destroyed 1860 ff. Included Barrières (customs houses) de Chartres, d'Enfer, de la Villette, du Trône. XIIa, XIVa

Feuillantines, convent. Rue des Feuillantines. 1623. Destroyed 1813-50. Xc

Feuillants, monastery. Rue de Castiglione. Begun 1587. Church 1606. Portal 1624 by F. Mansart. Gardens 1666 by Le Nôtre. Monumental gate 1677. Destroyed 1804-30. IXb, Xc, XIe, XIIId

Fieubet, Hl. 2 Quai des Célestins. 1676 by J. Hardouin-Mansart. Altered 19th and 20th c. XId

Figaro, Hl du. 26 rue Drouot. After 1870. Destroyed. XVIc

Filles anglaises, convent, called de Notre-Dame de Sion. 19-31 rue des Boulangers. 1631. Destroyed 1860. Xc, XIVc

Filles anglaises de la Conception. 40-60 rue de Charenton. 1635. Destroyed 1800 ff. Xc

Filles Bleues, see Filles de l'Annonciade.

Filles de la Croix, convent. 8 rue de Charonne. 1641. Destroyed 1906. Xc, XVId

Filles de la Croix, convent. Rue St-Antoine, rue des Tournelles, rue des Vosges, Impasse Guéménée. 1643. Destroyed 1790-97. XIe, XIId

Filles-de-la-Croix, country house. 19-21 rue Daubenton. 1656. Destroyed 1967. XIe

Filles de Ste-Agathe, convent. 39 rue de l'Arbalète. 1700. Destroyed 1859. XIe

Filles de la doctrine chrétienne, or "Ursulines," convent. Rue des Ursulines. 1612 Destroyed 1799 ff. Xc

Filles de la Madeleine, or "Madelonnettes," convent. 14-16 rue des Fontaines-du-Temple. 1620. Destroyed 1866 ff. Xc, XIVc

Filles de l'Annonciade, convent, or "Filles bleues," Site of Lycée Victor-Hugo. Rue Payenne. 1622. Destroyed. Xc

Filles de la Passion, convent, called Capucines. 360-364 rue St-Honoré, Place Vendôme. Installed 1604 in Hôtel de Mercœur-Vendôme. Destroyed 1685-88. Xc

Filles de la Passion, convent, called Capucines. Rue de la Paix. 1687-88, by d'Orbay. Destroyed 1806. XIe

Filles de la Providence de Dieu. 38 rue de l'Arbalète. 1651. Destroyed 1859. XIe

Filles de la Visitation Ste-Marie, or "Visitandines," convent. 17 rue St-Antoine. 1628 Destroyed 1796. Chapel survives (1632-34 by F. Mansart). Became Protestant church, 1802. Xc

Filles de la Visitation Ste-Marie, or "Visitandines," convent. 187-193 rue St-Jacques. 1626. Destroyed 1793. Xc

Filles de l'ordre de la Trinité, called Mathurines, convent. 12 rue Erard. 1713. Destroyed 1793. XIe, XIIId

Filles de l'Union chrétienne, convent. Was Hl de St-Chaumont. 226 rue St-Denis. 1683 Rebuilt 1780. Destroyed 1906. Vestiges. XIe, XIIe, XVId

Filles de la Charité, convent, or "Sœurs Grises." Intersection rue du Fbg-St-Denis, blvd de Magenta. 1642. Destroyed 1797. Xc

Filles de la Congrégation de Notre-Dame, convent. Rue de Navarre. 1673. Destroyed 1883. XIe

Filles de Ste-Elizabeth, convent. 195 rue du Temple. 1628-30. Destroyed: Chapel, church of Ste-Elizabeth (1646, enlarged 1826) survive. Xc

Filles de Ste-Geneviève, called Miramiones, convent. 47 quai de la Tournelle. Installed 1691 in Hôtel de Miramion (1636). Now Musée des Hôpitaux de Paris. XIe

Filles de St-Joseph, convent. 10-12 rue St-Dominique. 1641. Now ministry of National Defense. Xc

Filles de St-Michel, convent. 48-54 rue Lhomond. 1724. Destroyed. XIIe

Filles de St-Thomas, convent. Place de la Bourse. 1642. Destroyed 1808. Xc, XIIId

Filles de St-Thomas-de-Villeneuve, convent. Rue de Sèvres, blvd Raspail. 1660. Destroyed 1906. XIe

Filles-Dieu, convent. First 71 rue du Fbg-St-Denis (1226), withdrew to rue du Caire in 1360. Destroyed 1799. VI, VIIb, XIIId

Filles du Bon Pasteur, convent. 38 rue du Cherche-Midi. 1688. Destroyed 1855. XIe

Firemen's barracks, see Mesnil, 8 rue.

Flandre, see Flanders.

Flandres, Hl of the counts of. Hôtel des Postes rue Coquillière, rue du Louvre. 1285-93. Destroyed 1545. VIIa

Flesselles, Hl de (called). 52 rue de Sévigné. 1680 by Delisle-Mansart. Destroyed 1908. XId

Fleury; Hl de. 28 rue des Sts-Pères. 1768 by Antoine. Enlarged 1868-79. Now Ecole des Ponts et Chaussées. XIIc

Flower market (Marché aux fleurs). 1809. XIIIa

Folie Beaujon. Av. des Champs-Elysées, Hoche, rue du Fbg-St-Honoré, rue de Washington. 1784 by Girardin. Destroyed 1822 ff. XIId

Folie Bertin, first Hôtel de Julienne. 47-49 rue Raynouard. 1750. Destroyed. XIIc

Folie Boutin. 102 rue St-Lazare. 1766. Destroyed 1826. XIIc

Folie Bouxière. 88 rue de Clichy. 1760 by Le Charpentier. Destroyed ca. 1840. XIIc

Folie Brancas. 77-93 rue St-Lazare. 1725. Destroyed 1854. XIIc

Folie d'Artois, see Bagatelle.

Folie de Chartres. Blvd de Courcelles, rues du Rocher, de Monceau, de Courcelles. 1778 by Carmontelle. See Monceau, Parc. XIId

Folie-Favart, see Carré de Beaudoin.

Folie Marbeuf. Between rues Marbeuf, François-I, Quentin-Bauchart, and the Champs-Elysées. 1760. Destroyed 19th c. XIId

Folie Rambouillet. 172 rue de Charenton. 1633-35. Destroyed 18th c. Xc

Folie Regnault. Rue de la Folie-Regnault. 14th c. Destroyed VIIa

Folie Richelieu. 18 rue de Clichy. 1730. Destroyed 1826. XIIc

Folie Sainte-James. 34 Av. de Madrid. 1779-85 by Bellanger. XIId

Folie Titon. 31 rue de Montreuil. 1673. Destroyed 1880. XId

Fondation internationale. Cité Universitaire. 1935 by Larsen. XVIIc

Fontaine Boucherat. 133 rue de Turenne. 1962 by J. Beausire. XIa

Fontaine Cuvier. Corner rue Linné, rue Cuvier. 1840 by Vigoureux. XIIIb

Fontaine de Birague. Intersection rue St-Antoine, rue de Sévigné. 1577. Rebuilt 1627, 1707. Destroyed 1856. IXa

Fontaine de Joyeuse. 41 rue de Turenne. 1687. XIa

Fontaine de la Place Maubert. 1674. Destroyed. XIa

Fontaine de l'Observatoire. 1875 by Davioud. XVIa

Fontaine de Mars. 129 rue St-Dominique. 1806 by Bralle. XIIIa

Fontaine de Necker. Rue de Jarente, Impasse de la Poissonnerie. 1783 by Caron. XIIa

Fontaine des Haudriettes. Corner rues des Archives, des Haudriettes. ca. 1636. Destroyed and rebuilt 1764 by Moreau-Desproux. XIa, XIIa

Fontaine des Innocents, see Innocents fountain.

Fontaine des Quatre-Evêques. Place St-Sulpice. 1844 by Visconti. XIIIb

Fontaine des Quatre-Saisons. 57-59 rue de Grenelle. 1739-46 by Bouchardon. XIIa

Fontaine des Trois-Lions. First Place de la République, now Place Félix-Eboué. 1862 by Davioud. Displaced 1881. XIVa

Fontaine du Château-d'Eau, first Place de la République, reinstalled at Marché aux bestiaux de la Villette (La Villette animal market). 1811 by Girard. XIIIa

Fontaine du Fellah. Rue de Sèvres, opposite 97. 1806 by Bralle. XIIIa

Fontaine du Palmier. Place du Châtelet. 1808 by Bralle. XIIIa

Fontaine du Ponceau, later de la Reine. 142 rue St-Denis. End 12th c. Rebuilt 1642 and 1732. V

Fontaine du square Notre-Dame. 1843 by Vigoureux. XIIIb

Fontaine du Trahoir. Intersection rues St-Honoré, de l'Arbre-sec. 1635. Rebuilt 1776 by Soufflot. XIIa

Fontaine Gaillon. Corner rues de la Michodière, de Port-Mahon. 1707. Rebuilt 1827 by Visconti. XIIIb

Fontaine, HI de, called de Maillebois. 102 rue de Grenelle. ca. 1720 by Delisle-Mansart. Remodeled 1771 by Antoine. XIIc, XIId

Fontaine Louvois. Square Louvois. 1844 by Visconti. XIIb

Fontaine Maubuée. 122 rue St-Martin (section razed 1934 ff.). Known 1320. Rebuilt 1733, dismantled 1934. VIIa, XIIa

Fontaine St-Michel. Place St-Michel. 1860 by Davioud Destroyed 1840 (see Fontaine Cuvier). XIa

Fontaine St-Victor Corner rues Linné, Cuvier. 1671. Destroyed 1840 (see Fontaine Cuvier). XIa

Fontaine Trogneux. 61 rue du Fbg-St-Antoine. 1710. XIa

For-l'Evêque (Tribunal and prison de l'Evêque). 19 rue St-Germain-l'Auxerrois. 1161. Rebuilt 1652. Destroyed 1783. IV

Force (Grande Force and Petite Force), prisons. Rues de Sévigné, du Roi-de-Sicile, Pavée. Created in 1782, using old hôtels. Destroyed 1853. XIIa

Ford building. 36 blvd des Italiens. 1931 by Roux-Spitz. XVIIc

Forez, Hl de. Rue du Fer-à-Moulin. 14th c. Destroyed. VIIa

Fortet, Collège de. 21 rue Valette. 1394. Destroyed 1806, cellars survive. VIIIb

Forum. Base of Rue Soufflot, between rue St-Jacques, rue Cujas, and blvd St-Michel. Built 2nd c., fortified end 3rd c., ruined by successive invasions, excavated during Charles V during digging of moats for his wall. II, III

Fossés jaunes (yellow trenches), front with bastions, called. begun in 1566, resumed 1633-36, never really ended, abandoned under Louis XIV, disappeared about beginning 18th c. It really existed only at the west of the Tuileries. IXa

Fossé-le-Roi, first sewer following bypassed riverbed of Seine (reign of St-Louis). VI

Fountains, Rond-Point des Champs-Elysées, see Rond-Point des Champs-ELysées.

Foyer franco-libanais, see Franco-Lebanese center.

France, Collège de, see Lecteurs royaux, Collège des.

France, Place de. Project of Henri IV. To have been at intersection of rues de Bretagne, de Poitou, de Turenne. Xa

Franciscan Missions, monastery. 20 rue de la Tombe-Issoire. 1936. XVIId

Franco-Lebanese center (Foyer franco-libanais). 15 rue d'Ulm. 1963 by Dgenangi. XVIIIb

Franklin, 25 bis rue. Building. 1903 by A. Perret. XVIc

Frères de la Charité-Notre-Dame, called Billettes, monastery. 22 rue des Archives. 1299. Cloister 1415. Replaced by Carmelite Friars 1633 (see Carmes-Billettes). VIIb, VIIIb

G

Gaignières, HI de. 95 rue de Sèvres. 1685. Destroyed 1715. XId

Gaillard, HI. 1 Place Malesherbes. 1862 by Février. Now branch of Banque de France. XIVb

Gaité Lyrique, Théâtre de la, see Prince Impérial, Théâtre du.

Galerie des Machines (exhibition hall). Champ-de-Mars. 1889 by Dutert and Contamin. Destroyed 1910. XIVb

Galeries Lafayette (department store). Blvd Haussmann. 1912 by Chanut. Partial reconstruction 1926. XVIb, XVIIb

Galitzin, HI de. 7 rue St-Florentin. 1787. XIId

Galliera Palace, 10 Av. Pierre-I-de-Serbie. 1878-88 by Ginain, XVIc

Gallifet, HI de. 73 rue de Grenelle. 1775 by A. Legrand. XIId

Garde-Meuble, now Ministry of the Navy. Place de la Concorde. 1760-75 by J.-A. Gabriel. XIIb

Gare, Piscine de la (swimming pool). 45-47 blvd de la Gare. 1927. XVIIc

Garigliano, Pont du. On site of Auteuil viaduct. 1964-66. XVIIIa

Garlande enclosure (Clos de). Vineyards. Rue Galande, Place Maubert. IV

Garnelles, Château de, see Grenelle, Château de.

Gasworks, 1st in Paris. 129 rue du Fbg-Poissonnière. 1819. XIIIb

Gas, see Gasworks.

Geoffrin, HI de Madame. 374 rue St-Honoré. 1750. XIId

George V, HI. 29, 31 Av. George-V. 1931 by Lefranc and Wybo. XVIIc

Gesvres, Quai de. 1642. Xa

Gobelins, 48 Av. des. Lycée technique et école maternelle (technical high school and nursery school). Project by J. Rousselot and C. Aigrenault. XVIIIb

Gobelins royal tapestry factory (Manufacture royale des Gobelins). Rue Berbier-du-Mets, 42 Av. des Gobelins. 1667. Partly burned 1871. Enlarged during Third Republic. XIb, XV, XVIIb

Gondi, HI de. Place Vendôme, rue St-Honoré. 1561. Destroyed 1603. IXa

Goret de St-Martin, HI. Rue Lagrange. 1650. Destroyed 1887. XIc

Gouffier de Thoix, HI de, called de la Galaizière. 56 rue de Varenne. 1760. XIIc

Gourgues, HI de, see Montrésor, HI de.

Gournay, HI de, called de Tingry Mortemart. 1 rue St-Dominique. 1695 by Boffrand. XId

Gramont, Pont de, over a Seine channel, now Blvd Morland. 17th c. XIa

Grand Maître de l'artillerie, HI du, see Arsenal, Grand. Xa

Grand Pont, later (14th c.) Pont au Change. 11th c. Rebuilt 12th c., destroyed 1280. Rebuilt and duplicated in 1296: Pont au Change and Pont aux Moulins (or aux Meuniers) 1296-1595, then Pont Marchant 1608. Destroyed 1621. Pont au Change rebuilt 1637-47, rebuilt 1858. IV, V, VIIa, Xa, XIVa

Grand-Prieur, HI du. Square du Temple. 15th c. Rebuilt 1667 by F. Mansart. Destroyed 1853. XId, XIVb

Grand-Prieuré "du Temple" (in fact of the Order of Malta, formerly Hospitallers of St. John) see Knights Templars.

Grand-Veneur, HI du, see Boucherat, HI.

Grandes Carrières (plaster quarries). Montmartre. Closed 1860. XIVa

Grands-Augustins, monastery, first called Ermites de St-Augustin. NE corner quai and rue des Grands-Augustins. 1293. Church 14th c. Destroyed 1797 ff. VIIb, VIIIb, XIIId

Grands-Augustins, Quai des. 1313. VIIa

Grange-aux-Merciers, Château de la. Rue Gabriel-Lamé. 14th c. Destroyed. VIIIa

Grange "bataillée" (fortified barn of the Ste-Opportune canons. 9 rue Drouot. 1243. Destroyed. VI

Grange Batelière, see Grange "bataillée."

Grassins, Collège des. 12 rue Laplace. 1569. Destroyed 1790. IXb

Grenelle, 54 Blvd de. Office building. 1960 by Fayeton. XVIII

Grenelle, artesian well (puits artésien of. Corner rues Valentin-Hauy and Bouchut. 1841. XIIIb

Grenelle (earlier Garnelles), Château de. Caserne (barracks) Dupleix. Rue Desaix. 10th, 11th c. Powder store-house 1792, blown up 1794. IV, XIIIc

Grenelle, Pont de. 1875 by Vaudrey and Pesson. Destroyed 1967. New bridge 1968. XVIa, XVIIIa

Grenelle, provisional hospital of. South of Champ-de-Mars. 1580. IXa

Grenelle slaughterhouses (abattoirs). Place de Breteuil. Built 1808-10. Destroyed end 19th c. XIIIa

Grenelle, 134 rue de. Building. 1903 by Lavirotte. XVIc

Grenelle, 151 rue de. Building. 1898 by Lavirotte. XVIc

Grenier à Sel (salt storehouse). 6 rue St-Germain-l'Auxerrois. 1698. Destroyed 1909. XIb

Grenier d'abondance (warehouse). Blvd Bourdon, rue de l'Arsenal. 1810. Burned 1871. Vestiges. XIIIa

Grève, Place de, later Place de l'Hôtel-de-Ville (1830). Enlarged 1778 and 1853. IV, XIIa, XIVa

Grève, Pont de la, see Arcole, Pont d'.

Grimod de la Reynière, HI. 1,5 rue Boissy-d'Anglas. 1769 by Barré and Bellanger. Destroyed 1928. XIId

Gros Caillou, military hospital of. Rues St-Dominique, des Loges. 1765. Destroyed 1899. XIIb

Gros-Caillou pumping station. 67 quai d'Orsay. 1786. Destroyed 1858. XIIa

Grüyn des Bordes, HI, called de Lauzun. 17 quai d'Anjou. 1656 by Le Vau. XIc

Guénégaud des Brosses, HI de 60 rue des Archives. Ca. 1650 by F. Mansart.

Guénégaud, Petit HI, called de Sillery, de Caumont. 13 quai Conti. 1659 by F. Mansart. XIc

Guénégaud, Théâtre. 42 rue Mazarine. 1671. Destroyed ca. 1900. XIb

Guérard, Maison. 137 rue Vieille-du-Temple. 1775. XIId

Guimard, HI de Mlle. 11 rue Meyerbeer. 1773 by Ledoux. Destroyed 1862. XIId

Guimet, Musée. 6 Place d'Iéna. 1888. XVIb

Guise, HI de. Rues des Archives, des Quatre-Fils, Vieille-du-Temple, des Francs-Bourgeois. 1553. Destroyed 1704. IXa

Guynemer, 14 rue. Building. 1928 by Roux-Spitz. XVIIc

Gymnase, Théâtre du. 38 Blvd Bonne-Nouvelle. 1820. Renovated 1850 and 1887. XIIIc

Halle à la Volaille (poultry market), succeeded monastery of Grands-Augustins. 1808. Destroyed 1867. XIIIa

Halle au vieux linge (used-clothing market). Carreau du Temple. 1808-11 by J. Molinos. Destroyed 1905. XIIIa

Halle aux blés, see Halle aux farines.

Halle aux cuirs (leather market). Rues de Santeuil, du Fer-à-Moulin. 1865. Destroyed 1964. XIVa

Halle aux farines (flour market) or aux blés. Bourse de Commerce. 1763-66 by Le Camus de Mézières. Metal roof by Bellanger 1808-13. Destroyed 1889. XIIa, XIIIa

Halle aux Vins (wine market). Corner quai St-Bernard and rue des Fossés-St-Bernard. 1664. Rebuilt 1808-19, much enlarged over St-Victor monastery. Evicted 1962 ff. by new Faculté des Sciences. XIa, XIIIa, XVIIIb

Halle Barbier, see Halle du Pré-aux-Clercs.

Halle du Pré-aux-Clercs or Halle Barbier (Market hall). 13-17 rue du Bac. 1630. Destroyed 1659. Xa

Halles, Les (market halls). On site of Champeaux market, under Philippe-Auguste, 1183. Enlarged ca. 1269 and ca. 1284. Six halls destroyed 1553 and rebuilt by Henri II, 1553 ff. Enlarged over Innocents' cemetery 1788. Total renovation: 1852-66 by Baltard (present Halles). Enlarged 1936 rue Coquillière. Destruction planned. VI, VIIa, IXa, XIIIa, XIVa, XVIIa, XVIIIa

Hallwyll, HI d'. 28 rue Michel-le-Comte. Transformed by Ledoux in 1787. XIId

Hamelin, 11 rue. Town house. 1894 by L.-C. Boileau fils. XVIc

Harcourt, Collège d'. 40-42 Blvd St-Michel. 1280. Rebuilt 1675. Destroyed 1795. See St-Louis, Collège. VIIb

Harcourt, HI d'. Rue Champollion. 13th c. Destroyed from 17th c. to 1852. VIIa

Hauts-de-Seine, Préfecture des (district administration). Nanterre. 1968 by Wogensky. XVIIIf

Hélène-Boucher, Lycée (high school). 71-85 Cours de Vincennes. 1938 by J. Sallez. XVIIb

Héliport de Paris. Blvd Victor. Formerly Issy-les-Moulineaux airfield. XVIIIa

Helvétius, HI de Mme. 59 rue d'Auteuil. 1720. Destroyed 1871. XIIc

Hénault de Cantobre, HI. 82 rue François-Miron. 1706. XId

Henri-Heine, 3 rue. Building. 1956 by P. Vivien. XVIIIc

Henri-Martin, 115 Av. Building. 1931 by Roux-Spitz. XVIIc

Henri IV, Collège, later lycée (high school), was also Lycée Napoléon and Corneille. Rue Clovis. Installed 1796-1800 in abbey of Ste-Geneviève. XIIIc

Hercule, HI d'. 5-7 rue des Grands-Augustins. 1470. Destroyed beginning 17th c. VIIIa

Hérouet, HI. 54 rue Vieille-du-Temple. ca. 1510. VIIIa

Hersant, Pont, over the marshes of the bypassed Seine riverbed. Known 1351. VIIa

Hesselin, HI. 24 quai de Béthune. 1640 by Le Vau. Destroyed 1935. Xb

Hestomesnil, HI d', see Sens, HI of the archbishops of.

Hillerin, HI de, "de Transylvanie." 9 quai Malaquais. Ca. 1622-28. Xb

Hilton, Hotel. Av. de Suffren, rue Jean-Rey. 1966 by Dufau. XVIIIc

Holy Trinity (American cathedral). 23 Av. George-V. Ca. 1920. XVIId

Honoré de Balzac, Lycée (high school). 2 Av. de la Porte-Clichy. 1950-54 by Paquet. XVIIIb

Hôpital St-Jean-de-Jérusalem, Chevaliers de l', see Hospital of St. John of Jerusalem, Knights of the.

Hôpital universitaire, see University hospital.

Horse markets, see Markets, horse.

Hospice for children affected by venereal diseases (Hospice des enfants atteints de maladies vénériennes). Between 355 and 371 rue de Vaugirard. 1780. Destroyed 1792. XIIb

Hospital of St. John of Jerusalem, Knights of the (Chevaliers de l'Hôpital de St-Jean-de-Jerusalem), later called St-Jean-de-Latran. Between rues St-Jacques, Jean-de-Beauvais, Sommerard, des Ecoles. Church ca. 1170, rebuilt end 15th c., destroyed 1823-55. Keep (donjon) 13th c. Destroyed 1854. IV, VI, VIIIb, XIVc

Hospital for skin diseases (Hôpital des Teigneux), see Ste-Reine, Hospice.

Hospitalières (hospitaller sisters) de Notre-Dame, convent. 35 rue des Tournelles. 1624. Destroyed. 1906. Xc, XVId

Hospitalières (hospitaller sisters) de St-Joseph, convent. 142 rue de la Roquette. 1639. Destroyed 1818. Xc

Hospitaliers (hospitallers) de St-Jacques-du-Haut-Pas. 254 rue St-Jacques. 13th c. reconstructions. Institut des sourds-muets (school for deaf mutes) since 1794. See St-Jacques-du-Haut-Pas, church. VI

Incurables, Hospice des. 42 rue de Sèvres. 1634. Chapel by Gamard. Laënnec hospital since 1874. Xa, Xc, XVIb

Incurables, Hospice des. 150 rue du Fbg-St-Martin, hospice des Récollets. Installed 1802-60 in former convent of Récollets (q.v.). Now Villemin military hospital. XIIIc

Hôtel de Ville (city hall), succeeded Maison aux Piliers (q.v.) 1533-52 by D. da Cortona. Enlarged 1803, 1837, 1841. Burned 1871. Rebuilt 1872-82 by Ballu and Deperthes. IXa, XIIIc, XV, XVIb

Hôtel de Ville, Place de l', see Grève, Place de.

Hôtel-Dieu (hospital). South side of Parvis de Notre-Dame. 1200. Enlarged 1250-60 (Ste-Agnès chapel). St-Christophe chapel rebuilt 1380-94. Burned 1772. Rebuilt. Total destruction 1878. V, VI, VIIIb, XIIb, XIIe, XVIb, XVId. Branch built quai de Montebello (1629, destroyed 1909) and Pont St-Charles (1651, destroyed 1878). Xa

Hôtel-Dieu. North of Parvis de Notre-Dame. 1868-78 by Diet. XIVb

Hôtel populaire d'hommes (workmen's residence). 96 rue de Charonne. 1911 by La Bussière. Transformed. Now Palais de la femme (Salvation Army women's residence). XVIc

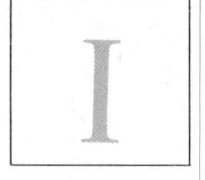

Iéna, Pont d'. 1809-13. Widened 1914, 1936. XIIIa, XVIIa

Ile aux Juifs, former islet, now quai des Orfèvres. VIIa

Ile des Cygnes, see Allée des Cygnes

Imécourt, HI d'. Square de l'Opéra. 1789. Destroyed. XIId

Innocents, cemetery of the Sts. Square des Innocents, rue de la Lingerie, rue de la Ferronnerie. Cemetery since Merovingian period. Enclosed by wall 1186. Ossuaries built beginning 14th c. Opened on rue de la Ferronnerie 1669. Destroyed 1780-86. V, XIIa

Innocents fountain. Formerly corner rues St-Denis, Berger; now Square des Innocents. 1548-49 by J. Goujon. Displaced and changed 1786 by Pajou (sculptor). IXa, XIIa

Institut agronomique (agricultural school). 16 rue Claude-Bernard. 1880. XVIb

Institut catholique (Catholic university). 21 rue d'Assas. In former convent of Carmes déchaussés. 1875. Renovated 1930. XVId, XVIId

Institut d'art et d'archéologie. 3 rue Michelet. 1927 by Bigot. XVIIb

Institut de France, Palais de, see Quatre-Nations, Collège

Institut de paléontologie humaine, see Institute of human paleontology.

Institut d'hygiène dentaire (dental school). Rue Eastman 1936 by Crevel. XVIIb

Institut d'optique. Rue de Sèvres, Blvd Pasteur. 1924-27 XVIIb

Institut du radium. Rues Pierre Curie, d'Ulm, Lhomond. 193[?] by Danis. XVIIb

Institut médico-légal (morgue). Quai de la Rapé[e] 1914 by Tournaire. XVIb

Institut national des sport[s] (physical education institute) 11 Av. du Tremblay. Work b[e]gun 1936. Stadium and swim[-]ming pool 1963 by Bovet XVIIIb

Institut océanographique, se[e] Oceanographic Institute.

Institute of human paleonto[-]logie humaine). 21 Blvd St-Marcel. 1913 by Pontremol[i] XVIb

Invalides, Esplanade des, se[e] Invalides, HI des.

Invalides, Gare des. Esplana[de] des Invalides, now Gare ae[-]rienne (air terminal) (q.v. End 19th c. by Lisch. XVI[]

Invalides, HI des. 1671-76 b[y] L. Bruant. Esplanade 1704[-]20 by R. de Cotte. XIa, XI[]

Invalides, Pont des. 1827-29[.] Rebuilt 1854-56, rebuilt 1880[.] XIIIb, XIVa, XVIIa

Irlandais, Collège des. 5 rue de[s] Irlandais. 1755-69 by Bella[n-]ger. XIIe

Issy-les-Moulineaux, Centr[e] sportif (sports center). On sit[e] of airport land. By L. Arretch[e,] H. Bourdon. XVIIIa

Issy-les-Moulineaux incinér[a-]tion plant (usine d'incinér[a-]tion). 1962-65 by Homber[g] XVIIIf

Issy-les-Moulineaux Military Ground (Champ de Manœuvre). Aerodrome since 1905. XVIa

Italie district, Place d' (Quartier Italie). Renovation project by Ascher, Holley, Braunsarda, Micol, Solotareff. XVIIc

Italie' Maison de l' (Italian students' center). Cité Universitaire. 1958 by Klein. XVIIc

Italie, Quartier, see Italie district, Place d'.

Ivry cemetery. Opened during Second Empire. XIVa

Ivry pumping station. 23 quai d'Austerlitz. 1788. Destroyed 1866. XIIa

J

Jabach, Hl. 110 rue St-Martin. 1659 by Bullet. Destroyed 1934. XIc

Jablines, Lac de (lake). By Vigo and Longepierre. XVIIIf

Jacobins, see Dominicans (rue St-Jacques) and Dominicans (rue du Marché St-Honoré).

Jacques-Cœur, Hl. Rues des Archives, du Plâtre. Ca. 1440. Destroyed. VIIIa

Jacques-Decour, Lycée, see Rollin, Lycée.

Janson-de-Sailly, Lycée (high school). 46 Av. Georges-Mandel. 1885. XVIb

Janvry, Hl de. "de Narbonne." 45 rue de Varenne. 1785 by Antoine. XIId

Jardin d'acclimatation (exotic animals and plants). Bois de Boulogne. 1854. Now playground and zoo. XIVa

Jardin des apothicaires, see Christian charity, House of.

Jardin des Plantes, see Jardin du roi.

Jardin du roi (king's garden), later Jardin des Plantes (botanical garden) or Muséum national d'histoire naturelle (Museum of natural history). 1626. Galerie de minéralogie (mineralogy dept.) 1841. Galerie de zoologie (zoological dept.) 1886. Galerie d'anatomie-paléontologie (paleontological dept.) 1896. Galerie de botanique (botanical dept.) 1935. New library 1964. Xa, XIIIa, XIIIc, XVIb, XVIIb

Jarnac, Hl de. 8 rue Monsieur. 1784 by A. Legrand. XIId

Javel, Quai de, later André-Citroën. 1837. XIIIb

Jean-Bouin Stadium. Av. du Général-Sarrail. XVIIa

Jean-Debray, Hl de. 57 rue Cuvier, in the Jardin des Plantes. 1650, later reconstructed by Bullet. XIc

Jean-Sarrailh, see Centre sportif universitaire.

Jeannin, Hl du Président. Former Hl St-Nicaise, Place du Carrousel. 1611. Destroyed 18th c. Xb

Jesuit novitiate. 82 rue Bonaparte. 1610. Church 1630-42 by Martellange. Destroyed 1806. Xc, XIIId

Jesuits, estate and country house, called Mont-Louis. Cimetière du Père-Lachaise (see Cemetery, east). Acquired 1626. Sold 1763. Xc

Jesuits, House of ordained. 99-101 rue St-Antoine. 1580-1763. Monastery (17th c.) became Lycée Charlemagne 1804, its chapel St-Paul-St-Louis (see St-Louis-des-Jésuites). IXb, XIIIc

Jeu de Paume. Tuileries gardens. 1851. Now museum. XIVb

Jeunes aveugles, Institution des, see Young Blind, Institution for the.

Jouffroy, 85 rue. Building. 1955 by Albert. XVIIIc

Juigné, Hl de, see Aubert de Fontenay, Hl.

Juillet, Colonne de, see July, Column of.

Juillet, Hl. 73 rue de Varenne. 1735 by Boffrand. XIIc

Jules-Ferry, Lycée (high school). Blvd de Clichy, rue de Douai. 1913 by Paquet. XVIb

Julienne, hunting lodge (pavillon de chasse) of M. de. 9 rue Berbier-du-Mets. 1732. In ruin. XIIc

July, Column of. Place de la Bastille. 1833-40 by Alavoine, later Duc. XIIIb

K

Knights Templars, Commanderie. Rues du Temple, de Bretagne, de Picardie. End 12th c. Keep 1265. Assigned to Knights of the Hospital of St-John of Jerusalem (q.v.) 1312. Walls and Hl du Grand-Prieur (q.v.) destroyed 17th c. Total destruction 1796 ff. (keep 1808). IV, VI, XIIId, XIIId

Küss, 8 rue. School. 1934 by Expert. XVIIb

L

Laas, area called. Land between Petit-Pont and village of St-Germain. IV

La Bazinière, Hl ("de Chimay"). 17 quai Malaquais. ca. 1640 by F. Mansart. Xb

"Labyrinthe." Petit Jardin des Plantes, former dump. 1303 ff. VIIa

La Chesnay, Hl de, see Rieux, Hl du Maréchal de.

Laënnec hospital, was Hospice des Incurables, (q.v.). 42 rue de Sèvres. 1878. XVIb

La Fayette, Pont. 1928. Caquot engineer. XVIIa

La Ferté-Sennetere, Hl de, see La Monnoye, Hl.

La Feuillade, Hl. 2-4 place des Victoires. 1686. XId

La Fontaine, Lycée (high school). Porte Molitor. 1938 by Héraud. XVIIb

La Fontaine, 17, 19, 21 rue. Buildings. 1911 by H. Guimard. XVIc

La Fontaine, 60 rue. Private residence. 1911 by H. Guimard. XVIc

La Galazière, Hl de, see Gouffier de Thoix, Hl.

La Marche, Collège de, was Collège de Constantinople (rue Frédéric-Sauton, Impasse Maubert), became Collège de la Marche 14th c. Moved farther south (rue des Ecoles, rue de la Montagne-Ste-Geneviève) in 1422. Destroyed 1852. XIVc

La Marck, Hl de, called Berthier de Sauvigny. rue Béranger. 1728. Destroyed 1950. XIIc

La Meilleraie, Hl. 56 rue des Saints-Pères. 1640 by Gittard. Now Ecole Nationale d'Administration. Xb

La Monnoye, Hl de, called La Ferté-Sennetere and Clérambault. 24 rue de l'Université. 1700. XId

Langres, Hl of the bishops of. 123 rue St-Jacques. Beginning 15th c. 1561 turned into Collège de Clermont. VIIIa

La Pérouse, 7 rue. Building. 1950 by Graveraux and Lopez. XVIIIc

La Planche, Hl de. Intersection Raspail-Varenne. 1628. Destroyed 1907. Xb

La Poupelinière, Hl de. 62 rue de la Chaussée-d'Antin. 1747. Destroyed 1952 except façade. XIId

Lariboisière hospital. Rue St-Vincent-de-Paul. 1846-54. XIIIc

La Roche-Guyon, Hl de. Square court of Louvre, north wing. 14th c. Destroyed 1664. VIIa

La Roche-Guyon, Hl de. 21 rue des Bons-Enfants. 1636. Xb

La Saïda, rue de. Workers' houses. 1912 by Labussière. XVIc

Lassay, Hl de. 35 quai d'Orsay. 1722-24 by Aubert. XIIc

La Tourette, Hl de, called Petit-Luxembourg. 17 rue de Vaugirard. 1546. Remodeled 1627 ff. by Lemaire. Remodeled 1701 ff. by Boffrand. IXa, Xb

La Trémoille, Hl. 15 rue de Vaugirard. 1620. Destroyed. Xb

Lauzun, Hl de ("de Lamballe"). 19 rue Raynouard, 17 rue Berton. 1692-1800 (Hl Delessert). XIb

Laval, Hl de. Place du Palais-Royal. 1420. Destroyed. VIIIa

La Vallière, Hl. 136 rue du Bac. 1760. XIIc

La Vaupalière, Hl. 86 rue du Fbg-St-Honoré. 1775 by Colignon. XIId

La Vieuville, Hl. 4 rue St-Paul. 1628-1928. Xb

La Vrillière, Hl. 1-3 rue la Vrillière. 1635-38 by F. Mansart. Remodeled 1713-19 by R. de Cotte. Now in Banque de France (q.v.). Xb

Le Bouthilier de Chavigny. 7 rue de Sévigné. 1630 by Mansart. Rebuilt 1700, by Bullet. XId

Le Brun, Hl. 49 rue du Cardinal-Lemoine. 1700 by Boffrand. Xb

Le Charron, Hl. 13-15 quai de Bourbon. 1652. XIc

Le Coigneux, Hl. 116 rue de Grenelle, now town hall of 7th arrondissement. 1650. Redone 1709 by Boffrand (Hl de Villars). Xb

Lecteurs royaux, Collège des, later Collège de France. Place Marcellin-Berthelot. 1610 ff. by Cl. Chastillon. Finished 1778 by Chalgrin. Enlarged 1930 ff. by A. and J. Guilbert. Xb, XIIb, XV, XVIIb

Le Fèvre de la Boderie, Hl, called Châlons-Luxembourg. 26 rue Geoffroy-l'Asnier. 1608. Xb

Legendre, Hl, wrongly called La Trémoille. 31 rue des Bourdonnais. 14th c. Destroyed 1841. VIIIa

Légion d'honneur, Palais de la, see Salm Kyburg, Hl de.

Le Juge, Hl. 66 rue des Archives. 1687 by de Cotte. Destroyed 1897. XId

Le Lièvre, Hl. 4-6 rue de Braque. End 17th c. XId

Le Nain, Hl. 77-79 rue de Richelieu. Before 1655. Destroyed 1719. XIc

Léo-Lagrange stadium. XVIIa

Le Peletier, Château des, called St-Fargeau. Between rues de Romainville, Pelleport, du Surmelin, des Glaïeuls, des Fougères. 1695. Destroyed 1763-1850. XId

Le Peletier de Souzy, Hl. 29 rue de Sévigné. 1686 by Bullet. XId

Le Prestre de Neufbourg, Hl. 68 Blvd Auguste-Blanqui. 1762 by Peyre. Destroyed 1909. XIIc

Le Tasse, 7 rue. Building. 1905 by Sorel. XVIc

Le Tellier, Hl. 70 rue J.-J. Rousseau. 1652. Destroyed 19th c. XIc

Letters, School of (Faculté des Lettres). Rues de la Clef, du Fer-à-Moulin, de Santeuil. (Halle aux Cuirs land.) 1965. XVIIIb

Lettres, Faculté des, see Letters, School of.

Leusse, Hl de. 7 bis rue Jean-Goujon. Restoration. XIIIc

Le Vayer, Hl, first "de Vassé." 44 rue du Bac. 1725. XIIc

Liancourt, Hl de. 14-16 rue de Seine. 1623 by Le Mercier. Destroyed 1825. Xb

Liban, Maison du (Lebanese students' center). Cité Universitaire. 1962 ff. by Vernon and Philippe. XVIIc

Libéral Bruant, house of. 1 rue de la Perle. 1685 by L. Bruant. XId

Lieutenants de Police, Hl des (police hq). 12 rue des Capucines. Ca. 1770. Destroyed 1854. XIIc

Lignerais, Hl de, later de Kernevenoy, later called Carnavalet. 23 rue de Sévigné. 1544 by P. Lescot ?. Remodeled 17th c. See Carnavalet. IXa

Lombards, Collège des. Called Maison des pauvres écoliers italiens de la Charité de la bienheureuse Marie. 15 rue des Carmes. 1334. Destroyed. Rebuilt 1738-60 as Collège des Irlandais (since 1677). VIIb

Longchamp, Abbey of. Bois de Boulogne, Carrefour de Longchamp. 1256. Destroyed 1795. VI

Longchamp, Hippodrome de (racetrack). Bois de Boulogne. 1857. Modernized 1965. XIVa, XVIIIa

Longjumeau, Hl of the prior of. Place St-Michel, rue St-Séverin. 1531. Destroyed. IXa

Louis de France, count of Evreux, Hl de, called de Navarre. 17 rue du Four. Ca. 1317. Destroyed. VIIa

Louis-le-Grand, Collège, later Lycée (high school). 123 rue St-Jacques. Was Collège de Clermont. 1814-20. Rebuilt 1885-93. XIIIc, XIVb

Louis-le-Grand, Place, called Place Vendôme. 1686 ff. by J. Hardouin-Mansart. XIa, XIIa, XV

Louis-XV, Place, later Place de la Concorde. 1757-72 by J.-A. Gabriel. Modified 1836-40. XIIa, XIIIb, XVIIIa

Louis-XVI, Pont, later Pont de la Concorde. 1787-90 by Perronet. XIIa, XVIIa

Louis-Philippe, Pont. 1833. Rebuilt 1862. XIIIb, XIVa

Lourcine hospital, or Sainte-Valère, or Hôtel-Dieu du Patriarche. 3-17 rue Broca. 1320. Became House of Christian charity (q.v.) 1578. VI

Louviers, Ile. Attached to north bank in 1844 by filling branch of Seine. Now Blvd Morland. XIIIb

Louvois, Hl de. Square Louvois. 1669. Destroyed 1784. XId

Louvois, Square. 1839. XIIIb

Louvre, area called. Zone to west of St-Germain-l'Auxerrois. IV

Louvre, Château du, later Palais du (palace). 1190 ff. Renovated (E and N wings) ca. 1360 by R. du Temple. Keep razed 1527. W face rebuilt 1546-63 by P. Lescot, J. Goujon. Enlarged 1594-1627 by J. Androuet du Cerceau, L. Métezeau, Le Mercier, S,E, and N faces 1661-80 by Perrault. Modifications and completion of merger with Tuileries, 1806-16 by Percier and Fontaine. 1853-67 by Visconti and Lefuel. East moat 1965-67. V, VIIa, IXa, Xb, XIIa, XIIIc, XIVa, XIVb, XVIb, XVIIIb

Louvre, Quai du. Ca. 1450. VIIIa

Louvre, 16 rue du. Building. 1912 by F. Jourdain. XVIc

Lude, Hl du. 8-10 rue du Boulol. 1652. XIc

Lude, Hl du. 13 rue Payenne. 1677. XId

Lulli, Hl. 45 rue des Petits-Champs. 1671 by Gittard. XId

Luna Park, amusement park. Porte Maillot. 1903. Destroyed 1946. XVIIa

Lutetia Arena, called Amphitheater. 49 rue Monge. 1st c. Ruined end 3rd c. (used as quarry for Cité ramparts), restored under Merovingians, still visible end 12th c. Excavated 1869, 1883-85, restored 1917-18. II, XVIa

Lutetia, Hl. 43 Blvd Raspail. 1911 by Boileau and Tauzin. XVIc

Luxembourg, Gare du (RR station). Corner Blvd St-Michel, rue Gay-Lussac. 1895. Renovated 1967. XVIa

Luxembourg, Hl. de. 38 Av. Gabriel. 1780. XIId

Luxembourg palace, see Médicis palace.

Luxembourg, Petit, see La Tourette, Hl de.

Luynes, Hl de, see Chevreuse, Hl de.

Lycée technique et école maternelle, see Gobelins, 48 Av. des.

Lyon, Gare de (RR station). First "Embarcadère de Lyon." Blvd Diderot. 1847-52. Rebuilt 1899 by Denis. Remodeled 1927. XIIIb, XVIa

M

Madeleine du Traisnel, convent. 100 rue de Charonne. 1644. Vestiges. XIe

Madeleine, La, see Ste-Marie-Madeleine.

Madelonnettes, see Filles de la Madeleine.

Madrid, Château de. Porte de Madrid. 1528-50 by G. Della Robbia, then Philibert Delorme. Destroyed 1793. IXa, XIIIc

Magasins des Menus Plaisirs du Roi (theatrical storage). Rue du Conservatoire. 1763-65. Destroyed 1788. XIIb

Magny, Hl de, see Jean-Debray, Hl de.

Mail, Quai du. Blvd Morland. 1750. XIIa

Maillé, Hl de, so called. 10 rue Charles V. 1550. Destroyed. IXa

Maillebois, Hl de, see Fontaine, Hl de.

Maillot, Porte. 17th c. Redone 1780 by Soufflot and Coustou. Project for new sector by G. Gillet. XIa, XIIa, XVIIIa

Mailly, Hl de, called de Brienne. 14 rue St-Dominique. 1730 by Aubry. XIIc

Maine, Gare du (RR station): Place Bienvenue. First "Embarcadère de l'Ouest" (1840), then annex of Gare Montparnasse, again made major station in 1966. See Montparnasse, Gare. XVIIa, XVIIIa

Maine, Hl du Duc du, called de Chanaleilles and du Prat. 24 rue Vanneau. 1770? XIId

Maine, 53, 59 Av. du. Building. 1956 by Lecaisne. XVIIIc

Mairie, see Town Hall.

Maison aux Piliers (town hall). Site of Hôtel de Ville. Bought 1357. Destroyed 16th c. VIIa

Maison de la Mutualité. Rue St-Victor. 1931. XVIIa

Maison de la Santé (hospital). 42 rue de la Santé. After 1270. Destroyed 1607. VIIb

Maison des Sciences de l'Homme (social sciences institute). NW corner Blvd Raspail, rue du Cherche-Midi. 1967-69 by Marcel Lods. XVIIIb

Maisons, Hl de, see Duret, Hl du Président.

Malakoff, 131-133 Av. Building. By Gras and Rendu. XVIIc

Malassis, Hl de. 20 rue de Condé. 1612. Xb

Mall (Mail). Promenade between Arsenal and Seine, created under Henri IV, now Blvd Morland. Xa

Mallet-Stevens, Cité and Rue. 1925 by Mallet-Stevens. XVIIc

Manège (riding school). Tuileries, rue de Rivoli at No 230. 1720. Destroyed 1811. XIIb

Mans, Hl des Evêques du. Impasse Chartrière. 14th c. Turned into college in 1519. VIIIa

Mansart de Sagonne, Hl. 28 rue des Tournelles. 1680 by J. Hardouin-Mansart. XId

Manufacture royale des Glaces, see Royal Glass Factory.

Manufacture royale des Gobelins, see Gobelins royal tapestry factory.

Marbeuf, Garage. 32 rue Marbeuf. 1929 by Laprade and Bazin. Completely altered. XVIIc

Marbeuf, Hl, see Blouin, Hl.

Marceau, 23 Av. Office building. 1961 by Ginsberg. XVIIIc

Marceau, 30 Av. Building. 1914 by Granet. XVIc

Marché aux chevaux, Poste de police du (police station). 5 rue des Fossés-St-Marcel. 1760. Restored 1877. XIIa

Marché aux fleurs, see Flower market.

Marchés, see Markets

Marché aux chevaux, see Markets, horse.

Marie-Médiatrice, church of Porte du Pré-St-Gervais. 1954 by H. Vidal. XVIIId

Marie, Pont. 1618-35 by Marie. Xa

Markets, district, see Blancs-Manteaux, Maubert, Popincourt, St-Germain, St-Honoré, St-Joseph, St-Martin.

Markets horse (Marché aux chevaux), see Tournelles, Terrains des; Molière, rue; St-Marcel, Blvd

Marmousets, Hl des, see Prévôt de Paris, Hl du.

Martyr, Mémorial to the Unknown Jewish (Mémorial du Martyr juif inconnu). Rue Geoffroy l'Asnier, rue Grenier-sur-l'Eau. 1957 by Goldberg, Persitz and Arretche. XVIId

Martyrs, Chapel of the. 9 rue Antoinette. 9th c. Restored 1147. Rebuilt 15th c. Destroyed 1795. Modern chapel of the Martyrs built in 1885 on about the same site (Couvent des Dames auxiliatrices du Purgatoire). III, IV, VIIIb, XIIId

Martyrs of the Deportation, Memorial to the. Square de

l'Ile-de-France. 1962 by Pingusson. XVIIId

Massa, Hl de, see Thiroux de Montsauge, Hl.

Masséna, Caserne de pompiers (firemen's barracks). 33-47 Blvd Masséna. 1966 by Willerval. XVIIIb

Masséna stadium. 81 Blvd Masséna. 1964-65 by Lefol. XVIIIa

Masserano, Hl. 52 Blvd des Invalides. 1787 by Brongniart. XIId

Mathurin-Régnier, 5, 15 rue. Building. 1960 by Candilis. XVIIIc

Mathurins, see Ste-Trinité, monastic hospice of.

Maubert, Marché (market). Place Maubert. 1813. XIIIa

Maubert, Place. Known 1224. Widened and displaced 1806 and 1855. V, XIIIa, XIVa

Mauconseil, Hl de, called des Carnaulx. Rues Daubenton, Mouffetard, du Fer-à-Moulin, Geoffroy-St-Hilaire. 13th c. Became Hl (Séjour) d'Orléans (q.v.) in 1388. Destroyed. VIIa

Maulevrier, Hl de. 252 Blvd St-Germain. 1700. Destroyed 1855 ff. XId

Mauregard, Hl, later de la Reine-Isabeau, called Hl Barbette. Rue Barbette. 1388. Destroyed 1563. VIIIa

Maxim's Restaurant. 3 rue Royale. Décor 1900. XVIc

Maxin, Hl. 8 rue d'Anjou. 1726. XIIc

Mayenne, Hl de, called d'Ormesson. 21 rue St-Antoine. 1613 by J. Androuet du Cerceau ? Remodeled 1709 by Boffrand. Xb, XId

Martyrs, Chapel of the. 9 rue Antoinette. 9th c. Restored 1147. Rebuilt 15th c. Destroyed 1795. Modern chapel of the Martyrs built in 1885 on about the same site (Couvent des Dames auxiliatrices du Purgatoire). III, IV, VIIIb, XIIId

Mazarin palace. In part Bibliothèqua nationale. 1645 by F. Mansart. XIc

Mazas, Prison of. Rue Emile-Gilbert. 1845 ff. Destroyed 1902. XIVa

Médecine, Faculté de, see Faculté de Médecine, Ecole de Médecine.

Médicis palace, called Luxembourg. Rue de Vaugirard. 1615-25 by S. de Brosse. Painting museum since 18th c. Remodeled 1804 ff. by Chalgrin. Enlarged 1836-41 by de Gisors. Modified under Napoleon III for the Senate. Xb, XIIb, XIIIc, XIVb

Ménilmontant slaughterhouses (abattoirs). Square Gardette. Built 1808-10. Destroyed 1868. XIIIa

Mercœur, Hl de, later de Vendôme. 356, 358 rue St-Honoré. 1603. Destroyed 1685 ff. Xb

Mère de Dieu, Orphelines de la (orphanage). 11 rue du Vieux-Colombier. 1680. XIe

Merri de Vic, Hl. 203 bis rue St-Martin. 1621-1708. Rebuilt 1708: Hl du Trésorier Schupin, q.v.) Xb

Mesme Gallet, Hl, later de Sully. 62 rue St-Antoine. 1624 by Jean Androuet du Cerceau. Garden wing 1660 by Lambert. Xb, XId, XVIIIb

Mesmes, Hl de. Place St-Michel, rue St-Séverin. 1523. Destroyed. IXa

Mesmes, Hl de. 27 rue St-Guillaume. 1587. Destroyed. IXa

Mesnil, 8 rue. Firemen's barracks. 1936 by Mallet-Stevens. XVIIb

Métropolitain (RR). 1898 ff., Fulgence Bienvenüe engineer. XVIa, XVIIa

Mirabeau, Pont. 1895, Résal engineer. XVIa

Miramiones, see Filles de Ste-Geneviève.

Missions étrangères (Foreign Missions), seminary. 128 rue du Bac. 1663. Chapel from 1693. Rebuilt 1736. XIe, XIIe

Missions franciscaines, see Franciscan Missions.

Mobilier national (state furniture repository). 1 rue Berbier-du-Mets. 1935 by A. Perret. XVIIb

Modern Art, Museum of, see Museum of Modern Art.

Mines, Ecole des, see Estrées, Hl d', called de Vendôme.

Minimes de Chaillot, monastery, called Bonshommes de Chaillot. Rues Beethoven, Le Nôtre, Blvd Delessert. Was Manor of the dukes of Brittany (q.v.). Rebuilt 16th c. Destroyed 1796 ff. VIIIb, IXb, XIIId

Minimes "de la Place Royale," monastery. Rue des Minimes. 1611. Destroyed 1926. Church 1630-79 by d'Orbay. Destroyed 1805. Xc

Ministère, see Ministry.

Ministry of Finances. Rues de Rivoli, du Mont-Thabor, de l'Isle. 1811-22. Burned 1871. XIIIc, XV

Ministry of Foreign Affairs. 37 quai d'Orsay. 1845-53 by Lacornée. XIVb

Ministry of the Merchant Marine. Place de Fontenoy. 1932 by Ventre. XVIIb

Ministry of National Education. Site of the Prison de la Santé. Project by Faugeron. XVIIIb

Ministry of the Navy, see Garde-Meuble.

Ministry of P. and T. (Post and Telegraph). Av. de Saxe and de Ségur. 1935-38. XVIIb

Ministry of War. 231 Blvd St-Germain. 1867-77 by Bouchot. XIVb

Molière, Lycée (high school). 71 rue du Ranelagh. 1888. XVIb

Molière, Rue (horse market). 1605-33, and rue Louis-le-Grand, 1633-87. Xa

Molitor swimming pool. XVIIa

Monaco, Hl de la princesse de. 59 rue St-Dominique. 1777 by Brongniart. XIId

Monceau, Château de. Place de Lévis, rue Legendre. 16th c. or before. Destroyed 1830 ff. IXa

Monceau, Parc, remains of the Folie de Chartres (q.v.). 1861 by Alphand. XIVa

Monnaies, Hl des (Mint). 11 quai Conti. 1768-75 by Antoine. XIIb

Montaigne, Collège de, first called des Aycelins. Site of Bibliothèque Ste-Geneviève and adjacent Place. 1314. Destroyed 1844. VIIb, XIIId

Montaigne, Lycée (high school). 17 rue Auguste-Comte. 1890 by Lecœur. XVIb

Montaigne, 33 Av. Building. Ca. 1930 by Bodecher. XVIIc

Mont-de-Piété (municipal brokerage). 55 rue des Francs-Bourgeois. 1785. XIIb

Montesquiou, Hl de. 20 rue Monsieur. 1781 by Brongniart. XIId

Montfaucon gallows. Between Cité Jacob, rue des Ecluses-St-Martin, rue de la Grange-aux-Belles, rue Louis-Blanc. Beginning 13th c. Abandoned 1627. Destroyed 1760. V

Montfaucon, 2nd gallows. 46 rue de Meaux. 1761. Destroyed 1790. XIIa

Montfermeil, Hl de. 68 rue de la Chaussée-d'Antin. 1789 by Ledoux. Destroyed. XIId

Montholon, Hl. 23 Blvd Poissonnière. 1775 by F. Soufflot. XIId

Mont-Louis, see Jesuits, estate and country house.

Montmartre, 142 rue. Building of "La France" newspaper. 1883 by Bol. XVIc

Montmartre slaughterhouses (abattoirs). Lycée J.-Decour Built 1808-10. Destroyed 1868. XIIIa

Montmor, Hl de. 79 rue du Temple. 1623. Remodeled 1750 ff. Xb, XIIc

Montmorency, Hl de. 5 rue de Montmorency. Known 1292. Rebuilt 17th c., remodeled 18th c. VIIa, XIIc

Montmorency, Hl de, or Bouret de Vézelay. 1 rue de la Chaussée-d'Antin. 1775 by Ledoux. Destroyed. XIId

Montmorency, Hl de, called d'Albret. 31 rue des Francs-Bourgeois. Ca. 1550. Rebuilt 1640 by F. Mansart. Façade 18th c. IXa, XIIc

Montmorency, later Matignon Hl de. 57 rue de Varenne. 1721 by Courtonne, then Mazin. XIIc

Montmorency, new Hl de. 62 rue du Temple, rue Braque, rue des Archives. 1557 Destruction completed 1838. IXa

Montmorency-Bours, Hl de. 89 rue du Cherche-Midi. 1756. XIIc

Montmorin, Hl, see Rambouillet de la Sablière, Hl de.

Montparnasse, Gare (RR station). First "Embarcadère de l'Ouest" (left bank), Place de Bienvenüe 1840. New station 1852, Place du 18-Juin-1940. Destroyed 1967 ff. Rebuilt Place Bienvenüe, 1966 by Lopez, Baudoin, de Marien. XIIIb, XVIIIa

Montparnasse, 126 Blvd. Residence and building. 1925 by Huillard. XVIIc

Montrésor, Hl, called also de Gourgues. 52-54 rue de Turenne. Beginning 17th c. Xc

Montsouris, Parc. 1875-78 by Alphand. XVIa

Montsouris, Réservoir de, Vanne, Réservoir de la.

Morfontaine, Hl de, see Romans, Hl.

Morillons, 64-82 rue des. School. 1935 by Pierre Sardou. XVIIb

Mortagne, HI de. 51-53 rue de Charonne. 1650 by Delisle-Mansart. XIc

Mortemart, HI de. 27 rue St-Guillaume. End 17th c. Now Institut national des sciences politiques. XId

Mortemart, HI de. 14 rue St-Guillaume. End 17th c. XId

Mosque. Place du Puits-de-l'Ermite. 1922-26 by Heubès, Fournez, Mantout. XVIId

Moulins, Pont aux, later aux Meuniers. Footbridge downstream from Pont au Change (see Change, Pont au), or Grand Pont. Destroyed 1596. Rebuilt 1608. Destroyed 1621. Xa

Mousquetaires gris, HI des. 13, 17 rue du Bac. 10 rue de Beaune. 1660-71. Destroyed 1781-1960. XIb

Mousquetaires noirs, barracks. Became Hospice des Quinze-Vingt (q.v.) 1780. 28 rue de Charenton. 1699-1701 by R. de Cotte. Destroyed 1957 (vestiges). XIb, XIIe, XVIIIb

Mozart, 122 Av. Apartment building. 1910 by H. Guimard. XVIc

Mozart, Square. Building. 1956 by Mirabaud. XVIIIc

Muette, Château de la. 20 Chaussée de la Muette. 16th c. by Philibert Delorme. New château 1716, destroyed 1764. Third château 1764, destroyed 1926. IXa, XIIc

Municipal arsenal. Rue de l'Arsenal. 1512. Became royal arsenal 1551 (see Arsenal, Grand). VIIIa

Municipal arsenal. 29 rue de Sévigné. 1551. Destroyed. IXa

Musée de la Chasse (hunting museum), in the HI Guénégaud (q.v.). 60 rue des Archives. 1967. XVIIIb

Musée de l'Industrie du Bois (wood products). Bois de Vincennes, near Lake Daumesnil. Was Togo-Cameroon pavilion (1931 Colonial Exposition). XVIIb

Musée des arts et traditions populaires (folk arts). Bois de Boulogne, Jardin d'acclimatation. By Dubuisson and Jausserand. Construction in progress. XVIIIa

Musée d'Orléans. 43 bis rue de Buffon. 1929. Destroyed 1962. XVIIb

Musée Napoléon, beginning of Louvre Museum. XIIIa

Museum d'histoire naturelle, see Jardin du roi.

Museum of Modern Art (Palais d'Art moderne). Av. du Président-Wilson. 1935-37 by Dondel, Aubert, Viard, Dastugue. XVIIb

Museum of Natural history, see Jardin du roi.

Museum, see also Musée.

Mutuelle du bâtiment et des travaux publics (public-works contractors' assn.). 120 Av. Emile-Zola. 1966 by Pottier and Leroy. XVIIc

N

Nanterre University (Faculté des Lettres). 1964 by Chauliat. XVIIIf

Napoléon barracks. Place St-Gervais. 1852. XIVb

Napoléon Circus. Place Pasdeloup. 1852 by Hittorf. Now Cirque d'Hiver. XIVb

Napoléon, Lycée (high school), see Henri IV, Lycée.

Napoléon, Pont, later Pont National. 1852. Widened 1939-42. XIVa

Narbonne, HI de, see Janvry, HI de.

National, Pont, see Napoléon, Pont.

NATO Headquarters (Palais de l'OTAN). Porte Dauphine. 1955-59 by Jacques Carlu. XVIIIb

Navarre, Collège de. Site of Ecole polytechnique. 1304. Rebuilt 15th c. Destroyed 1811-75. VIIb, VIIIb, XIIId, XVId

Navarre, Collège de, see Louis de France, HI.

Navarre, HI du roi de. 47-49 rue St-André-des-Arts. 1260-65. Destroyed. VI

Necker, HI. 7 rue de la Chaussée-d'Antin. 1777 by Cherpitel. Destroyed 1862. XIId

Necker hospital. 151 rue de Sèvres. 1802, reconstructed 1840. C.H.U. 1968 by Wogensky. XIIIc, XVIIIb

Néerlandais, Collège (Dutch students' center). Cité Universitaire. 1927 by Dudok. XVIIc

Nélaton, 7 rue. P. and T. (post and telegraph) office. 1961 by Dufau. XVIIIb

Nesle, HI de. Rue de Viarmes, Bourse de Commerce. End 12th c. Destruction completed 1571 ff. V

Nesle, HI de, "Grand Nesle." Quai de Conti, Hôtel des Monnaies. 13th c. (ca. 1270). Destroyed 1552. VIIa

Nesmond, HI de. 55 quai de la Tournelle. 1636. Xb

Neuilly, Pont de. Wooden bridge after 1606. Stone 1768-72 by Perronet. Destroyed 1935 and rebuilt. XIIa

Nevers, HI de, was Grand-Nesle. Quai de Conti, Hôtel des Monnaies. After 1552. Destroyed 1641. IXa

Nicolas Flamel, house of. 51 rue de Montmorency. 1407. VIIIa

Noirmoutiers, HI de, or de Sens. 138-140 rue de Grenelle. 1722 by Courtonne. XIIc

Nonce, HI du. 84 rue du Bac. 1713. Destroyed. XId

Nord, Gare du (RR station). First "Embarcadère du Nord." Blvd de la Chapelle, Place de Roubaix, under Louis-Philippe Then new station, place de Roubaix, 1846, taken down 1863. New station 1863 ff. by Hittorf. XIIIb, XIVa

Notre-Dame, Cathedral. 6th c. destroyed 9th c. New church 10th c. destroyed 12th c. New church ca. 1163-1250. Modified 13th-14th c. By Jean de Chelles, Pierre de Montreuil, Jean Ravy, Jean Le Bouteiller, Raymond du Temple. Altered end 17th and 18th c. Restored 1844-64 by Lassus, then Viollet-le-Duc. IV, V, VI, VIb, XIe, XIIe, XIIId, XIVc, XV

Notre-Dame, Cloître. Enclosed district, residence for canons of Notre-Dame. IV

Notre-Dame-d'Auteuil, church. Place d'Auteuil. 12th c. Enlarged 16th-17th c. Destroyed 1877-92 by Vaudremer. V, Xc, XVId

Notre-Dame-de-Bercy, church, see Notre-Dame-de-la-Nativité.

Notre-Dame-de-Bonne Nouvelle, chapel then church. 23 bis rue de la Lune. Chapel 1563, destroyed 1591. Church 1624, destroyed 1823. New church 1823-30 by Godde. IXb, Xc, XIIId

Notre-Dame-de-Grâce, see Bénédictines de la Ville-l'Evêque.

Notre-Dame-de-la-Consolation, see Bénédictines du Cherche-Midi.

Notre-Dame-de-la-Croix-de-Ménilmontant. Place de Ménilmontant. 1863-69 by Héret. XIVc

Notre-Dame-de-la-Délivrance, church, later St-Pierre-du-Gros-Caillou. 92 rue St-Dominique. 1738. Destroyed 1822. XIIe

Notre-Dame-de-la-Gare. Place Jeanne-d'Arc. 1855-64 by C. Naissant. XIVc

Notre-Dame-de-la-Grâce, chapel, later church. 10 rue de l'Annonciation. 1666. Rebuilt 1846-59 by Debressenne. XIe, XIIId

Notre-Dame-de-la-Miséricorde convent. 61 rue Mouffetard. 1656. Destroyed, vestiges (barracks of the Garde Républicaine). XIe

Notre-Dame-de-la-Miséricorde hospital, called Les Cent-Filles. 21-25 rue Censier. 1623. Destroyed 1863. Xc

Notre-Dame-de-la-Nativité. Place Lachambeaudie. 1826 by André Chatillon. Destroyed 1871. Rebuilt by Hénard. XIIId, XV

Notre-Dame-de-la-Salette, chapel. 27 rue de Dantzig. 1855. XIVc

Notre-Dame-de-Lorette, chapel then church. Rue de Châteaudun, rue Notre-Dame-de-Lorette. Ca. 1654. Destroyed 1796. New church 1823-36 by Lebas. XIe, XIIId

Notre-Dame-de-Lourdes. 128 rue Pelleport. 1910. 2nd church 1936-37 by Hombert. XVId, XVIId

Notre-Dame-des-Blancs-Manteaux, church. 16 rue des Blancs-Manteaux. Was chapel of monastery of the Blancs-Manteaux 1258. Rebuilt 1685, enlarged 1865 by Baltard. XIe

Notre-Dame-des-Bois, see Ste-Opportune. III

Notre-Dame-des-Champs, chapel, later priory. 20 rue Henri-Barbusse. Before 700. Church rebuilt 12th-13th c. Reconstruction 1604, installation of Carmelite nuns. 1797, general destruction except church crypt, much restored. III

Notre-Dame-des-Champs, church. 91 Blvd du Montparnasse. 1867-76 by Ginain. XIVc

Notre-Dame-de-Sion, convent, see Filles anglaises, convent.

Notre-Dame-d'Espérance. 51 bis rue de la Roquette. 1928-30 by Barbier. XVIId

Notre-Dame-des-Victoires, church, earlier chapel of Augustins déchaussés. 1629. New church 1666 by Le Muet, L. Bruant, Le Duc. Portal 1740 by Cartaud. Xc, XIIe

Notre-Dame-du-Bon-Secours, convent. 95-99 rue de Charonne. 1648. Vestiges. XIe

Notre-Dame-du-Rosaire, church. 194 rue Raymond-Losserand. 1909-11 by Pierre Sardou. XVIId

Notre-Dame-du-Travail, church. 59 rue Vercingétorix. 1899-1901 by Astruc. XVId

Notre-Dame, Pont. Roman bridge, later footbridge called de la Planche-Mibray. Pont Notre-Dame built 1413. Collapsed 1499, rebuilt several times, rebuilt 1913. VIIIa, XIIa, XVIa

Notre-Dame pump. Between Notre-Dame and Pont-au-Change. 1670. Destr. 1856. XIa

Nouvelles catholiques, convent. Passage Ste-Anne. 1634. Destroyed 1792 ff. Xc

Nouvion, HI de. 50-54 rue des Francs-Bourgeois. 14th c. Destroyed. VIIIa

Novitiate of the Dominican Order in France, General, see Dominican, General Novitiate.

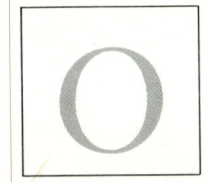

O

O, HI d', see Châteauvilain, HI de.

Observatoire météorologique, see Weather Observatory.

Observatory. Av. de l'Observatoire, rue Cassini. 1668-72 by Perrault. Modernized end 19th c. XIb, XIVb, XV

Oceanographic Institute (Institut océanographique). 195 rue St-Jacques. 1910 by Nénot. XVIb

Odéon, see Théâtre français.

Olier, seminary of M., see Seminary of M. Olier

Opéra, Place de l'. 1858-64. XIVa

Opéra, Théâtre de l'. 18 Blvd St-Martin. 1781 by Le Noir. Destroyed 1871. XIIb

Opéra, Théâtre de l'. 6 rue Le Peletier. 1821. Destroyed 1873. XIIIc

Opéra, Théâtre de l'. Place de l'Opéra. 1862-75 by Ch. Garnier. XIVb

Opéra-Comique. Place Boïeldieu. 1838. Burned 1887. Rebuilt 1898 by L. Bernier. XVIb

Opéra-Comique (Ventadour Hall). Rue Ventadour. 1826-29 by Huve. Was Théâtre-Italien 1843-70, Opéra 1873-75. Now annex of Banque de France. XIIIc

Oratoire, Congrégation de l' (Oratorians). 145 rue St-Honoré. Church 1621-30 by Métezeau and Lemercier. Portal 1745. Now Protestant church. Xc, XIIe

Oratoire, noviatiate (Oratorians). 70 bis-76 Av. Denfert-Rochereau. 1650. Vestiges in present Hospice des Enfants Assistés. XIe

Orléans, HI d'. 30 rue Descartes. 1742. XIIc

Orléans, HI d', first called des Carnaulx. Between rues Daubenton, Mouffetard, du Fer-à-Moulin, and Geoffroy-St-Hilaire. 13th c. Destroyed. VIIa

Orléans-Austerlitz, Gare d' (RR station), first "Embarcadère d'Orléans." Place Valhubert. 1835. Rebuilt 1869. Modified 1966 ff. XIIIb, XIVa, XVIIIa

Orliane, Folie d', called Hôtel Belgioso. 28 rue du Montparnasse. Ca. 1777. Now in Collège Stanislas. XIId

Orly Airport. 1946. Enlarged 1956-61. Air terminal 1961 by Vicariot and Becker. XVIIIa, XVIIIe

Orly-West Airport. Extension of Orly Airport. By Vicariot. XVIIIe

Orsay, Gare d' (RR station). Quai Anatole-France. 1898-1900 by Laloux. XVIa

Orsay, Gare d' (RR station). Quai Anatole-France. 1898-1900 by Laloux. XVIa

Orsay, Palais d'. Cour des Comptes. Quai Anatole-France, Gare d'Orsay. 1810-38 by Bonnard and Lacornée. Destroyed 1871. XIIIc, XV

Orsay, 89 quai d'. Building. 1929 by Roux-Spitz. XVIIc

Orsay University (Faculté d'Orsay). XVIIIf

O.R.T.F. Maison de l' (broadcasting center). 110 quai du Président-Kennedy. 1955-64 by H. Bernard. XVIIIb

O.T.A.N., see N.A.T.O.

Ourcq, Canal de l'. 1802 ff. XIIIa, XIIIb

Ourouer, HI d', called de Bauffremont. 87 rue de Grenelle. 1718-36. XIIc

Ozenfant, Maison. 53 Av. Reille. 1922 by Le Corbusier. XVIIc

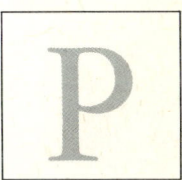

P

Païva, HI de la. 25 Av. des Champs-Elysées. 1860 by Maugain. XIVb

Palace of the Cité (Palais de la Cité), Palais de Justice. Palace since late Roman Empire or before. Capetian palace 11th c. Sainte-Chapelle (q.v.) 13th c. Enlargements, modifications 1301-15. 1350, Chambre des Comptes (q.v.). Grande Chambre beginning 16th c. Burned 1618. Grand' Salle, 1622, by S. de Brosse. Burned 1776. Rebuilt by Desmaisons and Antoine (Cour de Mai 1783-89). Restored 1840 ff. Cour de Cassation, west façade, by Duc. Burned 1871. Restored 1872-75 by Duc.

South face (Quai des Orfèvres) 1911-14 by Tournaire. II, III, IV, VI, VIIa, VIIIa, XIIb, XIIIc, XIVb, XV, XVIb

Palais Bourbon. Place du Palais Bourbon, Blvd St-Germain. 1722-28 by Giardini, then Lassurance, Aubert, and Gabriel. New north façade 1804-1807 by Poyet. Meeting hall by Gisors and Lecomte (1798) then by Joly (1828-32). XIIc, XIIIc

Palais-Bourbon, Place du. 1776. XIIa

Palais Cardinal, see Cardinal Palace.

Palais d'Art moderne, see Museum of Modern Art.

Palais de Glace (skating rink), or Patinoire des Champs-Elysées. Av. F.-Roosevelt, Champs-Elysées. 1893. Redone 1961. XVIIIb

Palais de la Cité, see Palace of the Cité:

Palais de la Découverte (science museum). Grand Palais. F.-Roosevelt, 1937. XVIIb

Palais de l'Industrie, gardens of Champs-Elysées. 1853. Destroyed 1900. XIVb

Palais des Sports (sports arena). Parc des Expositions, Porte de Versailles. 1960 by P. Dufau. XVIIIa

Palais, Grand. 1897-1900 by Deglane, Louvet, Thomas. XVIb

Palais, Petit. 1897-1900 by Ch. Girault. XVIb

Palais, Place du. 1785. XIIa

Palais Pompéien. 18 Av. Montaigne. 1860 by A. Normand. Destroyed 1892. XIVb

Palais Rose, see Sagan, HI de.

Palais-Royal, was Cardinal Palace (q.v.). Rebuilt 1752-58 by Cartaud. Burned. Newly rebuilt 1764-70 by Contant d'Ivry, Moreau, Louis. Circumference of gardens 1781 by Louis. Restored, cleared 1820 ff. by Fontaine. Partially burned 1871. Restored 1872-

76 by Chabrol and 1935 by Ventre. XIIc, XIId, XIIIc, XV, XVIb, XVIIb,

Panthéon, see Ste-Geneviève.

Panthéon, Place du. 1770. Realigned 1807. XIIIa

Pantin-Bobigny cemetery. Opened in 1886. XVIa

Parc des Expositions (exhibition grounds). Porte de Versailles. 1956-57. XVIIIa

Parc des Princes stadium. Blvd Murat. XVIIa, XVIIIa

Paris-North Airport. Project by Andrue, Vicariot. XVIIIe

Parking garage, see Bourse, Place de la.

Parloir aux Bourgeois. South side of Grand-Châtelet. 1246. Transferred to Maison-aux-Piliers 1357. VI

Parmentier, 155-159 Av. School, swimming pool, and gymnasium. 1966 by Brun. XVIIIb

Passy, Artesian well. Square Lamartine. 1855-66. XIVa

Passy, Château de. Rue de Boulainvilliers. 1660-68. Destroyed 1827. VIIIa, XId

Passy, 2 rue de. Building. 1903 by Klein. XVIc

Passy, Thermes de (mineral baths). 32 quai de Passy. 1719-1803. XIIb

Pasteur Institute. 25 rue du Docteur-Roux. 1888. XVIb

Patriarch of Alexandria, HI du. Place des Patriarches. 1320. Destroyed 1830. VIIa

Paul-Doumer, 1 Av. Building. 1936 by J. Filder. XVIIc

Paul-Valéry, Lycée (high school). 38 Blvd Soult. 1958-60 by Dhuit. XVIIIb

Pavillon de Flore. Louvre, Grande Galerie. 1608 by Jacques Androuet du Cerceau. Rebuilt 1860-70 by Lefuel. Burned 1871. Restored 1871-76 by Lefuel. Xb, XIVb, XVIIIb

Pavillon de Hanovre. 34 rue Louis-le-Grand. 1760 by Chevautet. Reassembled in Parc de Sceaux. XIIc

Pavillon de Marsan. Louvre. Galerie-Nord. 1659 by Le Vau. Burned 1871. Rebuilt 1874 by Lefuel. XIb

Pavillon d'Ermenonville. Entrance to Cours-la-Reine on Place de la Concorde. 1760 by J.-A. Gabriel. Destroyed 1854. XIIa

Pavillon Perronet. Entrance to Av. Gabriel on Place de la Concorde. 1760 by J.-A. Gabriel. Destroyed 1854. XIIa

Peilhon, HI de. 12 rue Boissy-d'Anglas. 1760. Destroyed 1911. XIId

Pénitents réformés du Tiers-Ordre-de-St-François, monastery. 61 rue de Picpus. 1600. Destroyed 1796. Xc

Pentémont, abbey church (abbatiale), or Panthémont. 37-39 rue de Bellechasse. Church 106 rue de Grenelle, 1747-56, by Contant d'Ivry. Now Protestant church. XIIe

Pépinière royale, see Royal nursery.

Père-Lachaise cemetery, see Cemetery, East.

Pères - de - la - Doctrine - chrétienne, see Enfants Rouges hospital.

Perrichont, 14 Av. Apartment building. 1911 by Deneu. XVIc

Perrin, Pont. Over bypassed riverbed, Place de la Bastille. Known in 1170. Destroyed. IV

Petit-Pont. Roman bridge. Rebuilt 12th c. Collapsed and rebuilt some 10 times. Rebuilt 1853. V, XIIa, XIVa

Petit-Pont, Place du. 1782 Enlarged 1909. XIIa

Petite-Roquette, see Youth Detention House.

Petite Seine (canal from the Seine to St-Germain-des-Prés). 13th c.? Filled 16th c. VI

Petites-Maisons hospital. Square Boucicaut, rue Velpeau, Bon Marché. 1557. Destroyed 1864. IXa

Petits-Augustins, country house of. 342-348 rue de Vaugirard. 1653. Destroyed 1845. XIe

Petits-Augustins, monastery. 14 rue Bonaparte. 1609. Absorbed in Ecole des Beaux-Arts. Xc

Petits-Pères, see Augustins déchaussés.

Peyrenc de Moras, HI called Biron. 77 rue de Varenne. 1728-31 by J. Gabriel and Aubert. XIIc

Phelypeaux de la Vrillière, HI. 2 rue St-Florentin. 1767 by Chalgrin. XIIc

Philippe - Auguste, wall of. 1190 (right bank), 1210 (left bank). Reinforced under Charles V (left bank), see Tournelle, Château de la. Gates destroyed ca. 1550. Never officially destroyed, it disappeared primarily in the 17th c. V

Philippe-le-Bel, Château de, at Passy. Perhaps 86 rue de la Tour (much-restored vestige). VIIa

Picpus, 56 rue de. School. 1966 by Secart. XVIIIc

Pidoux, HI. 6 rue des Sts-Pères. 1640. XIc

Pierre Crozat, HI. 91-93 rue de Richelieu. 1706 by Cartault. Destroyed 1780 ff. XId

Pierre de Coubertin stadium. Porte de St-Cloud. 1936-38 by Crevel, Carré, and Schlienger. XVIIa

Pinon de Quincy, HI. 9 rue Drouot. Ca. 1750 Destroyed 1847. XIIc

Pitié (La) hospital. 1 rue Lacépède and Mosquée. 1612. Destroyed 1912. Xa, Xc

Pitié (La) hospital, 2nd. 83 Blvd de l'Hôpital. 1911 by J. Rochet. XVIb, XVIIb

Pitié-Salpêtrière (La), hospital. C.H.U. 1965 by Rideberger. See Pitié (la) and Salpêtrière (La) hospitals.

Planche-Mibray, Pont de la, see Notre-Dame, Pont

Pleyel Hall. 252 rue du Fbg-St-Honoré. 1927 by Auburtin, Granet, and Mathon. XVIIc

Pocherons, HI des, later changed to "Porcherons." 77-93 rue St-Lazare. 1310. Destroyed 1725. VIIa

Pompes, HI des (central fire station). 30 rue Mazarine. Beginning 18th c. XIIa

Pont-Neuf. 1578-1606 by J.-B. Androuet du Cerceau and des Iles. Restored 1848-53. IXa, Xa, XIVa

Pontigny, HI of the abbots of. 15 rue de la Huchette. 1292. Destroyed. VIIa

Popincourt, Marché (market). Rue du Marché Popincourt. 1809. Destroyed 1860. XIIIa

Porcherons, HI des, see Pocherons, HI des.

Port-Royal. Paris branch of convent of Port-Royal-des-Champs, later Port-Royal-de-Paris. 119 Blvd de Port-Royal 1625. Church 1646-48 by Lepautre. Now Maternity hospital. Xc, XIe

Porte des Lilas reservoir. 1963 XVIIIa

Porte Maillot. Installation project by G. Gallet. XVIIIa

Porte Neuve. Quai des Tuileries, between Pont du Carrousel and Pont-Royal. 1537. Destroyed 1670. IXa

Porte Pouchet. Buildings. 1961 by Lopez. XVIIIc

Porte St-Antoine (Arc de triomphe). Rue de la Bastille-Blvd Beaumarchais. 1573. Rebuilt 1585. Rebuilt 1660-72 by Blondel. Destroyed 1789. IXa

Porte St-Martin, Théâtre de la, see Opéra.

Poste Parisien building, Le (broadcasting center). 116 bis Av. des Champs-Elysées. 1929 by Debouis. XVIIc

Postes, HI des (central post office). 48-52 rue du Louvre.

1880 by Guadet.

Potocki, HI. 27 Av. de Friedland. 1882. XVIc

Poullain, HI, called de Vendôme. 5 rue Béranger. 1752. XIIc

Préfecture de la Seine, annex. Blvd Morland. 1960-62 by Laprade, Fontaine, Fournier. XVIIIb

Préfecture de Police (police hq), see Cité barracks.

Prémontrés, Collège des. East of Ecole de médecine, rue de l'Ecole de médecine. 1252. Rebuilt 1618 and 1672-76. Destroyed 1878. XVId

Présentation de Notre-Dame au Temple, priory. 42 rue Lhomond. 1671. Destroyed. XIe

Président-Wilson, 18 Av. du. Building. 1913 by Tauzin. XVIc

Preuilly, HI of the abbots of. 19 rue Geoffroy-l'Asnier. 1239. Destroyed. VI

Prévôt de Paris, HI du, called des Marmousets. Passage Charlemagne 1367. Destroyed little by little until 1908. VIIa

Prince de Galles, HI. 33 Av. George-V. 1929 by Arfvidson. XVIIc

Prince Impérial, Théâtre du, now "de la Gaité Lyrique." Rue Papin. 1861 by Hittorf. XIVb

Printemps (Le) department store. Rue du Havre, Blvd Haussmann. 1889 by P. Sédille. 2nd store 1908 by R. Binet. Burned. Rebuilt by Wybo. XVIb, XVIIb

Printemps (Le) department store. Nation branch. 21 Cours de Vincennes. 1963 by Grimm. XVIIIb

Prison des jeunes détenus, see Youth Detention House.

Prison, New. Fleury-Mérogis. Will replace La Santé prison. 1964 ff. by Gillet, Vagne, Durant, Bœuf. XVIIIf

Protestant cemetery, see Cemetery, Protestant.

Public Works, Museum of (Musée des Travaux publics). Place d'Iéna. 1937-38 by G. Perret. XVIIb

Pumping station (pompe à feu), see Chaillot, Gros-Caillou, Ivry.

Q

Quatre-Nations, Collège des. Quai Conti. 1663-91 by Le Vau, then d'Orbay. Restored 1961-62. Now palace of the Institut de France. XIb, XIe

Quinze-Vingts, Hospice des. Place du Théâtre-Français, Hôtel du Louvre. 1260. Destroyed 1781. VI, XIIe

Quinze-Vingts, Hospice des. 28 rue de Charenton. Was barracks of Mousquetaires noirs (q.v.) 1780. Rebuilt 1957. XIIb, XVIIIb

R

Radix de Ste-Foy, HI, see Deshays, HI.

Raffet, 41 rue. Residence. 1922 by Lecœur. Destroyed. XVIIc

Rambouillet de la Sablière, HI de, later de Montmorin. 27 rue Oudinot. 1700. Now Ministry of Overseas Finance. XId

Rambouillet, HI de. Former rue - St - Thomas- du- Louvre. Place du Carrousel, Pavillon Richelieu. 1618. Destroyed 18th c. Xb

Rannes, HI de. 21 rue Visconti. 1713. XId

Rapp, 23 Av. Building. 1898 by Balleyguier. XVIc

Rapp, 29 Av. Building. 1901 by Lavirotte. XVIc

Rapp, 3 square. Building. 1899 by Lavirotte. XVIc

Raspail, 96 Blvd. Offices. 1952 by Provelenghios. XVIIIc

Raspail, 137 Blvd. Building. Ca. 1930 by Sauvage. XVIIc

Raymond-Poincaré, 96 Av. Building. 1892 by Plumet. XVIc

Raynouard, 51-55 rue. Building. 1929-32 by A. Perret. XVIIc

Réaumur, 39 rue. Building. 1899-1900 by Salard. XVIc

Réaumur, 124 rue. Office building. 1903-1905 by P. Chédanne. XVIc

Récollets, monastery. 150 rue du Fbg-St-Martin. 1604. Became Hospice des Incurables in 1802 (q.v.). Xc

Récollettes, convent. 85 rue du Bac. 1627. Façade survives. Xc, XIVc

Reims, HI of the archbishops of. 62 rue Beaubourg. 12th c. Destroyed. IV

Reims, HI of the archbishops of. Former rue du Bac. Cour du Commerce St-André, Blvd St-Germain. 13th c. Destroyed. VIIa

Reine (Catherine de Médicis), HI de la. Bourse de Commerce. Succeeded HI de Nesle. 1572 by Ph. Delorme and J. Bullant. Destroyed 1748. See Soissons, HI de. IXa

Reine Blanche, HI de la, at Bourg St-Marcel. 17 rue des Gobelins. End 13th c. Destroyed 1404. Rebuilt end 15th c., beginning 16th c. VIIa, IXa

Reine Blanche, HI de la. Blanche de Navarre, widow of Philippe VI de Valois. 37 rue de la Verrerie, rue des Archives, rue de Rivoli. 1376. Destroyed. VIIa

Reine Marguerite, HI de la. 2-10 rue des Beaux-Arts, up to rue des Saints-Pères. 1606. Destroyed 1623 ff. Xb

Religieuses du calvaire, convent. 19 rue de Vaugirard. 1622. Vestiges. Xc

Religieux de la Ste-Trinité, Hospice des, see Ste-Trinité, Monastic hospice of.

Renard, 8 rue du. Etablissements Rousseau. 1924 by Bocage. XVIIc

Renard, 12 rue du, see Syndicat de l'épicerie française.

René Le Gall, Square. 1938 by J.-Ch. Moreux. XVIIa

République, Place de la, see Château-d'Eau, Place du.

République, 21 Av. de la, School. 1936. XVIIb

Revel, HI de, later "de Broglie." 35 rue St-Dominique. 1711 by Boffrand. XId

Richelieu, HI de. 21 Place des Vosges. 1620. Xb

Richelieu, 2 rue de. Building. 1908 by Lemaire. XVIc

Rieux, HI de, "de Soudéac." 8 rue Garancière. 1640-46 by Bobelini. Xb, XIc

Rieux, HI du Maréchal de, later de la Chesnaye. 47 rue Vieille du Temple. 1939, rebuilt 1482. Destroyed 1638. VIIIa

Rivoli, Rue de. 1806 ff. by Percier and Fontaine. XIIIa, XIVa

Rochechouart, HI de, see Courteilles, HI de.

Rochechouart, 22-24 bis. Swimming pool, sports field, youth center. Finished 1969 by Chappey. XVIIIb

Rochefort, 11-19 rue de. Hôtels. 1870s. XVIc

Rohan, HI de. 87 rue Vieille-du-Temple. 1705-10 by Delamair. XId

Rohan-Montbazon, HI de. 29 rue du Fbg-St-Honoré. 1719 by Lassurance. XIIc

Rollin, Lycée (high school), later Jacques-Decour. Blvd Rochechouart, 12 Av. Trudaine. 1876. XVIb

Romans, HI. 20 rue Ste-Croix-de-la-Bretonnerie. 1696. Destroyed. XId

Rond-Point des Champs-Elysées, new fountains. 1958 by Ingrand, master glassmaker. XVIIIa

Roquelaure, HI de. 246 Blvd St-Germain. 1722 by Lassurance. XIIc

Roquelaure: HI de, later de Beringhen. Former rue St-Nicaise, cour du Carrousel. 1670. Destroyed. XId

Roquette, Château de la. Rue Pache, 142 rue de la Roquette. 1545 ff. Sold 1636 to Hospitalières de Notre-Dame (see Hospitalières de St-Joseph). IXa

Roquette, Grande, see Depot for condemned prisoners.

Roquette, Petite, see Youth Detention House.

Rose, HI de la. Former rue St-Thomas-du-Louvre, place du Carrousel. 15th c. Destroyed. VIIIa

Rothelin, HI de, called de Charolais. 101 rue de Grenelle. 1700-1704 by Lassurance. XId

Rotschild hospital. 15 rue Santerre. XVIIb

Rouault, HI de. 22 rue d'Anjou. 1763. Destroyed. XIId

Rouen, HI of the archbishops of. Cour de Rohan. 14th c. Destroyed 1584. VIIa

Rouge, Pont, see Barbier, Pont.

Rouge, Pont, see St-Louis, Pont.

Roule (Le) leper house. Outskirts of St-Philippe-du-Roule. Ca. 1200. Destroyed. V

Roule, Pont du. Over bypassed riverbed, rue du Fbg-St-Honoré at about rue Jean-Mermoz. Known in 1222. Destroyed. V

Roule (Le) slaughterhouses (abattoirs). Rue de Téhéran-Blvd Haussmann. Built 1808-10. Destroyed 1868. XIIIa

Royal Academy of Music (Académie royale de musique). Corner rue de Valois rue St-Honoré. 1763-70 by Moreau. Destroyed 1781. XIIb

Royal Glass Factory (Manufacture royale des Glaces). 20 rue de Reuilly. 1634. Destroyed 1846. Xa

Royal nursery (Pépinière royale). Rue du Fbg-St-Honoré, Champs-Elysées, rue de Berri, rue La Boétie. Ca. 1640. Destroyed 1720. Xa

Royal, Pont. 1685-89 by R.P. Romain, J. Gabriel. XIa

Royale, Place, later place des Vosges. Xa, Xb, XVIIIa

Royaumont, HI of the abbots of. 4 rue du Jour. 1326. Rebuilt 1612. Destroyed 1950, replaced by a reconstruction. VIIa, Xb

Roye, HI de, later Jacques Samuel-Bernard. 46 rue du Bac. 1741-44. XIIc

Rungis national market (Marché d'intérêt national de Rungis). XVIIIa, XVIIIf

Russian church, see St-Alexandre-Nevsky.

S

Sablons, Château des, see Ternes, Château des.

Saclay Atomic Research Center. 1949-51 by Perret. XVIIIf

Sacré-Cœur basilica. Montmartre. 1876-1919 by Abadie. Bell tower 1905-10 by L. Magne. XVId

Sagan, HI de, "Palais Rose." 50 Av. Foch. 1896 by E. Sanson. XVIc

"Salé," HI, see Aubert de Fontenay, HI.

Salle Pleyel, see Pleyel Hall.

Salm Kyburg, HI de. 64 rue de Lille. 1782 by P. Rousseau. Burned 1871, restored. Now Palais de la légion d'honneur. XIId, XV

Salpêtrière, see Arsenal, Petit.

Salpêtrière (La) general hospital. Blvd de l'Hôpital. 1657 ff. by Le Vau, then L. Bruant. XIb

Salvation Army, see Armée du Salut.

Samaritaine department store Quai du Louvre. 1905 by F. Jourdain. Modernized 1927 by Sauvage. XVIb, XVIIb

Samaritaine pumping station. North part of Pont-Neuf. 1608. Destroyed 1813. Xa

Samuel-Bernard, HI Jacques, see Roye, HI de.

Sandréville, HI de. 26 rue des Francs-Bourgeois. 1630. Xb

Santé, Maison de la. Hospital. 42 rue de la Santé. After 1270. Destroyed 1606. VIIb

Santé (La) prison. Blvd Arago, rue de la Santé. 1865 by Vaudremer. XIVb, XV

Sarah-Bernhardt Théâtre, see Théâtre lyrique.

Savoie, HI de, see Autun, HI of the bishop of.

Savonnerie, Maison de la (royal factory). 18 Av. de New-York. 1664. Destroyed 1855. XIa

Scarron, HI Michel Antoine, later d'Aumont. 7 rue de Jouy. 1646-49 by Le Vau. Modified 1656-62 by F. Mansart. XIc

Schupin, HI du Trésorier. 203 Blvd St-Martin. 1708. Destroyed. XId

Scipion Sardini, HI de. 13 rue Scipion. 1565. IXa

Sédillot, 18 rue. Building. 1899 by Lavirotte. XVIc

Séguier, HI. 133 rue St-Antoine. 1626. Xb

Séguier, HI du chancelier. 41-51 rue J.-J.-Rousseau. 1634, by J. Androuet du Cerceau. Xb

Ségur, HI de (called). 97 rue du Bac. 1720. XIIc

Seignelay, HI de. 80 rue de Lille. 1714 by Boffrand. XId

Seine front. Renovation of 15th arrondissement. Begun 1967 by Lopez and Pottier. XVIIIc

Seine-Saint-Denis prefecture. By Bobigny, Foliasson. XVIIIf

Seissac, HI de, called Boucher d'Orsay. 69 rue de Varenne. 1708 by Leblond. XId

"Séjour du roi" (king's residence, called). Rue du Jour. 1370. Destroyed before 1540. VIIa

Séminaire des Anglais, see English Seminary.

Seminary of M. Olier. 354-356 rue de Vaugirard, rue de Langeac. 1642. Destroyed 1806. Xc

Sens, HI de, see Noirmoutier, HI de.

Sens, HI of the archbishops of. 2 quai des Célestins. 1296. Destroyed 1365. VIIa

Sens, HI of the archbishops of. 1 rue du Figuier. 1365 (earlier HI d'Estomesnil). Destroyed 1474. New hôtel 1475-1519. VIIa, VIIIa

Sentier de Justice. Road over Pré-aux-Clercs, now rue de Varenne. VIIIa

Service technique des constructions navales (shipbuilding institute). 8 Blvd Victor. 1930 by A. Perret. XVIIb

Seurat, Cité. 101 bis rue de la Tombe-Issoire. 1926 by A. Lurçat. XVIIc

Sicily, HI of the king of. Between rues de Sévigné, Pavée, du Roi de Sicile, des Francs-Bourgeois. 1266. Rebuilt 1545 ff. became HI du cardinal de Meudon (q.v.), later HI de Birague. VI

Sillery, HI de. Place du Palais-Royal. 1608. Destroyed 1643. Xb

Sillery, HI de, see Guénégaud, Petit HI.

Société de géographie, HI de la. 184 Blvd St-Germain. 1880 by Leudière. XVIc

Sœurs grises, see Filles de la Charité.

Soissons, HI de. Site of Bourse de Commerce. Was HI de la Reine, modified starting in 1606. Destroyed 1748. Xb

Solférino, Pont de. 1859. Destroyed 1961. XIVa, XVIIIa

Sorbon, Collège de, or Sorbonne. Rues des Ecoles, de la Sorbonne, Cujas, St-Jacques (present expanse). (The Sorbonne of 1256 hardly covered the court of the present Sorbonne.) 1256. Rebuilt 1627-42 by Lemercier. All but church destroyed (see Ste-Ursule) 1880 ff. Rebuilt 1885-1901 by Nénot. VI, Xc, XV, XVIb

Sorbonne, Collège de, see Sorbon, Collège de.

Sorbonne, Place de la. 1639. Enlarged under Napoleon III. Xa

Soubise, HI des. 60 rue des Francs-Bourgeois. 1705-1709 by Delamair. Enlarged 1735-45 by Boffrand, and in 19th c. Now Archives nationales. XId, XIIc

Sourdéac, HI de. 12 rue de Condé. 1713. XId

Sourdis, HI de. 21 rue de l'Arbre-Sec. 1573. Destroyed. IXa

Soyecourt, HI de, see Duret, HI du Président.

Suger, HI de. 76 rue de la Verrerie. 1122. Destroyed. IV

Suisse, Fondation (Swiss students' center). Cité Universitaire. 1930 by Le Corbusier and P. Jeanneret. XVIIc

Sully, HI de, see Mesme-Gallet, HI.

Sully, Pont. 1874-76. XVIa

Surgeons' Amphitheater (Amphithéâtre des Chirurgiens). 5 rue de l'Ecole-de-Médecine. 1655. Reconstructed 1691 by Joubert. XIb

Synagogue. Rue de la Cité, Hôtel-Dieu. Merovingian? Became church of Ste-Marie-Madeleine (q.v.) in 1183. III

Synagogue. 44 rue de la Victoire. 1865-76 by Aldrophe. XIVc

Synagogue. 21 bis rue des Tournelles. 1861. XIVc

Synagogue. 10 rue Pavée. 1913 by Guimard. XVId

Syndicat de l'épicerie française (grocers' assn.). 12 rue du Renard. 1901 by Barreau and Bohain. XVIc

St

St-Aignan, church. 19 rue des Ursins. 1116-17. Still exists. IV

St-Aignan, HI de, see Avaux, HI d'.

St-Alexandre-Nevsky. Russian church. 12 rue Daru. 1859-61 by Kouzmine and Strohm. XIVc

St-Ambroise, church. 71 bis Blvd Voltaire. 1863-69 by Ballu. XIVc

St-Ambroise, church. 71 bis Blvd Voltaire. 1863-69 by Ballu. XIVc

St-Andéol, chapel. Place St-André-des-Arts. Before 1070. Destroyed ca. 1210. IV

St-André-des-Arcs, later des-Arts, church. Place St-André-des-Arts, ca. 1210-20. St-André-des-Arts. Destroyed 1808. V, XIIId

St-André-des-Arts, see St-André-des-Arts.

St-Antoine, Château, see Bastille.

St-Antoine-de-Padoue. 52 Blvd Lefebvre. 1934-36 by Azema. XVIId

St-Antoine-des-Champs, abbey. 184 rue du Fbg-St-Antoine. Known 1191. Church in 1220. Church destroyed 1796. Abbey became hospital in 1795. V, XIIId

St-Antoine des Quinze-Vingts, church. 66 rue de Lyon. 1903 by Lucien Roy. XVId

St-Antoine hospital. 184 rue du Fbg-St-Antoine. Installed 1795 in abbey of St-Antoine-des-Champs (q.v.) Successive modernizations. C.H.U. (q.v.) built 1965. XIIIc, XVIb, XVIIIb

St-Augustin, church. Place St-Augustin, 1860-71 by Baltard. XIVc

St-Baque, see St-Benoit-le-Bestourné.

St-Barthelemy, church. Blvd du Palais, Tribunal de Commerce. 9th c. Chapel of St-Magloire monastery, which moved out in 1138. Rebuilt 14th c. Renovated 18th c, then collapsed. Reconstruction begun before 1789. III, XIIe

St-Benoit-le-Bestourné, or St-Baque, church. First "Sts-Serge et Bacchus" (q.v.). Sorbonne, corner rues St-Jacques and des Ecoles. 2nd church 11th-12th c. Destroyed. 3rd church 14th c. New choir 1678 by Cl. Perrault. Destroyed 1854. IV, VIIb, IXb, XIe, XIVc

St-Bernard, chapel and collège, called des Bernardins. 24 rue de Poissy. 1230, chapel. 1244, collège. 1338, general Cistercian seminary. 1346 ff., totally rebuilt. Destroyed 1797-1869, except refectory. VI, VIIb

St-Bernard, Porte. About 17-19 quai de la Tournelle. Opened 15th or 16th c. Rebuilt 1606. Rebuilt 1670 by Blondel. Destroyed 1790. Xa, XIa

St-Bond, church. 6-8 rue St-Bon. Before 1136. Destroyed 1692. IV, XIe

St-Charles (de Monceau), church. 22 bis rue Legendre. 1907. XVId

St-Charles, Pont. Connected to Hôtel-Dieu. 1651. Destroyed 1878. XIa

St-Christophe, chapel of Hôtel Dieu. Parvis Notre-Dame. 1380-94. Destroyed 1802. VIIIb

St-Christophe, church and hospice. Hôtel-Dieu, Parvis Notre-Dame. 5th c. Destroyed 1747. III, XIIe

St-Christophe de Javel, church. 28 rue de la Convention. 1926-34 by Besnard. XVId

St-Cosme et St-Damien, church. South corner Blvd St-Michel, rue de l'Ecole-de-Médecine. 1213. Rebuilt 1427. Destroyed 1836. V, XIIId

St-Denis, abbey. 475. Rebuilt 630. Rebuilt 775. Rebuilt 1137-1444 (choir). Finished 1231-81 by P. de Montreuil. III, IV, VI

St-Denis canal. 1802-25. XIIIb

St-Denis de la Chapelle, church, earlier chapel of Ste-Geneviève. 16 rue de la Chapelle. 1204. Remodeled 1670. Portal 1757. Restored 1856. Enlarged 1895. V, XIe, XIIe

St-Denis-de-la-Chartre, see St-Symphorien.

St-Denis-de-la-Chartre, church. Rue de la Cité, Hôtel-Dieu. 12th c. Successive modifications. Destroyed 1808. IV, XIIId

St-Denis-du-Pas, oratory, then church of Cloître Notre-Dame. Chevet de Notre-Dame, Square de l'Archevêché. 9th c. Rebuilt 1148. Destroyed after 1786. III, XIIId

St-Denis, oratory, see St-Pierre de Montmartre. III

St-Denis, Porte. Blvd St-Denis, Blvd Bonne-Nouvelle. 1672 by Blondel. XIe

St-Denis-du-St-Sacrement. 68 rue de Turenne. 1826-35 by Godde. XIIId

St-Dominique, church. 20 rue de la Tombe Issoire. 1913-21 by Gaudibert. XVId

St-Eloi, abbey, earlier St-Martial. Rue de Lutèce. 635. Ruined beginning 1631. Destroyed 1862. III, XIVc

St-Eloi, chapel. 8 Rue des Orfèvres. 14th c. Rebuilt 1550-

66 by Ph. Delorme. Destroyed after 1786. Façade survives. VIIb

St-Eloi, church. 36 rue du Fbg-St-Antoine. 1856, rebuilt 1880. Rebuilt 1967 by Leboucheur. XIIIb, XVId, XVIIId

St-Esprit, church. 186 Av. Daumesnil. 1928-35 by Tournon. XVIId

St-Esprit, seminary. 30 rue Lhomond. 1732. Chapel from 1768-80 by Chalgrin. XIIe

St-Etienne, cathedral. Site of choir of Notre-Dame. 4th c. Destroyed ca. 1000. III

St-Etienne "des Grès," church. 5 rue Cujas. Faculty of law. Known since 700. Rebuilt 14th c. Restored 17th or 18th c. Destroyed 1808. III, VIIb, XIIId

St-Etienne "du Mont," church. 1225. Rebuilt 1492-1584. Façade from 1606-22 by Cl. Guérin. VI, VIIIb, IXb, Xc

St-Eugène, church, earlier chapel of Ste-Agnès. ca. 1180. Church before 1223, enlarged 1432. New church 1532-1640. Façade 1754-88 by Mansart de Jouy, then Moreau. V, IXb, XIIe, XV

St-Fargeau, see Le Peletier, Château des.

St-Ferdinand-des-Ternes, church. Place Tristan-Bernard. 1845. Enlarged 1877. New church 1937 by Théodon, F. Bertrand, P. Durand. XVIId

St-Ferdinand, 17 Place. Building. 1954 by Le Caisne. XVIIIc

St-François d'Assise. 7 rue de la Mouzaia. 1926 by P. and A. Courcoux. XVIId

St-François-de-Sales, church. 6 rue Brémontier. 1876. XVId

St-François-Xavier, church. Place du Président-Mithouard. 1861-75 by Lusson and Uchard. XIVc

St-Gabriel, church. 69-71 cours de Vincennes. 1937 by Murcier. XVIId

St-Georges. 114 Av. Simon-Bolivar. 1875. XVId

St-George-St-Magloire, chapel, see St-Magloire, monastery.

St-Germain, 195 Blvd. Building. Ca. 1880 by Garnier. XVIc

St-Germain "de Charonne," church. 119 rue de Bagnolet. 11th c. Repaired 12th-13th c. Rebuilt 15th c. IV, V, VIIIb

St-Germain-des-Prés, abbey, earlier St-Vincent-Ste-Croix (see). Blvd St-Germain, Place St-Germain-des-Prés. 543. Ravaged 861. Restored 869. Church rebuilt 1000 ff. New choir 1163. Monastery rebuilt 1239-55 (chapel of the Virgin, cloister, etc.) by P. de Montreuil. Abbey walls 1368. Disappeared 17th c. Church portal 1607. South portal, vaults 1646 by Gamard. Monastery destroyed 1794 ff. Church restored 1819-22 by Godde, then 1843 ff. by Baltard. III, IV, VI, VIIa, Xc, XIIId

St-Germain-des-Prés, abbot's palace. 1-5 rue de l'Abbaye. 1586 by G. Marchant. Remodeled 1699. IXb, XId

St-Germain-des-Prés, country house. 335-353 rue de Vaugirard. 1256. Destroyed 1704 ff. VI

St-Germain, fair. Rue du Four, rue Mabillon. Market halls 1486. Burned 1762. Rebuilt 1763. Destroyed 1806. VIIIa, XIIa

St-Germain-l'Auxerrois, church, first St-Germain-le-Neuf or le Rond. Oratory 5th c. Merovingian church. 2nd church finished 1025. 3rd church 1250 ff. Porch 1435-39. Restored 1838 ff. III, IV, VIIb, IXb, Xe, XIIe, XIIId

St-Germain-le-Neuf or le Rond, oratory then church, see St-Germain-l'Auxerrois.

St-Georges. 114 Av. Simon-Bolivar. 1875. XVId

St-Germain-le-Vieux, church. Préfesture de Police. 561-84. Rebuilt 15th-16th c. Destroyed 1796. III, VIIIb, XIIId

St-Germain, Maladrerie. Square Boucicaut, rue Velpeau, Bon Marché. 13th c. Destroyed 1544. VI

St-Germain, Marché (market). Rue Clément. 1810. Reduced 1900. XIIIa

St-Gervais-St-Protais, church. Place St-Gervais. Chapel 6th c. Destroyed 1213. Church 1213 remodeled 1420, destroyed 1494. Church 1494-1620 by M. Chambiges, then P. Chambiges. Façade 1616-20 by Cl. Métezeau. III, V, VIIIb, Xc

St-Guillaume, 31 rue. see Dalsace, Dr., residence.

St-Hilaire-du-Mont, church. Corner rue Valette, rue de Lanneau. Known 1158. Destroyed 1795. IV, XIIId

St Hippolyte, church. 3,5,7, Blvd Arago. 1158. Destroyed 1807. IV, XIIId

St-Hippolyte, church. 25 Av. de Choisy. 1909-24 by Astruc. XVId

St-Honoré, collegiate church. 8 rue des Bons-Enfants. 1205. Destroyed 1790. V, IXb, XIIId

St-Honoré-d'Eylau, church. 9 place Victor-Hugo. 1852 by Debressenne. XIVc

St-Honoré, Marché (market). Rue du Marché St-Honoré. 1810. Rebuilt 1865. Destroyed 1958. XIIIa

St-Honoré, Porte. Rue St-Honoré, rue Royale. 1632-34 by Pidoux. Destroyed 1732. Xa

St-Jacques-aux-Pélerins hospital. 133 rue St-Denis. 1317. Destroyed 1808-23. VIIb, XIIId

St-Jacques "de la Boucherie," church. Square St-Jacques. 1st church 900-950. 2nd church then monastery of St-Martin? 2nd church 1060 ff. 3rd church 14th-16th c. South tower 1509-23. Destroyed 1797, ex-

cept for south tower. III, IV, VIIb, VIIIb, IXb, XIIId

St-Jacques "des Jacobins," church. Rues St-Jacques, Soufflot, Cujas. Church of Dominican or "Jacobin" monastery. 1221 ff. Destroyed 1800 ff. V, XIIId

St-Jacques-du-Haut-Pas, church. 252 rue St-Jacques. First chapel of Hospitaliers du Haut-Pas (q.v.), 1566. New church 1630-84 by Gittard and others. VI, IXb, Xc

St-Jacques hospital, see Cochin hospital.

St-Jacques-St-Christophe (de la Villette), church. 1st north corner rues de Flandres, de Nantes. 15th c.-1578. Destroyed. 2nd, place de Bitche 1841-44 by Lequeux. VIIIb, XIIId

St-Jacques-St-François, church. 6 ter rue Charlot. 1715, altered by Godde in 1830 and Baltard in 1855). From monastery of Capucins du Marais (q.v.). XIIId

St-Jean-Baptiste "de Belleville," Church. 139 rue de Belleville. Chapel 1548. Church 1635. Church 1854 by Lassus, then Truchy. IXb, Xc, XIVc

St-Jean-Baptiste "de Grenelle," chapel then church. Intersection of rues des Entrepreneurs, du Commerce. 1828 by Bontat. Enlarged 1924-26. XIIId

St-Jean-Baptiste-de-la-Salle. 9 rue du Docteur-Roux. 1908-10 by Jacquemin. XVId

St-Jean-Baptiste, St-Laurent, St-Sulpice, church, later St-Sulpice. Place St-Sulpice. Chapel since 10th c. Church before 1210, destroyed 1646. New church 1645 ff. by Gamard, Le Vau, Gittard, Servandoni, Maclaurin, Chalgrin. IV, XIe, XIIe, XV

St-Jean-Bosco, church. 75 rue Alexandre-Dumas. 1933-37 by Rotter. XVIId

St-Jean-de-Jerusalem, Chevaliers, Hospitaliers, see Hospital of St. John of Jerusalem, Knights of the.

St-Jean-de-Latran, see Hospital of St. John of Jerusalem, Knights of the. XIVc

St-Jean-en-Grève, church. Hôtel de Ville and rue Lobeau. First baptistry of St-Gervais-St Protais. Church 1212. Rebuilt 1326. Destroyed 1800. IV, VIIb, XIIId

St Jean "le Rond," baptistry 4th of 5th c. Site unknown (Parvis de Notre-Dame?). Rebuilt ca. 1100. Rebuilt and moved (entered from rue du Cloître-Notre-Dame) 13th c. Façade redone beginning 17th c. Destroyed 1748. III, V, XIIe

St-Jean-l'Evangéliste, church. Place des Abbesses. 1894-1904 by A. de Baudot. XVId

St-Jean-Porte-Latine, chapel. 60 rue du Fbg-Montmartre. 1760. Destroyed 1846. XIIe

St-Joseph. 161 rue de St-Maur. 1860 by Ballu. XIVc

St-Joseph-des-Carmes, church 74 rue de Vaugirard. Chapel of monastery of Carmes déchaussés 1613-20. Now chapel of Institut catholique. Xc

St-Joseph-des-Epinettes, church. 40 rue Pouchet. 1910, architect unknown. XVId

St-Joseph, Marché (market). 144 rue Montmartre. 1806. Destroyed 1860. XIIIa

St-Josse, chapel then church. 31 rue Quincampoix. 1235. Destroyed 1791. VI

St-Julien-des-Ménétriers, hospice and chapel. 168-170 rue St-Martin. 1330. Destroyed 1791. VIIb

St-Julien-le-Pauvre, oratory then church. Rue Galande, square René-Viviani. 6th c. Ruined by Normans. Church 1170 ff. Altered 1651. Restored 1826. III, IV, XIe

St-Lambert (de Vaugirard), first Notre-Dame. Intersection rues de Vaugirard, St-Lambert, Desnouettes. 1341. Destroyed 1853. New church 282 rue de Vaugirard. 1848-56 by Naissant. VIIb, XIVc

St-Landry, church. Rue d'Arcole, Hôtel-Dieu. 12th c. Destroyed 1829. IV, XIIId

St-Laurent, church. Intersection Blvd de Strasbourg, Blvd Magenta. 6th c. Rebuilt 1429 ff. Vaults, façade 1655-59. New façade 1862-66. III, IV, VIIIb, XIe, XIVc

St-Laurent, market halls of fair. Rue St-Laurent, Blvd de Strasbourg. 1663. Destroted 1790 ff. XIa

St-Laurent, market halls of fair. Rue St-Laurent, Blvd de First Place de l'Europe (1836) Rebuilt 1885-89 by Lisch. Renovated 1936. XIIIb, XVIa, XVIIa

St-Lazare, Gare (RR station), first "Embarcadère de l'Ouest." First Place de l'Europe (1836) then rue St-Lazare (1842). Rebuilt 1885-89 by Lisch. Renovated 1936. XIIIb, XVIa, XVIIa

St-Lazare, leper house. 107 rue du Fbg-St-Denis. Before 1122. Transformed into monastery (q.v.) 1632. IV

St-Lazare, monastery then prison. Rues du Fbg-St-Denis, Poissonnière, Paradis, de Dunkerque. Succeeded St-Lazare leper house 1632. Rebuilt end 17th c. (q.v.). Became prison in 1793. Destroyed 1940. XIe, XIIIc, XVIIb

St-Léon, church. Place Dupleix. 1925-34 by E. Brunet. XVIId

St-Leu-St-Gilles, church. 92 rue St-Denis. Chapel 12th c.? Church 1235. Rebuilt 1320 ff. Remodeled 1727. Remodeled 1858 by Baltard. VI, VIIb, XIIe, XIVc

St-Louis, church. Former rue St Thomas du Louvre, place du Carrousel. 1744. Destroyed 1810. XIIe, XIIId

St-Louis, Collège, later Lycée (high school). 40-42 Blvd St-Michel. Succeeded Collège d'Harcourt (q.v.) 1814. Enlarged 1908. XIIIc, XVIb

St-Louis-de-la-Salpêtrière, church. Blvd de l'Hôpital. 1670 by L. Bruant. XIe

St-Louis-des-Invalides. 1679-1708 by J. Hardouin-Mansart. XIe

St-Louis-des-Jésuites, church, now St-Paul-St-Louis. 99 rue St-Antoine. 1624-41 by R.P. Martellange and R.P. Derrand. Xc

St-Louis-en-l'Ile, chapel then church. 21 rue St-Louis-en-l'Ile. Chapel 1623. Destroyed. Church 1664-1726 by Le Vau then Le Duc. Bell tower 1765. Xc, XIe, XIIe

St-Louis hospital. 2 Place du Dr-Alfred-Fournier. 1607-11 by Cl. Vellefaux? Xa

St-Louis, Jesuit chapel. 99 rue St-Antoine. 1582. Destroyed 1627. IXb

St-Louis, Pont, formerly Pont Rouge and Pont de la Cité. Between La Cité and Ile St-Louis. 1627. Destroyed several times. Rebuilt 1862. Collapsed 1939. Provisional footbridge. Xa, XIIIa, XIVa

St-Louis, seminary. Rue de Médicis, opposite fountain. 1704. Destroyed 1853. XIe

St-Magloire, monastery. Blvd du Palais, Tribunal de Commerce. See St-Barthélémy. IV

St-Magloire, monastery. 82 rue St-Denis. First chapel of St-Georges, 9th c., then St-Georges-St-Magloire. Monastery of St-Magloire-de-la-Cité installed there 1138. Destroyed 1790-1838. III, IV

St-Marcel, Blvd (horse market). 1687-1857. XIa

St-Marcel (Bourg), walls. 10th c. New walls end 13th c. IV, VIIa

St-Marcel, church. Corner Blvd St-Marcel, rue Michel-Peter. Chapel 5th c. New church 871? New church 1050. Remodeled 13th c. Destroyed 1806. III, IV, VIIb, XIIId

St-Marcel, church. 82 Blvd de l'Hôpital. 1856 by A. Blot. Destroyed 1962. 1967 by Michelin and Corret. XIVc, XVIIId

St-Martial, see St-Eloi, abbey.

St-Martial, oratory. Rue de Lutèce. Merovingian. Destroyed 1791. III

St-Martin canal. 1802-26. XIIIb

St-Martin-des-Champs, monastery. Now Conservatoire des arts et métiers. 292 rue St-Martin. 1st church 1060. 2nd church 1130 ff. Monastery: walls 1140, then 1273. Buildings redone: refectory 13th c.; cloister 1702-20; dormitories end 18th c. by Antoine. IV, VI, VIIa, VIIb, XIe, XIIe

St-Martin-des-Champs, walls of priory. 12th c. New walls 1273. Vestiges. IV, VIIa

St-Martin-du-Cloître, church. Rue de la Collégiale. Merovingian? Rebuilt 1158? Rebuilt 1480. Destroyed 1790-1807. IV, VIIIb

St-Martin, Marché (market). Rue Montgolfier. 1806. Destroyed 1878. XIIIa

St-Martin, monastery. First site square St-Jacques ? 8th c. Destroyed by Normans. III

St-Martin, Porte. Blvd St-Martin, Blvd St-Denis. 1674 by Bullet. XIa

St-Maur, HI des Abbés de. 47-49 rue St-Antoine. 1210. Destroyed 1556. V

St-Médard. 141 rue Mouffetard. 11th c. Nave redone 15th c. Choir 1562-86. Choir altered 1784. IV, VIIIb, IXb, XIIe, XV

St-Merri, church. 78 rue St-Martin. Succeeded chapel of St-Pierre-aux-Bois (q.v.) ? 1st church end 9th c. 2nd church 13th c. 3rd church 1510-52. III, IV, IXb

St-Michel-des-Batignolles, church. 19 Av. de St-Ouen. Earlier provisional quarters 1858-1926. Church 1926 by B. Haubold. XVIIId

St-Michel fountain, see Fontaine St-Michel.

St-Michel, Place du Pont. 18th c. Widened 1809, 1840, 1860. XIIa

St-Michel, Pont. 1378. Rebuilt several times. Rebuilt 1857. VIIa, XIVa

St-Nicolas-des-Champs, church. 254 rue St-Martin. End 11th c. Rebuilt Ca. 1200. Rebuilt 1420-80. South portal 1575. Choir, extension of nave 1613-15. IV, V, VIIIb, IXb, Xc

St-Nicolas-du-Chardonnet, chapel then church. Rue Monge, rue des Bernardins. Shortly after 1230. Rebuilt 1243. Bell tower 1625. All but tower destroyed. New church 1656-1709 by Noblet and Levé. Façade 1934 by Halley. VI, Xc, XIe, XVIId

St-Nicolas-du-Chardonnet, seminary. 24-26 rue St-Victor. 1631. Destroyed 1906. Xc

St-Nicolas-du-Louvre, Collège. Former rue St-Thomas-du-Louvre, cour du Carrousel. 1212. Closed 1541. Destroyed. V

St-Paul-des-Champs, church. 32 rue St-Paul. Parish since 1080. Rebuilt 13th c. Enlarged under Charles V. Destroyed 1799. IV, VIIb, VIIIb, XIIId

St-Paul, HI, or St-Pol. Rues St-Antoine, St-Paul, Petit-Musc. 1361. Destroyed 1543. VIIa

St-Paul-St-Louis, church, see St-Louis-des-Jésuites.

St-Pol, HI, see St-Paul, HI.

St-Roch, church. 286 rue St-Honoré. Succeeded Ste-Suzanne-de-Gaillon rebuilt 1587. New church 1653-60 by Lemercier. Portal 1735 by J. de Cotte. IXb, XIe, XIIe

St Philippe (du Roule), chapel then church. Place Chassaigne-Goyon. Chapel of St-Jacques-St-Philippe-du-Roule made parish church. 1697. Destroyed 1739. New church 1774-84 by Chalgrin. Enlarged 1845 by Godde and 1860 b Baltard. XIIe

St-Pierre or **St-Père**, chapel. 49 rue des Sts-Pères. Before 1200. Destroyed 1732. Rebuilt 1732 by R. de Cotte. Now Ukrainian Catholic church, St-Vladimir-le-Grand. IV

St-Pierre-aux-Bœufs, church. Rue d'Arcole. 925. Rebuilt Ca. 1200. Destroyed 1837. III, V, XIIId

St-Pierre-aux-Bois, chapel. Site of St-Merri (q.v.) ? 6th c. Destroyed. III

St-Pierre-de-Chaillot, church. I: 1st church 26 rue de Chaillot, known 1097; 2nd church 1696, destroyed. II: 33 Av. Marceau. 1933-37 by Bois. V, XIe, XVIId

St-Pierre-de-Montmartre, church. 2 rue du Mont-Cenis. First oratory of St-Denis, Merovingian, destroyed 944. Then chapel of Benedictine convent of Montmartre (q.v.) 1133-47. Vaults 1470. Façade 1775. Tower beginning 19th c. Restored 1900-1908. III, IV, VIIIb, XIIe, XIIId

St-Pierre (de Montrouge). I: rue Thibaud, 1847, destroyed. II: Place Victor-Bash. 1864-72 by Vaudremer. XIVc, XV

St-Pierre-des-Arcis, church. Tribunal de Commerce. Merovingian. Rebuilt 15th c. Destroyed. III

St-Pierre (du Gros-Caillou), church. 92 rue St-Dominique. First Notre-Dame-de-Bonne-Délivrance, 1738. Destroyed 1822. 1822 by Godde. XIIe, XIIId

St-Roman, HI de. 48 rue de l'Arbre-Sec. 1680. XId

St-Sauveur, church. 183 rue St-Denis. First chapel of la Tour, 1214. 2nd building 16th c. Enlarged 17th c. Destroyed 1787. V, IXb, Xc, XIIe

St-Sépulcre, church and hospice. 60 rue St-Denis. 1325. Remodeled 17th c. Destroyed 1795. VIIb, Xc, XIIId

St-Séverin, oratory then church. Rue des Prêtres-St-Séverin. Oratory 7th c. Church 13th c. Widened 14th c. Burned and rebuilt 15th c. Ossuaries 15th, 17th c. Chapel of St-Sacrement, choir altered 17th c. III, VI, VIIIb, XIe

St-Simon, HI de. 3 rue Monsieur. 1783. Destroyed. XIId

St-Stéphane, Greek Orthodox church. 21 rue George-Bizet. 1895 by Vaudremer. XVId

St-Sulpice, church, see St-Jean-Baptiste, St-Laurent, St-Sulpice.

St-Sulpice, country house of clergy. 358-364 rue de Vaugirard. 1752. Disappeared. XIIe

St-Sulpice, country house of Petit Séminaire de. 276-299 rue de Vaugirard. 1756. Destroyed 1832-1913. XIIe

St-Sulpice, Place. 1754 by Servandoni. Enlarged 1803-11. XIIa

St-Sulpice, seminary, on Place St-Sulpice. 1645. Destroyed 1803. Rebuilt 1820 south of Place, by Godde. Now Direction des Contributions directes. XIe

St-Symphorien-des-Vignes, basilica. Collège Ste-Barbe. 7th c. Destroyed 1650. III, XIe

Ste-Agnès, chapel. Rue du Jour. Later church of St-Eustache (q.v.). Ca. 1180. Destroyed. V

St-Symphorien, oratory, first St-Denis-de-la-Chartre, then lost its name to nearby oratory, became Ste-Catherine-St-Symphorien-St-Luc. Rue de la Cité, Hôtel-Dieu. Merovingian. Destroyed 1868. III

St-Thomas-d'Aquin, church, see Dominicans, General Novitiate.

St-Thomas-du-Louvre, collegiate church. 1186-87. Collapsed 1739. V, XIIe

St-Victor canal, branch of Bièvre. Installed 1148 for abbey mills. Diverted (Rue des Fossé St-Bernard) 1361. Filled under Louis XIV. IV, VIIa, XIa

St-Victor, oratory then abbey. Rues Linné and Cuvier, Halle aux Vins, Faculté des Sciences. Oratory beginning 11th c. Monastery and church 1131 ff. Cloister and infirmary chapel 13th c. Church totally rebuilt 1517 ff. New portal 18th c. Total destruction 1811. III, IV, VI, IXb, XIIId

St-Vincent-de-Paul, church. Place La Fayette. 1824-44 by Lepère, then Hittorf. XIIId

St-Vincent-Ste-Croix, see St-Opportune hospital.

St-Vincent-Ste-Croix, abbey, St-Germain-des-Prés (q.v.) after 756, or "le Doré." 543. Ravaged 861. Restored 869. III

St-Vladimir-le-Grand, see St-Pierre, chapel.

St-Yves, chapel. NE corner rue St-Jacques. Blvd St-Germain. 1350. Destroyed. 1796. VIIb, XIIId

Ste-Agnès, see St-Eustache.

Ste-Anne-de-la-Maison-Blanche. 186 rue de Tolbiac. 1894-1921 by Robin and Sandoz. XVId

Ste-Anne hospital. 1 rue Cabanis. 1652. Rebuilt 1861-76 by Questel. XIb, XV

Ste-Anne-la-Royale, church. 13 quai Voltaire, 26-30 rue de Lille. Church of Théathins' monastery (q.v.) 1661 ff. by R.P. Guarini. Destroyed 1821 (vestiges 30 rue de Lille and 13 quai Voltaire). XIe, XIIId

Ste-Aure, community. 16 rue Tournefort. 1707. Now convent of Dames de l'Adoration perpétuelle du St-Sacrement. XIe

Ste-Barbe, Collège. 4 rue Valette. 1460. Destroyed 1798 (new collège 1802 ff.). VIIIb

Ste-Catherine-du-Val-des-Ecoliers, monastery. Rues de Jarente, d'Ormesson, place du Marché-Ste-Catherine. Before 1229. Destroyed 1783. VI, XIIe

Ste-Catherine hospital, see Ste-Opportune hospital.

Ste-Catherine-St-Symphorien-St-Luc, see St-Symphorien, oratory.

Ste-Chapelle. Palais de Justice. 1246-48 by Pierre de Montreuil? Façade redone 15th c. Restored 1837 ff. by Duban, Lassus, Viollet-le-Duc. Spire 1853 by Lassus. VI, XIIId

Ste-Chapelle (de Vincennes), Château de Vincennes. 13th c. New chapel 14th, 16th c. (finished 1552). VI, VIIb, IXa

Ste-Claire, church. Porte de Pantin. 1959 by Le Donné. XVIIId

Ste-Clotilde, church. Square Ste-Clotilde. 1846-56 by Gau and Ballu. XIIId

Ste-Croix, church. Marché aux Fleurs. Before 1136. Enlarged 15th c. Destroyed 1797-1847. IV, VIIIb

Ste-Croix-de-la-Bretonnerie, monastery. Rues de Moussy, Ste-Croix-de-la-Bretonnerie, des Billettes, de la Verrerie. 1258. Destroyed 1793. VI

Ste-Elizabeth, church, see Filles de Ste-Elizabeth.

Ste-Foix, HI. Théâtre de l'Opéra. 1775 by Brongniart. Destroyed 1858. XIId

Ste-Geneviève, abbey, first "des Sts-Apôtres-Pierre-et-Paul." "Site of Lycée Henri-IV and rue Clovis. 510. Burned 857. Restored. Church rebuilt 1180 ff. Kitchens, refectories rebuilt 13th c. Cloister, tower 15th c. Cloister redone 1744. Library beginning 18th c. Church destroyed 1802. III, IV, V, VI, VIIIb, XIe, XIIe, XIIId

Ste-Geneviève, Bibliothèque (library). Place du Panthéon. 1844-50 by H. Labrouste. XIIIc, XV

Ste-Geneviève, chapel, later St-Denis-de-la-Chapelle (q.v.). 16 rue de la Chapelle. 1204. IV

Ste-Geneviève, church, later called Panthéon. 1755-90 by Soufflot, then Rondelet. 1792 ff., alterations (bell towers destroyed, windows walled up) by Quatremère de Quincy. XIIe, XIIId, XV

Ste-Geneviève-des-Ardents, or la Petite, church. Parvis Notre-Dame. 6th c? Rebuilt 13th c. New portal 1402. Destroyed 1747. III, VI, VIIIb, XIIe

Ste-Hélène, church. 102 rue du Ruisseau. 1936 by G. Trévoux. XVIId

Ste-Jeanne-d'Arc, church. 16 rue de la Chapelle. 1932, architect unknown. Nave unfinished, after 1945. XVIId, XVIIId

Ste-Jeanne-de-Chantal, Porte de St-Cloud. Was chapel of Ste-Geneviève 1902-36. Rebuilt and ended after 1945 by Barbier, then Nicod and Blanc. XVIId, XVIIId

Ste-Marguerite, chapel then church. 36 rue St-Bernard. Ca. 1627. Xc

Ste-Marie (des Batignolles). Intersection of Rues Legendre and des Batignolles. 1828 by Lequeux. XIIId

Ste-Marie-l'Egyptienne, chapel. Rue de la Jussienne, rue Montmartre. Before 1290. Destroyed by Revolution. VIIb, XIIId

Ste-Marie-Madeleine, church. Rue de la Cité-Hôtel-Dieu. Synagogue until 1183. Restored 14th c. Enlarged 18th c. Destroyed 1790. V, VIIIb, XIIe

Ste-Marie-Madeleine (de la Ville-l'Evêque). 8 Blvd Malesherbes. 13th c. Rebuilt 1659. Destroyed 1797. VI, XIe, XIIId

Ste-Marie-Madeleine (de la Ville-l'Evêque), church. Place de la Madeleine. 1764-77 by Contant d'Ivry, unfinished. Destroyed 1777. 1777-90 by Couture Jr., unfinished. Destroyed 1806

Ste-Marie-Madeleine (de la Ville-l'Evêque), "La Madeleine," first Temple de la Gloire, then church. Place de la Madeleine. 1806-42 by Vignon and others. XIIId

Ste-Marine, church. Rue d'Arcole. Before 1045. Destroyed 1867. IV, XIVc

Ste-Odile, church. Av. Stéphane-Mallarmé, Blvd de la Somme. 1934-38 by Barge. XVIId

Ste-Opportune canons, Grange "bataillée," see Grange "bataillée."

Ste-Opportune, church. 21 rue St-Denis. Succeeded oratory of Notre Dame des Bois, Merovingian? Church before 1150. Destroyed 1797. IV, XIVc

Ste-Opportune, Fossés de, drainage ditch for bypassed riverbed of Seine. VIIa

Ste-Opportune hospital, later Ste-Catherine. 13th c. 20 rue St-Denis. Before 1188. Destroyed 1854. V

Ste

Ste-Opportune, Marais de (swamp). Bypassed riverbed of Seine. IV

Ste-Pélagie, convent and refuge. 11-15 rue Lacépède. 1665. Destroyed 1895. XIe, XVId

Ste-Perrine, convent. 61-65 rue de Flandre. 1646. Moved 1742 (Ste-Perrine de Chaillot). See Augustines de Nanterre, convent. XIe

Ste-Reine, Hospice, or Hôpital des Teigneux (hospital for skin diseases). Bon Marché department store. 15th c. Destroyed. VIIIa, VIIIb

Ste-Suzanne-de-Gaillon, chapel, later church of St-Roch (q.v.). 286 rue St-Honoré. 1521. Destroyed 1587. IXb

Ste-Trinité, monastic hospice of (Hospice des Religieux de la Ste-Trinité, called Mathurins). Rue de Cluny. 1229. Their chapel of St-Louis Enlarged 15th c. restored 18th c.) Destroyed 1855. VI, VIIIb, XIIe, XIVc

Ste-Ursule-de-la-Sorbonne, chapel. Place de la Sorbonne. 1326. Destroyed 1635. 1635-42 by Lemercier. Xc

Sts

Sts-Apôtres-Pierre-et-Paul, abbey, see Ste-Geneviève, abbey.

Sts-Innocents, church. Rue des Innocents. Ca. 1150. Destroyed 1786. IV

Sts-Pères, 76-76 bis rue des. Building. 1879-80 by Dupuis. XVIc

Sts-Serge-et-Bacchus, church. See St-Benoit-le-Bestourné. Sorbonne corner of Rues St-Jacques and des Ecoles. 6th-7th c. Destroyed. III

T

Tabacs, Manufacture des, see Tobacco factory.

Taillepied de Bondy, HI. 112 rue de Richelieu. 1771-89 by Brongniart. Destroyed 19th c. XIIc

Tallard, HI de, see Amelot de Chaillou.

Talon, HI du Président, called de Créqui. 16 rue St-Guillaume 1660-64 by Le Muet. XId

Tanneguy du Chatel, HI. 14-16 rue du Temple. 1413. Destroyed. VIIIa

Taranne, HI de. 1 rue du Dragon. 1412. Destroyed 16th c. VIIIa

Teigneux, Hôpital des, see Ste-Reine, Hospice.

Télévision, Cité de la (television center). Bry-sur-Marne. Project. XVIIIf

Templars, see Knights Templars.

Temple, see Knights Templars.

Temple de la Gloire, later church of the Madeleine, see Ste-Marie-Madeleine (de la Ville-l'Evêque). XIIIc

Temple of the reformed Church (Protestant church). Charenton. 1606 by S. de Brosse. New church 1623 by S. de Brosse. Xc

Templiers, see Knights Templars.

Tenon hospital. 4 rue de la Chine. 1878. XIVb

Ternes, Château des, or "des Sablons." Rue Bayen. 15th c. Rebuilt 1548 ff. Rebuilt 18th c. Destroyed 1781, except one façade. VIIIa, IXa, XIIc

Tessé, HI de. 59 rue de Varenne. 1704. Destroyed. XId

Tessé, HI de. 2 rue des Sts-Pères, 1 rue Voltaire. 1765 by Letellier. XIIc

Theater, Gallo-Roman. Blvd St-Michel (Lycée St-Louis), rue Racine. 2nd c. Destroyed 3rd c. II

Théatins, country house. 389 rue de Vaugirard. 1661. Destroyed. XIe

Théatins, monastery. 17 quai Voltaire, 26 rue de Lille. 1644 ff. Church of Ste-Anne-la-Royale (q.v.) 1662 ff. Destroyed 1821. XIe, XIIId

Théâtre de la Ville, see Théâtre lyrique.

Théâtre du Palais-Royal, see Beaujolais, théâtre de.

Théâtre-Français (Comédie-Française), see Variétés amusantes, Théâtre des.

Théâtre-Français, later called Odéon. Place de l'Odéon. 1779-82 by Peyre and Wailly. Burned 1799. Rebuilt identically by Chalgrin. XIIb, XIIIc, XV

Théâtre-Français, Place du Palais-Royal. 1786-90. Destroyed. VIIIa

Théâtre-Français, Place du Palais, Place de l'Odéon. 1779. XIIa

Théâtre-Français, Place du Palais-Royal. 1854. XIVa

Théâtre lyrique (Théâtre Sarah-Bernhardt). Place du Châtelet. 1862 by Davioud. Interior completely changed 1967 ff. (Théâtre de la Ville) by Perrotet. XIVb, XV, XVIIIb

Théâtre Marigny. Champs-Elysées gardens. 1885 (Diorama). Converted into theater 1894. Renovated 1925. XVIb

Théâtre Montansier, see Beaujolais, Théâtre de.

Théâtre Sarah-Bernhardt, see Théâtre lyrique.

Thélusson, HI de. Rue Laffitte, rue de Provence. 1776-83 by N. Ledoux. Destroyed 1823. XIId

Thermae (baths), Gallo-Roman. I: rue Gay-Lussac, near Blvd St-Michel. II: beneath Collège de France. III: Thermes "de Cluny," Blvd St-Germain, Blvd St-Michel, rue des Ecoles. II

Thermes, (Mineral baths), see Belleville, Passy.

Thiers, wall. 1839. Destroyed 1920-24. XIIIb

Thiers, HI. 27 place St-Georges. 1873 by Aldrophe. XVIc

Thiroux de Montsauge, HI, called de Massa. 60 Av. des Champs-Elysées. 1784 by Le Boursier. Moved in 1928 to 38 rue du Fbg-St-Jacques. XIId, XVIIc

Thomé, HI. 25 Blvd du Montparnasse and 132 rue de Vaugirard. 1712. XId

Thorigny, HI de. 78 rue Vieille-du-Temple. 1407. Destroyed 16th c. VIIIa

Tillet de la Bussière, HI du. 52 rue St-André-des-Arts. 1740. XIIc

Tingry-Mortemart, HI de, see Gournay, HI de.

Tiron enclosure (clos). Vineyards, east flank of Montagne Ste-Geneviève. IV

Titon, HI. 58 rue du Fbg-Poissonnière. 1776-83 by Delafosse. XIId

Tobacco factory (Manufacture des Tabacs). Rue Jean-Nicot, quai d'Orsay. 1810. Destroyed. XIIIc

Tocqueville, 36 rue de. Building. 1898 by Plumet. XVIc

Tolbiac, Pont de. 1879-84. XVIa

Tour, chapelle de la. 183 rue St-Denis. 1214. Destroyed. See St-Sauveur. V

Tour Schöffer. Project. XVIIIf

Tourelles (Les), swimming pool stadium (Stade nautique des Tourelles). Square du Dr-Variot. 1924 by Bévière. XVIIa

Tournelle, Château de la. About 17-19 quai de la Tournelle. Ca. 1370. Rebuilt 1554. Destroyed 1790. VIIa

Tournelle, Pont de la. 1369. Rebuilt 1656. Rebuilt 1851. Rebuilt 1926-28. VIIa, XIa XIVa, XVIIa

Tournelles (Les), royal house, first HI d'Orgemont. 1388. Destroyed 1563 ff. VIIa

Tournelles, Terrains des (horse market). Future Place des Vosges. 1563-1605. IXa

Tourville' HI du maréchal de. 199 rue St-Martin. 1728. Destroyed. XIIc

Tourville, 4 Av. de. Building. 1890. XVIc

Town Hall (Mairie) of 4th arrondissement. Place Baudoyer. 1866. Burned 1871. Rebuilt 1884. XIVb

Town Hall (Mairie) of 5th arrondissement. Place du Panthéon. 1844-50 by Hittorf. Rebuilt 1927-28, except façade. XIIIc, XVIId

Town Hall (Mairie) of 10th arrondissement. 76 rue du Fbg-St-Martin. 1892-96. XVIb

Town Hall (Mairie) of 12th arrondissement. 130 Av. Daumesnil. 1844. Burned 1871. Rebuilt 1874-77. XV

Town Hall (Mairie) of 14th arrondissement. Place Ferdinand Brunot. 1852. Enlarged 1888. XVIb, XVIIb

Town Hall (Mairie) of 15th arrondissement. 98 rue Péclet 1929 by H. Rapin. XVIIb

Town Hall (Mairie) of 18th arrondissement. Place Jules-Joffin. 1888-96. XVIb

Town Hall (Mairie) of 19th arrondissement. Place Armand-Carrel. 1876 by Davioud. XVIb

Transylvanie, HI de, see Hillerin, HI de.

Travaux publics, Musée des, see Public Works, Museum of.

Trente-Trois, Collège des. 34 rue de la Montagne-Ste-Geneviève. 1654. Rebuilt 18th c. Destroyed 1797 ff. XIe

Trente-Trois, country house of seminary of. 373-377 bis rue de Vaugirard. 1747. Destroyed 1635-1763. VI

Trésorier, Collège du. 8 Place de la Sorbonne. 1268. Destroyed 1635-1763. VI

Tribunal de Commerce. Blvd du Palais. 1860-65 by Ballu. XIVb

Trinité (La) church. Place d'Estienne d'Orves. 1861-67 by Ballu. XIVc

Trinité (La) hospital, was Aumônerie (alms house) de la Croix de la Reine, called Hospice des Enfants-Bleus (16th c. ff. 28 rue Greneta. Ca. 1200. Destroyed 17th c. V, IXb, XIIId

Trocadero, palace, gardens, and Place du. 1878 by Davioud. Palace encompassed by Palace of Chaillot (q.v.). XVIa, XVIIa

Trône, Barrière du (customs house), see Fermiers Généraux customs wall.

Tropical Institute (Centre technique forestier tropical, or Centre tropical). Av. de la Belle-Gabrielle (Bois de Vincennes). 1951 by Roux-Spitz. XVIIIb

Trousseau hospital. 158 Av. du Général Michel Bizot. 1901. XVIb

Tubeuf, HI, see Duret de Chevry.

Tuileries gardens. 1st laid out 1560s-1570s. New arrangement. 1665 by Le Notre. 1716, revolving bridge. IXa, XIb, XIIa, (bridge).VIIIa

Tuileries palace. Between Pavillon de Marsan and Pavillon de Flore. 1567 by Ph. Delorme, then J. Bullant. 1594-1610 by du Pérac, Métezeau, J. Androuet du Cerceau. 1659 ff. connected to Grande Galerie, theater, by Le Vau, d'Orbay. Burned 1871. Destroyed 1882-84. IXa, Xb XV, XVIa

Tuileries, Porte des. West end of quai des Tuileries. As early as 1583. Rebuilt 1633. See Conférence, Porte de la. IXa

U

Ukranian Catholic church, see St-Pierre, chapel.

UNESCO House (Maison de l'UNESCO). Place de Fontenoy. 1955-58 by Breuer, Nervi, Zehrfuss. XVIIIb

Union européenne des chemins de fer (European RR Union). Rue Jean-Rey. 1961. XVIIIb

Université, HI de l'. 25-31 rue du Bac. 25 rue de l'Université. 15th c. Destroyed. VIIIa

University hospital (Hôpital universitaire). 40-42 Blvd Jourdan. 1960 by Casan. XVIIIb

Unknown Soldier, tomb of the. Arc de Triomphe. 1921-23. XVIId

Ursins, HI des. 14th c. site of Hôtel-Dieu. Destroyed. 16th c. farther north, on Seine. Destroyed 1563. VIIIa, IXa

V

Vaches, Chemin aux, road in Pré-aux-Clercs (future rues St-Dominique and de Grenelle). VIIIa

Vagenende restaurant. 142 Blvd St-Germain. 1900 décor. XVIc

Val-de-Grâce, abbey. Rue St-Jacques, Place Alphonse-Laveran. Installed 1621. Rebuilt 1645-67 by F. Mansart, then Lemercier, Le Muet, Le Duc. Xc, XIV, XV

Val de Grâce military hospital. Installed in abbey in 1795. XIIIc

Val de Marne prefecture. Créteil. XVIIIf

Val d'Oise prefecture. Pontoise. 1967 ff. by Henry Bernard. XVIIIf

Valence-Timbrune, HI de. 52 rue de la Chaussée-d'Antin. 1769 by Brongniart. Destroyed XIId

Valhubert, Place. 1806. XIIIa

Valles, HI de. 70 rue de Vaugirard. Ca. 1545. Destroyed IXa

Valois fief. Val de Grâce. End 13th c. Destroyed 1621 ff. VIIa

Vanne, Réservoir de la, or Montsouris. 115 rue de la Tombe Issoire. 1860-74 by Belgrand. XIVa, XVIa

Varennes, 54 rue de. Residence. 1893 by Magnan' XVId

Variétés amusantes, Théâtre des, Now Théâtre Français or Comédie Française. 1786-90 by Louis. South façade 1850 by Chabrol. XIIb, XIVb

Vaudreuil, HI (called), called also Borghèse. 5-7 rue de la Chaise. 1763. XIIc

Vaugirard, wall. 1589. Disappeared 18th c. Xa

Vauvert, Château. South of Luxembourg gardens, Av. de l'Observatoire. 10th or 11th c. Destroyed 13th c. (see Chartreux). IV

Vavin, 26 rue. Building. 1912 by Sauvage. XVIc

Vélodrome d'Hiver (winter cycling track). Blvd de Grenelle, rue Nélaton, rue du Dr-Finlay. 1910. Destroyed 1959. XVIa, XVIIIa

Vendôme column, see Austerlitz column.

Vendôme, HI de. Former rue Fromenteau, Place du Carrousel. 1378. Destroyed. VIIa

Vendôme, HI de, first de Mercœur (q.v.).

Vendôme, HI de, see Poullain, HI.

Vendôme, HI de. Blvd St-Michel. See Estrées, HI d'

Vendôme, Place, see Louis-le-Grand, Place.

Ventadour Hall (Salle Ventadour), see Opéra-Comique.

Versailles, 25 Av. de. Building. 1932 by Ginsberg. XVIIc

Versailles, 42 Av. de. Building. 1934 by Ginsberg. XVIIc

Versailles, 54 Av. de. Building. 1960 by Ginsberg. XVIIIc

Vert-Galant Building (Immeuble du Vert-Galant). Quai des Orfèvres. 1932 by H. Sauvage. XVIIc

Vert-Galant, square du. Cité. End 19th c. XVIa

Vertus, HI de. 3 rue de la Chaise. 1640. Xb

Vézelay, HI of the abbots of. Bibliothèque Ste-Geneviève. North side Place du Panthéon. 13th-14th c. Destroyed. VIIa

Victoire, 37 rue de la. Office building. 1959 by Balladur, Lebeigle, Tostivint. XVIIIc

Victoires, Place des. 1685 by J. Hardouin-Mansart. XIa, XIc

Victor-Hugo, 39 Av. Building. 1913 by Plumet. XVIc

Villarceaux, Hl de. 75 rue de Richelieu. 1684. XId

Villars, Petit Hl de. 118 rue de de Grenelle. 1712 by Boffrand. XId

Ville- Neuve- St- Ladre: early name of La Villette. V

Villejuif slaughterhouses (abattoirs). Ecole des Arts et Métiers. Built 1808-10. Destroyed 1904. XIIIa

Villeroy, Hl de, see Desmares, Hl de Mlle.

Villetaneuse, Faculté de (University). Project by Fainsilber, Mme Anspach. XVIIIf

Villette, Barrière de la (customs house), see Fermiers Généraux customs wall.

Villette, Hl de, see Bragelongne, Hl de.

Villette (La) slaughterhouses (abattoirs). 28 Av. du Pont-de-Flandre. 1868 by Baltard. Rebuilt 1960 ff. by Sémichon, Valrand, Fournier. XIVa, XVIIIa, XVIIIe

Vincennes, Bois de (woods). Enclosure end 12th c. Replanted 1731. Laid out 1859-60 by Alphand. V, XIIa, XIVa

Vincennes, Château de. 12th c. or even 9th c. Rebuilt 13th c. Fortified 14th c. (keep, walls). New palace 1654 ff. by Le Vau. Walls "modernized" 1804-19. Restored 1930-39, 1944 ff. V, VI, VIIa, IXa, XIb, XIIb, XIIIc, XVIIb, XVIIIb

Vincennes Zoo, Bois de (Parc zoologique de Vincennes). 1934. Modified 1935-36 XVIIa

Viry-Chatillon, base nautique de (marina). 1958 by Vigor. XVIIIf

Visitandines, see Filles de la Visitation-Ste-Marie.

Voie express, see Expressway.

Volière, Pavillon de la. Tuileries gardens. End 16th c. Destroyed. Xb

Volta, 3 rue, House. Ca. 1300. VIIa

Vosges, Place des, see Royale, Place.

W

Weather Observatory (Observatoire météorologique). Parc Montsouris. Was Tunisian pavilion, 1867 Exposition. XVIa

Wepler-Pathé, Cinéma. 14 place Clichy. 1956 by Scop. XVIIIb

Y

Yellow tenches, see Fossés Jaunes.

Young Blind, Institution for the (Institution des Jeunes aveugles). 56 Blvd des Invalides. 1843 by Philippon. XIIIc

Youth Detention House (Prison des jeunes détenus), called Petite-Roquette. 143 rue de la Roquette. 1830. XIIIc

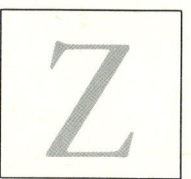

Z

Zamet, Hl, later de Lesdiguières. 10 rue de la Cerisaie. 1580 ff. Destroyed 1877. Xb

Following pages:

present names of streets, squares, and bridges shown in the book, and bibliography.

Photographic credits:

*The photographs in this book are by Editions Joël Cuénot, with the following exceptions: St-Paul-St-Louis (façade), colonnade of the Louvre, Place de la Concorde, the Louvre of Napoléon III, the autoroute south, Orly Airport: M. Laroche.
Hôtel de Beauharnais: R. Jacques.
Place de l'Etoile: R. Durandaud.
Métro tunnel, regional express system: with the kind permission of the RATP.
Patio of the Grand Mosque: Yvon.
La Villette interchange:
Direction de la Voirie parisienne (photo J.-C. Bollier).
Ministry of National Education: press service of the Ministry.
Hauts-de-Seine prefecture: IAURP.
Rungis National Market:
Direction de l'Urbanisme de la Ville de Paris. Défense ensemble:
EPAD (J. Biaugeaud).*

A 1 rue de Chanzy. 2 av. de la Marne. 3 pont d'Asnières. 4 rue de Colombes. 5 rue de Verdun. 6 rue A.-Sylvestre. 7 bd St-Denis. 8 pont de Levallois. 9 quai du Dr-Dervaux. 10 quai de Clichy. 11 rue de Neuilly. 12 rue Henri-Barbusse. 13 rue J.-P. Timbaud. 14 av. de la République. 15 quai Maréchal-Joffre. 16 quai Michelet. 17 pont de Courbevoie. 18 bd Bourdon. 19 rue P.-V. Couturier. 20 rue Kléber. 21 rue du Pdt-Wilson. 22 rue Jules-Guesde. 23 rue V.-Hugo. 24 rue de Bezons. 25 quai Paul-Doumer. 26 pont de la Jatte. 27 bd de la Saussaye. 28 bd V.-Hugo. 29 rue de Villiers. 30 rue Danton. 31 rue A.-France. 32 rue A.-Briand. 33 rue L.-Rouquier. 34 rue J.-Jaurès. 35 av. du Gal-de-Gaulle. 36 bd du Gal-Leclerc. 37 bd du Château. 38 bd Bineau. 39 rue Louise-Michel. 40 rue Octave-Mirbeau. 41 rue de Courcelles. 42 bd de Reims. 43 pont de Neuilly. 44 bd d'Argenson. 45 av. de la pte Champerret. 46 bd de la Somme. 47 bd Mallarmé. 48 bd Berthier. 49 av. du Roule. 50 bd J.-Mermoz. 51 bd Inkermann. 52 bd de l'Yser. 53 av. de Villiers. 54 bd du Gal-Kœnig. 55 av. de Madrid. 56 av. de Neuilly. 57 bd de Dixmude. 58 bd Gouvion-St-Cyr. 59 bd Pereire. 60 rue de Courcelles. 61 rue Cardinet. 62 bd M.-Barrès. 63 bd Maillot 64 bd Pershing. 65 av. Niel. 66 av. de Wagram. 67 av. des Ternes. 68 bd de Courcelles. 69 bd du Cdt-Charcot. 70 rte de Madrid à la pte Maillot. 71 allée de Longchamp. 72 av. de la Division-Leclerc. 73 bd de l'Amiral-Bruix. 74 av. Malakoff. 75 av. de la Gde-Armée. 76 av. Carnot. 77 av. Mac-Mahon. 78 rue du Fg-St-Honoré. 79 place de l'Etoile. 80 av. Hoche. 81 av. de Friedland.

B 1 route de la Reine-Marguerite. 2 allée de Longchamp. 3 route de Suresnes. 4 route de la pte des Sablons à la pte Dauphine. 5 av. Foch. 6 av. V.-Hugo. 7 av. des Champs-Elysées. 8 rue Washington. 9 rue de Berri. 10 av. Bugeaud. 11 place V.-Hugo. 12 rue Copernic. 13 av. d'Iéna. 14 av. Marceau. 15 rue François-Ier. 16 lac Inférieur. 17 av. du Mal-Fayolle. 18 bd Lannes. 19 route de Neuilly à La Muette. 20 bd Flandrin. 21 rue de la Pompe. 22 rue de Longchamp. 23 av. Raymond-Poincaré. 24 av. Kléber. 25 rue de Lübeck. 26 av. Pierre-Ier-de-Serbie. 27 av. du Pdt-Wilson. 28 av. George-V. 29 av. Montaigne. 30 route de la Gde-Cascade. 31 allée de St-Cloud. 32 av. H.-Martin. 33 av. G.-Mandel. 34 av. Albert-de-Mun. 35 quai de New-York. 36 passerelle de Solférino. 37 pont de l'Alma. 38 bd Jules-Sandeau. 39 rue de la Tour. 40 av. Paul-Doumer. 41 jardins du Trocadéro. 42 place de Varsovie. 43 pont d'Iéna. 44 quai Branly. 45 rue de l'Université. 46 av. du Gal-Maunoury. 47 bd Suchet. 48 av. Raphaël. 49 av. Prud'hon. 50 rue Franklin. 51 rue Delessert. 52 av. de La Bourdonnais. 53 av. Rapp. 54 av. Bosquet. 55 rue St-Dominique. 56 rue de Grenelle. 57 route des Lacs à Passy. 58 av. du Ranelagh. 59 bd de Beauséjour. 60 chée de la Muette. 61 rue de Passy. 62 rue de l'Annonciation. 63 rue Raynouard. 64 av. du Pdt-Kennedy. 65 pont de Bir-Hakeim. 66 av. de St-Cloud. 67 lac Supérieur. 68 av. du Mal-Franchet-d'Esperey. 69 bd de Montmorency. 70 av. Mozart. 71 rue de l'Assomption. 72 rue La Fontaine. 73 pont de Grenelle. 74 quai de Grenelle. 75 rue du Dr-Finlay. 76 bd de Grenelle. 77 rue Desaix. 78 av. de Suffren. 79 Champ-de-Mars. 80 av. du Mal-Lyautey. 81 place de la pte d'Auteuil. 82 rue d'Auteuil. 83 pont Mirabeau. 84 quai André-Citroën. 85 rue Ingénieur-Keller. 86 rue du Théâtre. 87 rue Rouelle. 88 place Charles-Michel. 89 rue Fondary. 90 place Dupleix. 91 av. de La Motte-Picquet. 92 place Cambronne. 93 av. de Lowendall. 94 bd Garibaldi. 95 rue Molitor. 96 rue Mirabeau. 97 quai Louis-Blériot. 98 av. E.-Zola. 99 rue St-Charles. 100 rue Frémicourt. 101 rue de Javel. 102 rue de Lourmel. 103 rue des Entrepreneurs. 104 rue Violet. 105 place Violet. 106 rue du Commerce. 107 rue de la Croix-Nivert. 108 rue Cambronne. 109 bd Murat. 110 rue Michel-Ange. 111 bd Exelmans. 112 av. de Versailles. 113 rue de la Convention. 114 rue des Cévennes. 115 rue Balard. 116 place Félix-Faure. 117 rue de l'Abbé-Groult. 118 sq. St-Lambert. 119 rue Lecourbe. 120 rue Blomet.

C 1 av. de la pte St-Cloud. 2 place de la pte St-Cloud. 3 av. de Versailles. 4 pont d'Auteuil. 5 rue Leblanc. 6 rue Balard. 7 rue St-Charles. 8 rue de Lourmel. 9 rue Duranton. 10 rue de la Convention. 11 rue de Javel. 12 rue de l'Abbé-Groult. 13 rue de Vaugirard. 14 av. Edouard-Vaillant. 15 quai du Point-du-Jour. 16 quai d'Issy-les-Moulineaux. 17 bd Victor. 18 place Balard. 19 rue Lecourbe. 20 rue St-Lambert. 21 av. Pierre-Grenier. 22 bd de la République. 23 quai du Pdt-Roosevelt. 24 rue de la pte d'Issy-les-Moulineaux. 25 rue Desnouettes. 26 place de la pte de Versailles. 27 rue Leriche. 28 rue de Vouillé. 29 pont d'Issy. 30 rue Camille-Desmoulins. 31 rue Rouget-de-l'Isle. 32 bd Gallieni. 33 bd Gambetta. 34 rue Guynemer. 35 rue Ernest-Renan. 36 av. de la pte de la Plaine. 37 bd Lefebvre. 38 rue Olivier-de-Serres. 39 rue de Dantzig. 40 rue des Morillons. 41 rue Brancion. 42 av. de la pte de Plaisance. 43 av. de la pte Brancion. 44 place de la pte de Vanves. 45 quai de Stalingrad. 46 rue Gouv.-Gal-Eboué. 47 rue V.-Hugo. 48 rue du Gal-Leclerc. 49 bd Voltaire. 50 rue J.-J.-Rousseau. 51 av. Victor-Cresson. 52 rue Auguste-Gervais. 53 bd de Stalingrad. 54 av. V.-Hugo. 55 rue Jean-Bleuzen. 56 av. du 12-Février-1934. 57 av. de Verdun. 58 rue Gabriel. 59 av. de Clamart. 60 rue A. Frattacci. 61 rue E.-Marcheron. 62 rue E.-Laval. 63 bd Gabriel-Péri. 64 av. de la Paix. 65 rue Larmeroux. 66 av. Augustin-Dumont. 67 av. J.-Jaurès. 68 rue des Garements. 69 bd du Colonel-Fabien. 70 bd de Stalingrad. 71 av. Pierre-Brossolette.

D 1 rue Henri-Barbusse. 2 bd du Mal-Leclerc. 3 bd V.-Hugo. 4 rue du Bois-des-Caures. 5 av. Gabriel-Péri. 6 rue Ch.-Schmidt. 7 rue des Rosiers. 8 av. Michelet. 9 rue du Dr-Bauer. 10 rue des Poissonniers. 11 autoroute du Nord. 12 bd J.-Jaurès. 13 av. de la pte de St-Ouen. 14 av. de la pte Montmartre. 15 av. de la pte de Clignancourt. 16 av. de la pte des Poissonniers. 17 av. de la pte de Clichy. 18 bd Bessières. 19 bd Ney. 20 rue Pouchet. 21 rue de la Jonquière. 22 av. de St-Ouen. 23 rue Ordener. 24 rue du Poteau. 25 rue du Mont-Cenis. 26 bd Ornano. 27 rue Cardinet. 28 rue Guy-Moquet. 29 av. de Clichy. 30 rue Marcadet. 31 rue de la Chapelle. 32 rue Saussure. 33 bd Pereire. 34 rue de Maistre. 35 rue Caulaincourt. 36 rue Custine. 37 rue Ramey. 38 bd Barbès. 39 rue Marx-Dormoy. 40 bd Malesherbes. 41 rue de Tocqueville. 42 rue de Rome. 43 rue des Abbesses. 44 sq. Willette. 45 rue Muller. 46 rue Christiani. 47 place Malesherbes. 48 rue de Levis. 49 av. de Villiers. 50 bd des Batignolles. 51 place Clichy. 52 bd de Clichy. 53 bd de Rochechouart. 54 rue de Clignancourt. 55 bd de la Chapelle. 56 rue de Prony. 57 bd de Courcelles. 58 rue de Constantinople. 59 rue de Léningrad. 60 rue d'Amsterdam. 61 rue de Clichy. 62 rue Blanche. 63 rue des Martyrs. 64 rue Rochechouart. 65 rue du Fg-Poissonnière. 66 bd Magenta. 67 rue de Maubeuge. 68 parc Monceau. 69 rue de Monceau. 70 rue du Rocher. 71 rue de Madrid. 72 place de l'Europe. 73 rue de Liège. 74 rue de Londres. 75 place d'Estienne-d'Orves. 76 rue St-Lazare. 77 rue de Châteaudun. 78 rue La Fayette. 79 rue de Dunkerque. 80 rue de Strasbourg. 81 rue de Courcelles. 82 bd Haussmann. 83 place St-Augustin. 84 rue de la Pépinière. 85 rue du Havre. 86 rue de la Chée-d'Antin. 87 rue du Fg-Montmartre. 88 rue de Paradis. 89 rue La Boétie. 90 rue du Fg-St-Denis.

E 1 rue de Berri. 2 av. Franklin-Roosevelt. 3 rue du Fg-St-Honoré. 4 bd Malesherbes. 5 rue Pasquier. 6 rue Tronchet. 7 rue Auber. 8 rue Scribe. 9 place de l'Opéra. 10 rue de la Chaussée-d'Antin. 11 bd des Italiens. 12 bd Haussmann. 13 bd Montmartre. 14 bd Poissonnière. 15 rue du Fg-Poissonnière. 16 rue du Fg-St-Denis. 17 bd de Strasbourg. 18 bd Magenta. 19 av. des Champs-Elysées. 20 rond-point des Champs-Elysées. 21 av. Matignon. 22 av. de Marigny. 23 rue de l'Elysée. 24 place de la Madeleine. 25 bd de la Madeleine. 26 rue Duphot. 27 bd des Capucines. 28 rue de la Paix. 29 rue du 4-Septembre. 30 place de la Bourse. 31 rue Montmartre. 32 bd Bonne-Nouvelle. 33 bd St-Denis. 34 rue du Fg-St-Martin. 35 bd St-Martin. 36 av. Montaigne. 37 av. Gabriel. 38 rue Boissy-d'Anglas. 39 rue Royale. 40 place Vendôme. 41 rue Danielle-Casanova. 42 av. de l'Opéra. 43 rue des Petits-Champs. 44 rue de Richelieu. 45 rue de Cléry. 46 rue Poissonnière. 47 rue Réaumur. 48 rue St-Denis. 49 rue St-Martin. 50 rue de Turbigo. 51 cours Albert-Ier. 52 rue François-Ier. 53 Cours-la-Reine. 54 place de la Concorde. 55 rue de Rivoli. 56 place N.-D.-des-Victoires. 57 rue Etienne-Marcel. 58 rue Montorgueil. 59 bd de Sébastopol. 60 rue des Gravilliers. 61 quai d'Orsay. 62 pont des Invalides. 63 pont Alexandre-III. 64 pont de la Concorde. 65 jardin des Tuileries. 66 rue de Valois. 67 rue du Louvre. 68 place St-Eustache. 69 rue Rambuteau. 70 rue Michel-Le-Comte. 71 rue du Temple. 72 rue des Archives. 73 rue de l'Université. 74 quai Anatole-France. 75 pont de Solférino. 76 quai des Tuileries. 77 place du Carrousel. 78 rue St-Honoré. 79 rue Berger. 80 rue St-Merri. 81 rue des Francs-Bourgeois. 82 rue St-Dominique. 83 place du Palais-Bourbon. 84 rue de Solférino. 85 pont Royal. 86 pont du Carrousel. 87 quai du Louvre. 88 place du Louvre. 89 rue de la Verrerie. 90 rue Vieille-du-Temple. 91 rue de Grenelle. 92 rue de Latour-Maubourg. 93 esplanade des Invalides. 94 rue de Bourgogne. 95 rue de Bellechasse. 96 bd St-Germain. 97 rue du Bac. 98 pont des Arts. 99 pont Neuf. 100 pont au Change. 101 pont Notre-Dame. 102 place de l'Hôtel-de-Ville. 103 rue François-Miron. 104 pont d'Arcole. 105 av. de La Motte-Picquet. 106 bd des Invalides. 107 rue de Varenne. 108 rue de la Chaise. 109 bd Raspail. 110 rue Bonaparte. 111 rue Mazarine. 112 rue Dauphine. 113 bd du Palais. 114 place St-Germain-des-Prés. 115 rue Jacob. 116 pont St-Michel. 117 petit Pont. 118 pont au Double. 119 pont Louis-Philippe. 120 pont St-Louis. 121 pont Marie. 122 av. de Tourville. 123 place Vauban. 124 rue de Babylone. 125 rue du Four. 126 rue St-André-des-Arts. 127 pont de l'Archevêché. 128 pont de la Tournelle. 129 pont Sully. 130 av. de Lowendall. 131 rue d'Estrée. 132 av. de Ségur. 133 av. Duquesne. 134 rue de Rennes. 135 place St-Sulpice. 136 rue Monsieur-le-Prince. 137 place Maubert. 138 av. de Saxe. 139 av. de Breteuil. 140 rue de Sèvres. 141 rue du Cherche-Midi. 142 rue de Vaugirard. 143 place de l'Odéon. 144 bd St-Michel. 145 rue St-Jacques. 146 rue des Ecoles. 147 rue des Fossés-St-Bernard. 148 av. de Suffren. 149 bd Garibaldi. 150 jardin du Luxembourg. 151 rue Gay-Lussac. 152 rue Soufflot. 153 place du Panthéon. 154 rue Linné. 155 rue Cuvier. 156 rue Lecourbe. 157 rue Blomet. 158 av. du Maine. 159 rue de l'Arrivée. 160 rue du Départ. 161 bd du Montparnasse. 162 rue Vavin. 163 av. d'Assas. 164 rue N.-D.-des-Champs. 165 av. de l'Observatoire. 166 rue Henri-Barbusse. 167 rue d'Ulm. 168 rue Mouffetard. 169 rue Monge. 170 jardin des Plantes. 171 rue du Docteur-Roux. 172 bd Pasteur. 173 bd de Vaugirard. 174 bd Edgar-Quinet. 175 rue Claude-Bernard. 176 rue Lhomond. 177 rue Geoffroy-St-Hilaire. 178 rue Buffon. 179 rue Poliveau. 180 rue Coquillère. 181 rue des Halles. 182 rue des Nonnains-d'Hyères. 183 rue St-Séverin. 184 rue de la Harpe. 185 rue Galande. 186 rue de l'Ecole de Médecine. 187 rue des Fossés St-Jacques.

F 1 rue de la Procession. 2 rue Dutot. 3 rue du Château. 4 av. du Maine. 5 rue de la Gaîté. 6 bd Edgar-Quinet. 7 bd Raspail. 8 av. Denfert-Rochereau. 9 av. de l'Observatoire. 10 rue du Fg-St-Jacques. 11 bd de Port-Royal. 12 rue de la Santé. 13 rue Broca. 14 bd St-Marcel. 15 rue Lebrun. 16 place d'Alleray. 17 rue de Vouillé. 18 rue de Gergovie. 19 rue Raymond-Losserand. 20 rue Froidevaux. 21 place Denfert-Rochereau. 22 place St-Jacques. 23 bd Arago. 24 rue L.M.-Nordmann. 25 av. des Gobelins. 26 bd de l'Hôpital. 27 rue d'Alésia. 28 av. du Gal-Leclerc. 29 rue de la Tombe-Issoire. 30 bd St-Jacques. 31 bd Auguste-Blanqui. 32 rue Croulebarbe. 33 place d'Italie. 34 bd de la Gare. 35 bd Brune. 36 rue Didot. 37 place Victor-Basch. 38 av. du Parc Montsouris. 39 rue Broussais. 40 rue Cabanis. 41 rue Barrault. 42 rue Bobillot. 43 av. de Choisy. 44 av. de la pte de Châtillon. 45 place de la pte de Châtillon. 46 av. de Châtillon. 47 rue Friant. 48 av. de la pte de Montrouge. 49 place du 24-août-1944. 50 av. de la pte d'Orléans. 51 av. Reille. 52 rue de Tolbiac. 53 rue de l'Amiral-Mouchez. 54 rue Boussingault. 55 av. d'Italie. 56 av. du Gal-Leclerc. 57 rue Nansouty. 58 rue du Gal-Deutch-de-la-Meurthe. 59 bd Jourdan. 60 rue Gazan. 61 place de Rungis. 62 bd Kellermann. 63 av. Gabriel-Péri. 64 av. Pierre-Brossolette. 65 rue M.-Arnoux. 66 av. Verdier. 67 av. de la République. 68 rue de Bagneux. 69 rue Barbès. 70 rue Paul-Vaillant-Couturier. 71 av. de la pte de Gentilly. 72 av. Aristide-Briand. 73 av. Gambetta. 74 av. Joseph-Staline. 75 av. J.-Jaurès. 76 autoroute du Sud. 77 av. Pasteur. 78 rue d'Arcueil. 79 av. J.-Jaurès. 80 rue de la Convention.

G 1 rue des Fillettes. 2 av. V.-Hugo. 3 canal St-Denis. 4 av. de la République 5 rue Diderot. 6 av. J.-Jaurès. 7 av. Edouard-Vaillant. 8 av. du Gal-Leclerc 9 bd Ney. 10 bd MacDonald. 11 rue d'Aubervilliers. 12 rue Corentin-Cariou 13 rue Delizy. 14 rue de Crimée. 15 bd d'Indochine. 16 rue Hoche. 17 rue V.-Hugo. 18 rue de Paris. 19 rue Riquet. 20 rue de Flandre. 21 canal de l'Ourcq. 22 place de la pte de Pantin. 23 rue des Sept-Arpents. 24 rue des Grilles. 25 rue Jules Auffret. 26 rue de Montreuil. 27 rue d'Aubervilliers 28 bd de la Chapelle. 29 bassin de La Villette. av. J.-Jaurès. 31 rue de Stalingrad. 32 rue du Pré-St-Gervais. 33 rue Gabriel-Péri. 34 rue Méhul. 35 bd Sérurier. 36 rue d'Estienne-d'Orves. 37 rue Danton. 38 rue du Château-Landon 39 place de Stalingrad. 40 rue de Meaux. 41 rue Manin. 42 rue du Gal-Brunet 43 av. du Belvédère. 44 av. Faidherbe. 45 rue La Fayette. 46 rue du Fg-St-Martin 47 quai Valmy. 48 bd de La Villette. 49 bd Secrétan. 50 rue Botzaris. 51 av. de la pte St-Gervais. 52 rue des Bruyères. 53 rue E.-Varlin. 54 quai de Jemmapes. 55 rue des Ecluses-St-Martin. 56 av. Simon-Bolivar. 57 rue Fessart. 58 rue de La Villette. 59 rue de Belleville. 60 av. Gambetta.

H 1 rue Lucien-Sampaix. 2 rue St-Maur. 3 bd de La Villette. 4 rue de Belleville. 5 rue Haxo. 6 bd Magenta. 7 quai de Valmy. 8 quai de Jemmapes. 9 rue du Fg-du-Temple. 10 rue des Couronnes. 11 rue des Pyrénées. 12 rue de Rigoles. 13 rue St-Fargeau. bd Mortier. 15 place de la République. 16 rue de la Folie-Méricourt. 17 rue Jean-Pierre Timbaud. 18 rue Oberkampf. 19 bd de Belleville. 20 rue de Ménilmontant. 21 rue de la Bidassoa. 22 rue Gambetta. 23 rue de Turenne. 24 bd du Temple. 25 bd Voltaire. 26 bd Richard-Lenoir 27 av. de la République. 28 rue du Chemin-Vert. 29 place Auguste-Métivier 30 av. Gambetta. 31 place M.-Nadeau. 32 place Gambetta. 33 rue Belgrand. 34 place de la pte de Bagnolet. 35 rue Vieille-du-Temple. 36 rue du Pont-aux-Choux. 37 rue du Parc-Royal. 38 bd Beaumarchais. 39 rue de la Folie-Regnault. 40 bd de Ménilmontant. 41 rue de Bagnolet. 42 bd Davout. 43 rue des Francs-Bourgeois. 44 rue St-Gilles. 45 rue St-Sabin. 46 rue Popincourt. 47 place Léon-Blum. 48 rue de la Roquette. 49 rue Mont-Louis. 50 bd de Charonne. 51 rue des Orteaux. 52 rue St-Antoine. 53 place des Vosges. 54 rue Léon-Frot. 55 rue de Charonne. 56 place de la Bastille. 57 rue de Lappe. 58 passage du Bureau. 59 av. Philippe-Auguste. 60 bd Henri-IV. 61 bd Morland. 62 bd Bourdon. 63 rue du Fg-St-Antoine. 64 rue St-Bernard. 65 rue de Montreuil. 66 rue de Boulets. 67 av. de Taillebourg. 68 rue d'Avron. 69 rue de Lagny. 70 quai Henri-IV. 71 bd de la Bastille. 72 rue de Charenton. 73 rue de Reuilly 74 place de la Nation. 75 cours de Vincennes. 76 av. de la pte de Vincennes 77 quai St-Bernard. 78 rue de Lyon. 79 av. Daumesnil. 80 bd Diderot 81 av. du Bel-Air. 82 bd de Picpus. 83 pont d'Austerlitz. 84 place Valhubert 85 rue Buffon. 86 bd de l'Hôpital. 87 quai d'Austerlitz. 88 quai de la Rapée 89 rue de Bercy. 90 rue de Rambouillet. 91 rue de Picpus. 92 av. de St-Mandé 93 av. du Dr-Arnold-Netter. 94 bd Soult. 95 square du Temple.

I 1 bd de l'Hôpital. 2 rue Sauvage. 3 quai d'Austerlitz. 4 pont de Bercy 5 rue de Bercy. 6 bd de Bercy. 7 bd de Reuilly. 8 place Félix-Eboué. 9 av. Daumesnil. 10 rue de Picpus. 11 av. du Gal-Michel-Bizot. 12 bd Soult. 13 rue Jenner. 14 rue Bruant. 15 bd de la Gare. 16 quai de la Gare. 17 quai de Bercy 18 rue de Dijon. 19 rue Proudhon. 20 rue Gabriel-Lamé. 21 av. de Charenton 22 rue Claude-Decaen. 23 bd Poniatowski. 24 av. Francis-Fresneau. 25 bd Carnot 26 rue Jeanne-d'Arc. 27 rue du Chevaleret. 28 pont de Tolbiac. 29 rue Château-des-Rentiers. 30 place Jeanne-d'Arc. 31 rue de Tolbiac. 32 pont National 33 av. de la pte de Charenton. 34 av. de Gravelle. 35 route du Bac. 36 route de la Ceinture-du-Lac. 37 rue de Patay. 38 bd Masséna. 39 quai d'Ivry. 40 quai de Bercy-Charenton. 41 av. de Choisy. 42 av. d'Ivry. 43 rue Regnault. 44 av. de la pte de Vitry. 45 av. de la Liberté. 46 rue de Paris. 47 av. de la pte d'Ivry 48 rue V.-Hugo. 49 quai M.-Boyer. 50 av. de la pte de Choisy. 51 rue Marceau 52 av. Pierre-Semard. 53 quai J.-Compagnon. 54 pont de Conflans. 55 quai des Carrières. 56 rue Barbès. 57 rue Louis-Bertrand. 58 rue Joseph-Staline 59 bd Paul-Vaillant-Couturier. 60 quai A.-Deshaies. 61 Passerelle. 62 rue Roger Salengro. 63 rue de Châteaudun. 64 route de Choisy. 65 rue Pierre-Curie 66 rue de Paris. 67 av. Danielle-Casanova. 68 bd Carnot. 69 bd du Colonel Fabien. 70 pont d'Ivry. 71 av. Paul-Vaillant-Couturier. 72 rue Paul-Andrieux 73 rue E.-V.-Raspail. 74 av. J.-Jaurès. 75 quai Henri-Pourchasse. 76 quai Blanqui.

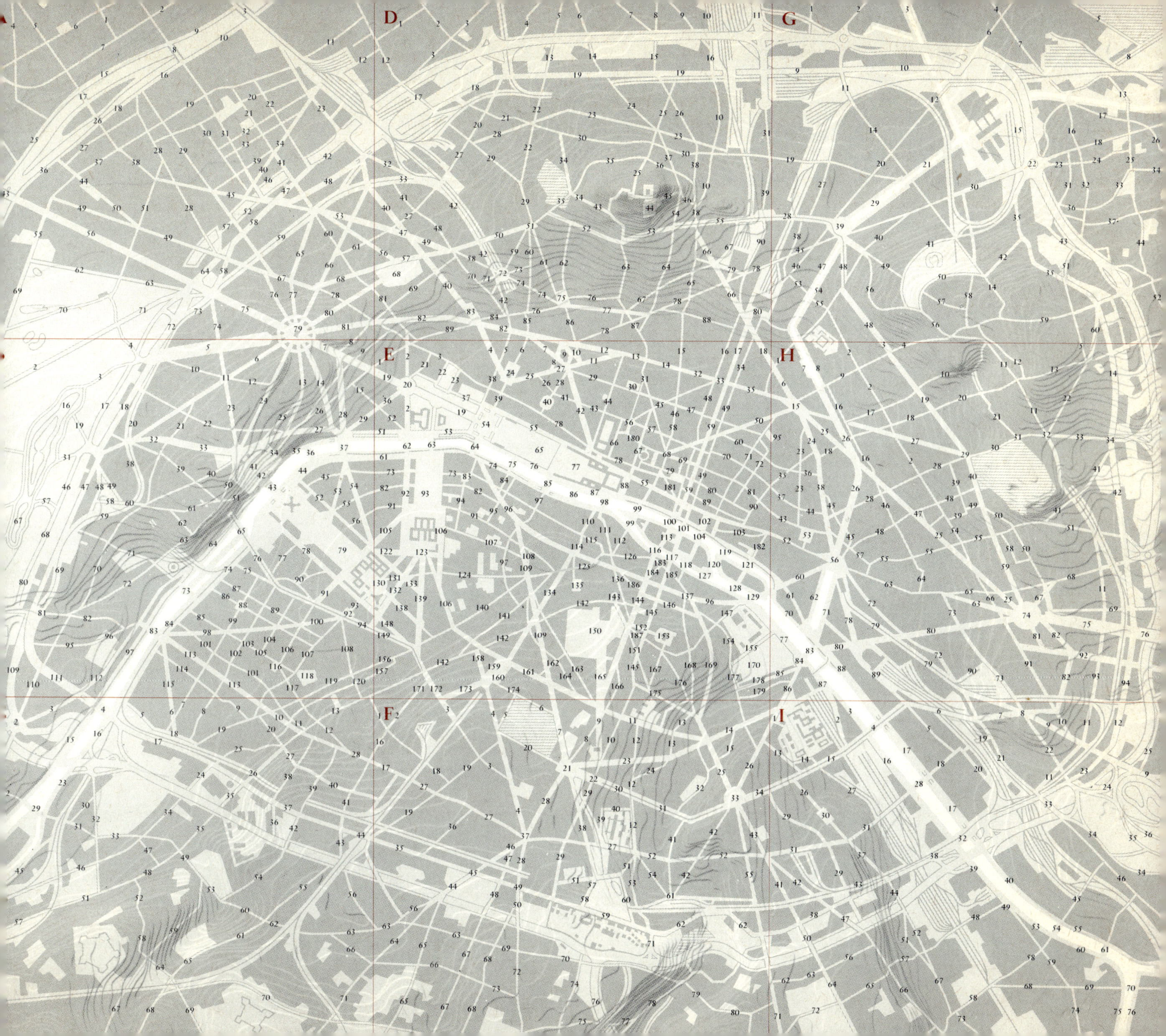
D
G
E
H
F
I

Bibliography

The enormous bibliography on Paris is very unequally distributed among the various historical problems. The works dealing with traditional aspects – description, architecture, major events – can easily be found in the long bibliography of the excellent Guide Bleu on Paris by G. Monmarché and G. Poisson (Paris: Hachette, 1963). Except for our attention to works on architectural and decorative styles which, because they are new, are too often excluded, we have tried here to give greater attention to the other bibliography, the one that aims at more fundamental data on the mechanisms of the city's evolution. Most of the works cited will complete this bibliography, as will the recent "Bibliographie d'histoire des villes de France" (Paris: Klincksieck, 1967), by Ph. Dollinger, G. Wolff and S. Guenée.

Architecture d'aujourd'hui (periodical). Especially n. 88. 1960. Urbanisme des capitales, n. 97, 1961. Paris and its region.

Babelon, J.-P. Demeures parisiennes sous Henri IV et Louis XIII. 1965, Le Temps. *Bardet, G.* Naissance et méconnaissance de l'urbanisme. 1951, Sabri. *Barroux, R.* Paris des origines à nos jours et son rôle dans l'histoire de la civilisation. 1951, Payot. *Barroux, R.* L'Evêque de Paris et l'administration municipale, jusqu'au XIIe siècle. Revue d'histoire de l'Eglise de France, n. 46, 1960. *Bastié, J.* Capital immobilier et marché immobilier parisien, Annales de géographie, n. 69, 1960. *Batiffol, L.* La Vie de Paris sous Louis XIII. 1932, Calmann-Lévy. *Bautier, R.* and *Mollat, M.*, Le Trafic fluvial sur la Seine au pont de Meulan au milieu du XVe siècle. Bulletin philologique et historique du Comité des travaux historiques. 1959. *Bazin, G.* L'architecture hospitalière, L'Œil 1963. *Belleville, G.* Morphologie de la population active à Paris, 1962. A. Colin. *Bergeron, L.* Approvisionnement et consommation à Paris sous le Premier Empire. Paris and Ile-de-France, n. 14, 1963. *Bertillon, J.* Essai de statistique comparée du surpeuplement des habitations à Paris et dans les grandes capitales européennes. Paris, 1894. *Bibliothèque nationale.* Paris d'hier et de demain. Exposition 1966. *Biver, M-L.* Le Paris de Napoléon. 1963, Plon. *Boinet, A.* Les Eglises parisiennes. 1958. Editions de Minuit. *Bonnefond.* Les colonies de bicoques de la région parisienne, La Vie urbaine. 1925. *Bonnoure, P.* Quelques aspects de l'évolution géographique de Paris. Les Etudes rhodaniennes, n. 19, 1944. *Bossuat, R.* La Pêche en Seine au XVe siècle, Bulletin de la Société de l'histoire de Paris et de l'Ile-de-France, n. 90. 1963. *Bourgeon, J.-L.* L'Ile de la Cité pendant la Fronde, structure sociale, Paris et Ile-de-France, n. 13, 1962. *Boutet de Monvel, N.* Les Demains de Paris. 1964, Denoël. *Braibant, C, Mirot, A, Le Moël, M.* Guide historique des rues de Paris. 1963, Hachette.

Caben, L. Ce qu'enseigne un péage du XVIIIe siècle. La Seine entre Rouen et Paris et les caractères de l'économie parisienne. Annale E.S.C. n. 3, 1931. *Carpentier, E.* and *Glenisson, J.* La Démographie française au XIVe siècle, Annales E.S.C. n. 17, 1962. *Champigneulle, B. Lavedan, P., Raval, M., Pillement, G., Auzelle, R., D'Espezel, P., Remaury, P.* Destinée de Paris. 1943, Editions du Chêne. *Chastel* and *Gloton, J.-J.*, L'Architecture en France autour de 1900, L'Information d'histoire de l'Art, n. 3, 1958. *Chastel* and *Pérouse de Montclos, M.* L'Aménagement de l,accès oriental du Louvre, Les Monuments historiques, n. 12, 1966. *Chelini, J.*, La Ville et l'Eglise. 1958, Ed. du Cerf. *Chevalier, L.* La formation de la population parisienne au XIXe siècle. 1950, P.U.F. *Chevalier, L.* Classes laborieuses et classes dangereuses à Paris pendant la première moitié du XIXe siècle. 1958, Plon. *Chombart de Lauwe, P.-H.* Paris et l'agglomération parisienne, 2 vol., 1952. P.U.F. *Christ, Y.* Eglises parisiennes actuelles et disparues. 1947, Tel. *Christ, Y.*, L'architecture parisienne de la fin du XIXe siècle. March, 1964, Jardin des Arts. *Clerc, P.* Grands ensembles, banlieues nouvelles. 1967, P.U.F. *Clouzot, F.* Les innondations à Paris du VIe au XXe siècle, Bulletin de la Société de géographie, n. 23, 1911. *C.R.H.A.M.* Les vestiges de l'Hôtel Legendre et le véritable Hôtel de la Trémoille, Bulletin monumental n. 124, 1966. *Crozet, R.* La Vie artistique en France au XVIIe siècle (1598-1661). 1954, P.U.F.

Daniel, Y. Aspects de la pratique religieuse à Paris. 1952, Ed. Ouvrières. *Daniel, Y.* L'équipement paroissial d'un diocèse urbain, Paris (1802-1956). 1957, Ed. Ouvrières. *Daumart, A.* and *Furet, F.* Structures et relations sociales à Paris au XVIIIe siècle. 1961, A. Colin. *Daumart, A.* La bourgeoisie parisienne de 1815 à 1848. 1963, S.E.V.P.E.N. *Daumart, A.* Maisons de Paris et propriétaires parisiens au XIXe siècle, 1809-1880. 1965, Cujas éd. *Defourneaux M.* La vie quotidienne au temps de Jeanne d'Arc. 1952, Hachette. *Desbruères, M.* Maisons 1900 de Paris, Bizarre n. 27, 1963. *Dion, R.* Les Frontières de la France. 1947, Hachette. *Dion, R.* Paris dans les récits historiques et légendaires du IXe au XIIe siècle. Tours, 1949, Arrault éd. *Dion, R.* Les Accroissements successifs de Paris et la configuration du sol, Revue des travaux de l'Académie des sciences morales. 1961. *Doehaerd, R.* Au temps de Charlemagne et des Normands. Ce qu'on vendait et comment on le vendait dans le Bassin parisien, Annales E.S.C. n.2, 1947. *Dollinger, Ph.* Le Chiffre de la population de Paris au XIVe siècle: 210,000 ou 80,000 habitants? Revue historique n. 215-216. 1956. *Dubech L.* and *D'Espezel, P.* Histoire de Paris, 1931, Ed. pittoresques. *Dufau, P.* Non à l'urbanisme. 1964, Flammarion. *Dumoulin, M.* Etudes de topographie parisienne, 1930, 3 vol. *Duon.* Evolution de la valeur vénale des immeubles parisiens (de 1840 à 1940), Journal de la Société de statistique de Paris. 1943. *Durand, Y.* L'Habitat parisien des Fermiers Généraux, Bulletin de la Société de l'histoire de Paris et de l'Ile-de-France, n. 89, 1962. *Durbec, J.-A.* La Grande Boucherie de Paris, Bulletin philologique et historique du Comité des travaux historiques et scientifiques. 1955-1956. *Duval, P.-M.* Paris antique, des origines au IIIe siècle. 1961, Hermann. *Duveau, G.* La Vie ouvrière en France sous le Second Empire. 1946, Gallimard.

Feillet, A. La Misère au temps de la Fronde et Saint Vincent de Paul. Paris, 1862. *Ferté, J.* La Vie religieuse dans les campagnes parisiennes au XVIIe siècle. 1962, J. Vrin éd. *Fourquin, G.* La population de la région parisienne aux environs de 1328, Le Moyen Age, n. 62, 1956. *Fourquin, G.* Paris, capitale économique à la fin du Moyen Age, Bulletin de la Société de l'histoire de Paris et de l'Ile-de-France, n. 87, 88. 1961. *Fourquin, G.* Les Campagnes de la région parisienne à la fin du Moyen Age. 1964. P.U.F. *Friedmann. A.* Paris, ses rues, ses paroisses. 1959, Plon: *Furet, F.* Structures sociales parisiennes au XVIIIe siècle, l'apport d'une série "Fiscale," Annales E.S.C. Sept.-Oct. 1961.

Gallet, M. Demeures parisiennes, l'Epoque de Louis XVI. 1964, Le Temps. *Ganshof, F.* Etudes sur le développement des villes entre Loire et Rhin au Moyen Age, Paris-Bruxelles. 1943, P.U.F. *Garreta, J.-C.* Le Quartier Saint-André-des-Arts à Paris des origines à 1600, Positions de thèses de l'Ecole des Chartes. 1957. *Gay, J.-L.* L'Administration de la capitale entre 1770 et 1789, Paris et Ile-de-France, n. 7 to 12. 1957-1961. *George, P., Randet, G., Bastié, J.* La Région parisienne. Paris 2nd ed. 1964, P.U.F. *Géraud, H.* Paris sous philippe le Bel. Paris, 1837. *Geremek B.* Najemna sixa robocza w rzemiosle Parysa XIII-XV w (salaried labor in the Paris working classes from the 13th to the 15th centuries). Warsaw, 1962, with French résumé. *Gille, B.* Industriels et industrialisation de la région parisienne sous la Révolution et l'Empire. Bulletin de la Société de l'histoire de Paris et de l'Ile-de-France, n. 89. 1962. *Girard, L.*, La Garde Nationale, 1814-1871. 1964, Plon. *Giraud Abbé.* Paris, hier, aujourd'hui ... et demain. 1967 Semaine religieuse de Paris éd. *Gravier, J.-F.* Paris et le désert français. 1958, Flammarion. *Griotteray, A.* L'Etat contre Paris. 1962, Hachette. *Guerout, J.* Le Palais de la Cité à Paris, des origines à 1417. 1953. *Guerrand, R.-H.* Mémoires du métro. 1961, La Table Ronde

Halbwachs, M. Les expropriations et le prix des terrains à Paris, 1860-1900. Paris, 1909. *Halbwachs, M.* Les Plans d'extension et d'aménagement de Paris avant le XIXe siècle, La Vie urbaine, 1920. *Halbwachs, M.* La population et les tracés des voies à Paris depuis un siècle. 1928, P.U.F. *Halfen, L.* Paris sous les premiers Capétiens. Paris, 1909. *Henry, L.* and *Levy, Cl.* Quelques données sur la région autour de Paris au XVIIIe siècle, Population n. 17. 1962. *Héron de Villefosse*, R. La Grande Boucherie de Paris, Bulletin de la Société de l'histoire de Paris. 1928. *Héron de Villefosse, R.* Histoire de Paris. 1955, B. Grasset. *Hillairet, J.* Evocations du Vieux Paris. 1959, Dictionnaire historique des rues de Paris. Editions de Minuit. *Horne, A.* The Fall of Paris. London, 1965. Macmillan. *Huisman, G.* Pour comprendre les monuments de Paris. 1950, Hachette. *Huisman, Poisson, G.* Les Monuments de Paris. 1966, Hachette. *Husson, A.* Les Consommations de Paris. 1856, 2nd ed. 1875.

Isay, R. Panorama des Expositions universelles. 1937, Gallimard.

Jacquart, J. La Fronde des princes dans la région parisienne et ses conséquences matérielles. Revue d'histoire moderne et contemporaine, n. 7, 1959. *Jardillier, A.* Les Carosses à cinq sols. 1962, R.A.T.P. *Jonas, I.* Groupement de la bourgeoisie commerçante et artisanale de Paris suivant le rôle des contributions pour 1313. Annales Universitatis scientiarum Budapestinensis. Sectio Historia. n. 5, 1963. *Jurgens, M.* and *Couperie P.* Le Logement à Paris aux XVIe et XVIIIe siècles. Annales E.S.C., 1962.

Kleindienst, Th. La Topographie et l'exploitation des "marais de Paris" du XIIe au XVIIe siècle. Paris et Ile-de-France, n. 14, 1963

Labatut, J.-P. Situation sociale du quartier du Marais pendant la Fronde parlementaire. XVIIe siècle, n. 38, 1958. *Lagarrigue, L.* Cent ans de transports en commun dans la région parisienne, 4 vol. R.A.T.P. *Lambeau, L.* Les logements à bon marché, Paris 1897. *Lambert, J.* Les conditions de logement dans l'agglomération parisienne (d'après le recensement de 1926). 1929, Journal de la Société de statistique de Paris. *De la Monneraye, J.* La Crise du logement à Paris pendant la Révolution. 1928, Champion. *Lavedan, P.* Histoire de l'urbanisme, Paris 1926-1952, 3 vol. H. Laurens. *Le Bras, G.* Paris, seconde capitale de la chrétienté, Revue d'histoire de l'Eglise de France, n. 37, 1951. *Leclercq, H.* Article Paris, Histoire," in Dictionnaire d'archéologie Chrétienne et de liturgie, vol. 13, 1938, Letouzey and Ané. *Le Grand, L.* .Les Maisons-Dieu et léproseries du diocèse de Paris. Nogent-le-Rotrou, 1899. *Leboux, F.* Le Bourg Saint-Germain-des-Prés depuis ses origines jusqu'à la fin de la guerre de Cent Ans. Paris, 1951, author. *Lemoine, H.* Manuel d'histoire de Paris, 1924. A. Michel. *Léon, P.* Histoire de la rue. Paris, 1947. La Taille-Douce, éd. *Lepointe, G.* Les Villes dans la France du XIXe siècle in La Ville, Recueil de la Société Jean Bodin, n. 7, 1955. *Longnon, A.* Paris pendant la domination anglaise (1420-1436). Paris, 1878. *Lot, F.* L'Etat des paroisses et des feux de 1328, bibliothèque de l'Ecole des Chartes, n. 90. 1929. *Lot, F.* Recherches sur la population et la superficie des cités remontant à la période gallo-romaine, 3 vol. 1945-1953, Champion. *Lucas, C.* Les Transports en commun à Paris. Paris, 1914.

Magne, E. Paris sous l'échevinage au XVIIe siècle. 1960, Emile Paul, éd. *Mallet, F.* Le quartier des Halles de Paris, Etude d'un héritage millénaire, Annales de géographie, n. 76, 1967. *Mandrou, R.* Les Consommations des villes françaises (viandes et poissons) au milieu du XIXe siècle. Annales E.S.C. n. 16, 1961. *Marnata, F.* Les loyers des bourgeois de Paris, 1860 1958, 1961, A. Colin. *Martineau J.* Les Halles de Paris, des origines à 1789. 1961 Eds. Montchrestien. *Meuvret, J.* Le Commerce des grains et des farines à Paris et les marchands parisiens à l'époque de Louis XIV, Revue d'histoire moderne et contemporaine, n. 3, 1956. *Michaelsson, K.* Le Livre de la Taille de Paris, l'an de grâce 1296, Acta Universitatis Gotoburgnesis, vol. 64. Göteborg, 1958. *Mollat, M.* Rouen avant-port de Paris à la fin du Moyen Age. Bulletin de la Société d'études historiques, géographiques et scientifiques de la région parisienne, n. 25, 1951. *Mollat, M.* Notes sur la mortalité à Paris au temps de la peste noire, d'après les comptes de l'œuvre de Saint-Germain-l'Auxerrois, Moyen Age, n. 69, 1963. *Mols, R.* Introduction à la démographie historique des Villes d'Europe du XIVe au XVIIIe siècle, Louvain, 1954-56, 3 vol. Publications Universitaires. *Mousnier, R.* Paris au XVIIe siècle, C.D.U. 1961, 3 vol. *Mousset, A.* Petite Histoire des Monuments de Paris. 1947, Amiot-Dumont. *Mumford, L.* The City in history, 1961.

Pacaut, M. Louis VII et son royaume. 1964, S.E.V.P.E.N. *Patchere (de) F.-G.* Paris à l'époque gallo-romaine. 1912. *Colloques, cahiers de civilisation,* Paris, croissance d'une capitale, 1961. Paris, fonctions d'une capitale, 1962. Paris, présent et avenir d'une capitale, 1964, Hachette. *Paris, 1960, Paris 1961,* Société de statistique de Paris, éd. *Philippe, R.* L'étude du ravitaillement de Paris au temps de Lavoisier, Annales E.S.C. n. 16, 1961. *Philipponeau, M.* L'Evolution historique de la vie rurale dans la banlieue parisienne. 1956, A. Colin. *Pillement, G.* Destruction de Paris. 1943, B. Grasset. *Pilliet, G.* L'Avenir de Paris, 1961, Hachette. *Pinkney, D.-H.*, Napoleon III and the rebuilding of Paris. 1958, Princeton University Press. *Plan d'urbanisme directeur de Paris.* Report, 1960. *Plouin, R.* Les Plans de Paris à travers les âges. L'information d'histoire de l'Art, n.4, 1959. *Poète, M.* Une vie de Cité, Paris de sa naissance à nos jours, 4 vol. 1924-31. Aug. Picard. *Poisson, G.* Fontaines de Paris. 1957, Le Centurion. *Poisson, G.* Napoléon et Paris. 1964, Berger-Levrault. *Poupardin, Cl.* Etude sur les fortifications de Charles V à Paris. Positions de thèses de l'Ecole des Chartes, 1963. *Pourcher, G.* Le Peuplement de Paris. 1964, P.U.F. *Pronteau, J.* Construction et aménagement des nouveaux quartiers de Paris (1820-26). Histoire des entreprises, n. 1, 1958.

Quenioux, G. Les Arts décoratifs modernes (France). 1925, Larousse.

Ragon, M. Paris hier, aujourd'hui, demain? 1965, Hachette. *Reinhard, M.* Les Divisions administratives de Paris et l'esprit de quartier pendant la Révolution. Bulletin de la Société de l'histoire de Paris et de l'Ile-de-France, n. 89, 1962. *Reinhard, M.* Paris pendant la Révolution. 1965, C.D.U. *Roblin, M.* Le Terroir de Paris aux époques gallo-romaine et franque. 1951, A. et J. Picard. *Roblin, M.* Cités ou Citadelles? Les Enceintes romaines du Bas-Empire d'après l'exemple de Paris. Revue des études anciennes, n. 53, 1951. *Roblin, M.* Les Juifs de Paris. 1952, A. et J. Picard. *Rochegude (de)* and *Dumoulin, M.* Guide pratique à travers le vieux Paris. 1923, Edouard Champion. *Rougerie, J.* La Commune de 1871, problèmes d'Histoire sociale, Archives internationales de sociologie de la coopération, n. 8, 1960. *Rude, G.E.* The motives of Popular Insurrection in Paris during the French Revolution. Bulletin of the Institute of Historical Research, n. 26, 1953. *Rupp, J.* Histoire de l'Eglise de Paris. 1948, R. Laffont. *Sauval, H.* Histoire et recherche des antiquités de la Ville de Paris, 1724.

Schein, I. Paris construit. Vincent et Fréal. *I.A.U.R.P.* Schéma directeur d'aménagement et d'urbanisme de la région de Paris., Paris 1965. Un siècle d'architecture. L'Architure d'aujourd'hui, n. 34, April-May, 1964. *Singer-Kerel, J.* Le Coût de la vie à Paris de 1840 à 1854, Recherches sur l'économie française, vol. 3. 1961, A. Colin. *Soboul, A.* Les Sans-Culottes parisiens en l'An II. 1958, Clavreuil. *Subilleau. J.-L.* Sociologie urbaine, Essai de synthèse, Urbanisme, n. 35, 1966.

Urbanisme (periodical). Especially n. 51 (1956) Paris et sa région. n. 55 (1957) Propos sur Paris, n. 84 (1964) Destin de Paris.

Vallée, L. Catalogue des Plans de Paris et des cartes de l'Ile-de-France. 1908, Bibliothèque nationale. *Valmy-Baisse,* Les Grands Magasins. 1924, Gallimard. *Vénard, M.* Bourgeois et paysans au XVIIe siècle. 1957, S.E.V.P.E.N. *Verne, H.* and *Chavance, R.* Pour comprendre l'art décoratif moderne en France. 1925, Hachette. *Vialay, A.* La Vente des biens nationaux pendant la Révolution française. Paris 1908. *Viard, J.* Paris sous Philippe le Bel, Bulletin de la Société de l'histoire de Paris et de l'Ile-de-France, n. 61. 1934. *Vidier, A.* Les origines de la municipalité parisienne, Mémoires de la Société d'histoire de Paris et de l'Ile-de-France, n. 49, 1927. *Vieillard-Troiekouroff, M., Fossard, D., Chatel, E., Lamy-Lassalle, C.* Les anciennes églises suburbaines de Paris (IVe-Xe siècles). Paris et l'Ile-de-France. 1960. *Vossen, F.* Du Paris de Quasimodo au Paris d'Haussmann. Annales E.S.C. n. 2, 1947.

Walter, G. La Vie de Paris sous l'occupation (1940-44). 1960, A. Colin. *Weiss, N.* La Seine et le nombre des victimes de la Saint-Barthelemy, Bulletin de la Société de l'histoire du protestantisme français, n. 46, 1897.